Frances Trollope and the Novel of Social Change

Recent Titles in
Contributions in Women's Studies

Victorian London's Middle-Class Housewife: What She Did All Day
Yaffa Claire Draznin

Connecting Links: The British and American Woman Suffrage Movements, 1900–1914
Patricia Greenwood Harrison

Female Journeys: Autobiographical Expressions by French and Italian Women
Claire Marrone

Excluded from Suffrage History: Matilda Joslyn Gage, Nineteenth-Century American Feminist
Leila R. Brammer

The Artist as Outsider in the Novels of Toni Morrison and Virginia Woolf
Lisa Williams

(Out)Classed Women: Contemporary Chicana Writers on Inequitable Gendered Power Relations
Phillipa Kafka

"Saddling La Gringa": Gatekeeping in Literature by Contemporary Latina Writers
Phillipa Kafka

Representing the Marginal Woman in Nineteenth-Century Russian Literature: Personalism, Feminism, and Polyphony
Svetlana Slavskaya Grenier

From the Field to the Legislature: A History of Women in the Virgin Islands
Eugenia O'Neal

Women and Domestic Experience in Victorian Political Fiction
Susan Johnston

African American Women and Social Action: The Clubwomen and Volunteerism from Jim Crow to the New Deal 1896–1936
Floris Barnett Cash

The Dress of Women: A Critical Introduction to the Symbolism and Sociology of Clothing
Charlotte Perkins Gilman, Michael R. Hill, Mary Jo Deegan

Frances Trollope and the Novel of Social Change

Edited by
Brenda Ayres

Contributions in Women's Studies,
Number 192

GREENWOOD PRESS
Westport, Connecticut • London

PR
5699
.T3
Z66
2002

Library of Congress Cataloging-in-Publication Data

Frances Trollope and the novel of social change / edited by Brenda Ayres.
 p. cm.—(Contributions in women's studies, ISSN 0147-104X ; no. 192)
 Includes bibliographical references and index.
 ISBN 0-313-31755-0 (alk. paper)
 1. Trollope, Frances Milton, 1780-1863—Criticism and interpretation. 2. Trollope,
Frances Milton, 1780-1863—Political and social views. 3. Literature and society—
England—History—19th century. 4. Women and literature—England—History—19th
century. 5. Social change in literature. I. Ayres, Brenda, 1953- II. Series.
PR5699.T3 Z66 2002
823'.7—dc21   2001023319

British Library Cataloguing in Publication Data is available.

Copyright © 2002 by Brenda Ayres

All rights reserved. No portion of this book may be
reproduced, by any process or technique, without the
express written consent of the publisher.

Library of Congress Catalog Card Number: 2001023319
ISBN: 0-313-31755-0
ISSN: 0147-104X

First published in 2002

Greenwood Press, 88 Post Road West, Westport, CT 06881
An imprint of Greenwood Publishing Group, Inc.
www.greenwood.com

Printed in the United States of America

The paper used in this book complies with the
Permanent Paper Standard issued by the National
Information Standards Organization (Z39.48-1984).

10 9 8 7 6 5 4 3 2 1

46240326

Copyright Acknowledgments

The author and publisher gratefully acknowledge permission for the use of the following material:

Anthony Trollope. *Can You Forgive Her?* 1864–65. *The Electronic Text Center*. Ed. David Kiton. 1994. Folio Society Ed. London: the Folio Society, 1989. U of Virginia. 8 March 2001. http://etext.lib.virginia.edu/

Excerpt adapted by the author from Chapter 1 of *Fanny Trollope: The Life and Adventures of a Clever Woman* by Pamela Neville-Sington, copyright © 1997 by Pamela Neville-Sington. Used with permission of Viking Penguin, a division of Penguin Putnam Inc.

Fanny Trollope. *Domestic Manners of the Americans*. Illust. Auguste Hervieu. 2 vols. London: Whittaker, Treacher, 1832. Edited by Pamela Neville-Sington (Penguin Classics, 1997). Editorial matter copyright © Pamela Neville-Sington, 1997. Reproduced by permission of Penguin Books Ltd. Text quoted is from the Preface.

Frances Trollope. *The Vicar of Wrexhill*. Illust. Auguste Hervieu. 3 vols. Stroud, England: Pocket Classics, Sutton Publishing, 1996.

Frances Trollope. *The Widow Barnaby*. 3 vols. London: Bentley, 1839. Stroud, England: Pocket Classics, Sutton Publishing, 1995.

Frances Trollope. *Hargrave; or the Adventures of a Man of Fashion*. 3 vols. London: Colburn, 1843. Introd. Teresa Ransom. Stroud, England: Pocket Classics, Sutton Publishing, 1995.

To
Harry W. McCraw
Professor of Victorian Literature at
the University of Southern Mississippi,
who passed away in 1996

Contents

Illustrations

Preface

Harry W. McCraw was one of the loveliest Victorians I have ever known, in or out of books. When I was a graduate student at Southern Mississippi and met him, I thought "Dickensian"; that was the only adjective that could approximate his uniqueness. More specifically, he was Pickwickian. After peddling a few miles on his bike to campus, he would assume a Buddha position on top of his desk, his cherub cheeks flushed. My first day in his class was "The first day of light which illumines the gloom, and converts into a dazzling brilliancy that obscurity in which the earlier history of the public career of the immortal Pickwick would appear to be involved. . . ," just like the introduction to Pickwick's oration inviting those "who had volunteered to share the perils of his travels, and who were destined to participate in the glories of his discoveries."

Forgive the sentimentality, but the man absolutely radiated with love for Victorian literature. With rapture, he tackled obscure works by men and women, never afraid to adventure into unknown territory, although I doubt if anything that came out of the nineteenth century struck him as unfamiliar or strange. Nonetheless, he often made it clear that he was reading assigned novels for the first time, right along with us. With the plethora of novels and poems written in that exquisitely pewter century, he just could not get his fill of reading and talking about them. And he, the Pickwickian, never traveled alone.

We were discussing *Is He Popenjoy?* when Harry (always Harry to everybody) mentioned that Trollope had had a mother who published oodles of novels. Then he scratched his head and looked up to the ceiling, which is where he always seemed to search for information. There he pulled out a figure of thirty-five novels. I jotted it down. How could Anthony Trollope, whose books take up more shelf space than any other Victorian in any store, have had a mother who wrote so many novels, and I had never heard of her? After all, as Harry would come to boast about me, I was majoring in extant Victorian women's writing (even though my dissertation would be on Dickens), but Frances Trollope was not a part of even that canon.

So Harry planted that tiny seed about Frances Trollope, and here I am, nearly a decade later, putting together a book that means to recognize a body of work that changed Britain and several parts of the rest of the world forever. *Frances Trollope and the Novel of Social Change* began with Harry. Alas, this kind, gentle, and good soul passed on just a few years after I received my doctorate at Southern Miss. But he is indelibly etched in my mind and heart as the Victorian with the eternal "juvenility of spirit" that "death will [not] terminate" (to quote again from *Pickwick Papers*).

Besides Harry, I would like to thank all of the contributors to this collection. They generously and happily wrote their chapters because, like me, they love Frances Trollope and her work. They believe in the merits of her written legacy, that it needs to be reprinted for contemporary consumption, and that it deserves serious scholarly attention. With a network of scholars focused on a single mission, producing a collection of criticism has been sheer delight. They have all been so encouraging and always laboring to produce a manuscript that would do honor to Fanny.

Unfortunately it requires a lot of work to get one's hands on a Frances Trollope novel. "Not *Domestic Manners of the Americans*," I keep telling Amazon.com. "I do not need another copy of that. Find me a Frances Trollope novel!" Most of them have not been reprinted in this century. Research university libraries that sequester their copies are reluctant to share, because, of course, the paper is so delicate and difficult to turn without tearing. However, I could not possibly lead a project extolling its virtues if I had not read the novels under query. This is where Paul Robards came in. He, the Technical Services Librarian at Middle Georgia College, has been my lifeline to the world of research. If not for his diligence in unearthing copies and his persuading/bribing/cajoling/ threatening library colleagues to lend me theirs, this manuscript could not have been possible. And if not for Paul and the Assistant Librarian for Public Services, Dr. Leslie Rampey, and all of our Wednesday lunches at the Middle Georgia Supper Club, I would not have been able to motivate myself enough to produce this manuscript alongside two others being published in the same year, all the while teaching at a two-year college.

I am in debt to their stimulating intellectual discussions over dumplings and their indefatigable love for reading and learning.

Finally, I must thank Frances Trollope, an obvious given in that the book is about her. After reading her biographies, especially those by Heineman, Ransom, and Neville-Sington, I will never forget this woman who constantly was given reasons for giving up, but who never did. She wrote her first book and embarked upon her world travels at age fifty-three. What a testimony to the rest of us who often feel that we cannot pull ourselves up again after being knocked down or that we are too old to start over. These thoughts never entered Fanny's mind. A number of the titles to her novels begin with "The Life and Adventures of." That is exactly how she perceived life: oodles of life and adventure, with no time for self-pity or doubt. She was a remarkable woman. If you would indulge me one more passage of Victorian sentimentality—I bet she and Harry are getting on famously.

Apis Trollopiana:
An Introduction to the Nearly Extinct Trollope

Brenda Ayres

In an 1838 review of *Vienna and the Austrians*, the *Spectator* identified Frances Trollope as an *apis Trollopiana*.[1] The scientific name refers to a species of honeybee, designating Mrs. Trollope as a satirist with a sting. Indeed Frances Trollope was a woman sensitive to social and legal injustices, and she used the pen to prick the conscience of her considerable readership. "Apis" without the italics refers to an ancient bull worshiped by the ancient Egyptians; Mrs. Trollope was often like a bull in a china closet. So spirited and passionate were her novels of protest, that most reviewers labeled her vulgar, indecent, unwomanly, unfeminine, profligate, vinegary, gross, coarse, and "Trollopian." Paradoxically, no statement so accurately summarizes Fanny's work as the one published in an 1839 issue of *New Monthly Magazine*: "No other author of the present day has been at once so much read, so much admired, and so much abused."[2]

Many caustic opinions would have already been printed about her by 1838 (the date of her travel book on Austria) in that Mrs. Trollope would have already induced controversy with three other travel books and five novels. Her first nonfiction work, a satire of America, threw her into the limelight. *Domestic Manners of the Americans* (1832) was written at a time when best-selling works were travel books. Hers outsold all of them to date, but critics railed it as coarse and indecent. One reviewer named her "a profligate woman" (qtd. in Heineman, *Mrs. Trollope* 94) and another called "the texture of her mind . . . essentially gross" (qtd. in 96). This calumny would become all too common as Trollope continued to write about what disturbed her and to write about it in a way that would disturb others.

The Refugee in America (1832) appeared on the wave of her success. A fictional version of her visit to America, it was not received very well. The critics then and perhaps more so now would agree that the narrative is contrived and the characters implausible—but no more than what one might expect from many of the domestic novels written by women in the nineteenth century. Jane Tompkins, in her well-known *Sensational Designs*, would have considered these as genre conventions, dismissed as nonliterary simply because they characterized many works by women (xi–xix). Early in the 1800s, Trollope's fictional work received as much attack as did many other women's novels on both sides of the Atlantic, and even more so because, beginning with *Refugee*, Trollope did not balk at dealing with social issues about which women were not supposed to know anything, much less have an opinion. Not only does her typical protagonist subvert domestic ideology by being a heroine who is independent and self-defining and is rewarded for being so, her other women do not aspire to a Victorian womanly ideal.

Her second novel, *The Abbess: a Romance* (1833), favors the gothic genre still popular at the time. In a narrative imbued with melodrama, an evil monk pursues an ingénue. That the novel was so characteristic of the genre may be the reason it met with positive reviews, which is ironic in that, like most gothic novels, it ripples with gender subversion. The story begins with a father who makes decisions for his daughter that nearly cost her life. He is the first of many patriarchs in the Trollope canon who, by simply being men, have the power to determine the destiny of women. These men, more often than not, are incompetent to make wise decisions. Trollope's women constantly suffer because of patriarchy, and if there are any saviors to be found in her novels, they are usually female.

Such is the case of *The Abbess*. The women, including the nuns, are believable, fully drawn characters who resort to fantasy in order to survive the constraints of convent life, constraints shared by most Victorian women and not by just those in convents. The abbess and her niece are the heroines who free themselves and other women from bonds of imprisonment.

From Ann Radcliffe's *The Mysteries of Udolpho* (1794) to Maria Edgeworth's *Castle Rackrent* (1800) to Mary Shelley's *Frankenstein* (1817) to Jane Austen's *Northanger Abbey* (1818), a number of women writers placed the evils of patriarchy under a magnifying glass. By the Victorian Period, it became essential to create and appoint an agent (a detective) to bring order to a battery of details that had left people feeling totally out of control and victims to evil wrongdoing. Making things right and making sure that the good were saved and the bad punished became the job and mission of the detective. Evolving from the gothic tradition came the truly first detective novels written, interestingly enough, by women. Moreover, the first true solver of crimes were not male detectives, but female characters. This is the case in Trollope's *Hargrave*, which was completed before Poe published *Murders in the Rue Morgue* and Catherine Crowe published her female detective novel, *Susan Hopley, or the Adventures of a Maid Servant*. Although Hargrave's women are victimized and a detective is hot on the trail of the villain, the women make all right for themselves and for society at large.

Tremordyn Cliff (1835) also subverts Victorian gender codes with its effeminate, incompetent patriarch who receives an inheritance in the place of a sister. This sister, Augusta, is much more capable of managing the family's financial and business affairs than is the brother. She schemes to murder him, a shocking, unacceptable form of behavior for a character that heretofore in this novel and in most sister-spouse stories by other writers, had been drawn as noble and admirable. When the plot is foiled, Augusta kills herself. Her desperation prefigures Kate Chopin's Edna Pontellier; the two are Victorians who learn that there is no place in society for an independent woman.

Of course, such a novel raised a number of eyebrows but not with the fervor and frequency that came with her next two novels. *The Life and Adventures of Jonathan Jefferson Whitlaw* (1836) her anti-slavery novel, predates Richard Hildreth's *The White Slave: or Memoirs of Archy Moore* as well as *Uncle Tom's Cabin* by fifteen years. Trollope's third novel, *The Vicar of Wrexhill* (1837), represents one of what would become several of her warnings about women's vulnerability being ruled and destroyed by religiously zealous men. A critic in *Gentleman's Magazine* accused her of seeing "many things no refined Englishwoman would have seen, or seeing would not have understood—still less have written and published" (qtd. in Heineman, *Frances Trollope* 96). With the release of every volume of her thirty-five novels, Mrs. Trollope would be deemed by critics as a traitor to her sex; no writer created as many heroines and stories that undermined Victorian gender politics. And no authoress attacked so many important social issues, such as slavery, evangelistic zeal, poor laws, the bastardy clause, labor, abuse and exploitation of laborers in industry, inheritance laws, hypocrisy, class pomposity, misdiagnosed/misunderstood mental illness, spinsterism, patriarchal oppression, and the dangers of marriage. If these were not fitting topics about which women should have been concerned, then what other issues could have had more direct bearing on their lives?

Apis Trollopiana sounds like an extinct species, and unfortunately, is another reason why the epithet befits Trollope. In the twentieth century, other than her *Domestic Manners* and two biographies, very few books have been reprinted and sold in a store like Barnes and Noble. This is a travesty because her novels have so much to contribute to Victorian studies. *Jessie Phillips* (1843), for one, strikes me as being much more realistic and knowledgeable than Dickens' *Oliver Twist* (1837) in its assault on the Poor Laws, especially in regard to the bastardy clause. Trollope's novel must have had a similar effect on many because one year after its release, the House of Commons returned rights to unwed mothers (Ransom, *Fanny Trollope* 152). Likewise *The Life and Adventures of Michael Armstrong* (1840) rings more true than *Hard Times* (1854), a novel about a factory class, about which Dickens has often been accused of knowing nothing. Trollope was a social commentator and provocateur of social change; the issues that she considered and often assailed put the modern reader closer to Victorian times. Furthermore, so many of her other novels offer perspectives not found in canonized works from the viewpoint of a woman who constantly had to deal with limitations placed upon her simply because she was a woman.

Aside from their own incisive and insight depictions of social plight, Trollope's groundbreaking texts greatly influenced other writers who are better known today than Trollope for their social satire. Yet Trollope is readily identifiable in works by her contemporaries and successors, such as Dickens, Thackeray, Charlotte Brontë, Stowe, Gaskell, and of course, her son, Anthony—as demonstrated by Heineman, Neville-Sington, Kissel Adams, and others in their chapters included in this collection.

Her novels also challenge domestic ideology, inviting immediacy with their characters and writer, so that the pain and betrayal that Trollope's women feel, the reader is to feel also. Although some modern readers may have trouble with the style of narrative in some of her novels—for example, with the frequent recap at different points in the novels, or another example, with the sentimentality and melodrama, or with, at times, lack of careful detail with setting and character development—nonetheless, these idiosyncrasies, I believe, can be explained within the literary context of nineteenth-century genre styles, a factor in itself of interest to Victorian scholars. Moreover, her style does often include beautiful lyrical description and powerful character development. Some of her caricatures and comic scenes are just as good as, if not better than, Dickens'. With an appropriate set of expectations, the modern reader will find Trollope's novels to be not only socially important to the study of Victorian culture, but also charming enough to give an enduring pleasure of the sort one expects from good literature. And some of the foibles of human nature that Trollope addressed in her century have not disappeared; Trollope still has something to say to the present-day reader.

The contributors to this collection share these sentiments. This is evident in the latest biography on Trollope by Pamela Neville-Sington. *Fanny Trollope: The Life and Adventures of a Clever Woman* is a critical biography that identifies the source for most of the key ingredients in each of Trollope's works. When one reads *Fanny Trollope*, one learns not only remarkable things about a remarkable woman, but one learns remarkable things about remarkable works by that woman. Neville-Sington's edition, introduction, and notes to Trollope's *Domestic Manners of the Americans* also bring Frances Trollope back to life. Unfortunately, this is the only book, nonfiction at that, that continues to be reprinted when Fanny's novels are simply delightful but dreadfully hard to find. Borrowing a title from one of Trollope's novels, *The Life and Adventures of a Clever Woman* (1854), Neville-Sington's chapter in this collection provides a brief biographical sketch of Fanny's life and publications. The chapter also estimates Fanny's influence on Anthony Trollope and the debt that he owed but never acknowledged. Chapter 1 additionally elaborates on Fanny and Charles Dickens as literary rivals and the effect of their work on each other's writing. Whether esteemed as a writer in her own right or as a writer that influenced others to great works, Frances Trollope deserves more than just a footnote in the annals of literary history.

No other scholar has written as much on Frances Trollope as Helen Heineman. She has authored *Mrs. Trollope: The Triumphant Feminine in the Nineteenth Century* and Trollope's biography for Twayne's *English Authors Critical Biography*. She also appreciates Trollope in *Restless Angels: The Friendship of Six Victorian Women*, as well as in *Three Victorians in the New World: Charles Dickens, Frances Trollope and Anthony Trollope*. Heineman's chapter, "Mrs. Frances Trollope: Triumphant Female Friendship in the Nineteenth Century," underscores Trollope's belief in the power of female friendships. Heineman hails Trollope's women as strong characters who undo the damage to the world caused by men who have been given power but lack the character and ethics to wield that power for good. Rarely do these women act alone and in pairs, in leagues, they pool their resources to combat issues that often affected Victorian women but rarely were within women's providence or legal arena to affect.

To the contrary, Priti Joshi finds Trollope's women morally and socially irresponsible and ineffective. "*Michael Armstrong*: Rereading the Industrial Plot" argues that the strength of Trollope's factory novel lies not in its plight of child-laborers but in its depiction and narration of one woman's struggle to know and understand the poor. Joshi draws a parallel between the exploitation of workers and the ignorance of middle-class Victorian women. Instead of portraying women as morally superior as did many other factory novelists, Trollope describes the painful discovery of women's collaboration with class privilege and brutality. Such perspective places the responsibility equally upon women of the upper classes for the deplorable conditions of factory workers. At the same time, Trollope's novel reflects ambivalence as to what women can do to effect change, being as much restrained by gender boundaries as were laborers by class.

Clearly Frances Trollope was outraged at factory conditions, especially pertaining to child labor. Perhaps she was, as Priti Joshi suggests, frustrated by class propensities that continued to exacerbate those conditions, and even more frustrated by gender dynamics that prohibited women from social, legal, and political activism. Yet, just as clearly, Frances Trollope was no woman to remain silent or complicit about the plight of the lower classes. Ann-Barbara Graff applauds Trollope's literary activism, her efforts to inform the social conscience of her readers, especially female readers. She transformed domestic fiction into protest against systemic weakness and inequity. On the heels of Joshi's treatment of *Michael Armstrong* comes this study of *Jessie Phillips*. "Fair, Fat and Forty" explores Trollope's attack on Poor Law reforms, and in particular, the bastardy clause. As in *Michael Armstrong*, Trollope finds as much wrong about attempts in British law to resolve social evils among the lower classes as she does about those same laws that impair mostly women. Just as the New Poor Law aimed to obliterate the poor by enclosing them in workhouses, thus both putting them out of sight and killing them—psychologically, socially, and physically—so did the bastardy clause enclose women in a mortal gridlock, placing on them the sole burden of providing for their children when they could not secure employment because of their gender, while fathers were excused from any obligations. Again, Trollope abhors the dependent status of women and the implications of gender restrictions.

One area in which women could exert power and legitimate influence was in religion. As Ann Douglas points out, here was a rare site for female power in a time when society viewed women as being spiritually superior to men. Even though nearly all denominations in Britain were controlled by men, women—viewed as the moral guardians of the empire—often exercised and mobilized aggressive political and social pressure through churches to bring about change. However, Fanny saw women's religious fervor also as a site of entrapment in which women often were exploited by men who took advantage of their earnestness to surrender all to God through "God's instruments," who were often unscrupulous and dissolute curates and priests. *Domestic Manners* (1832), *Vicar of Wrexhill* (1837), and *Father Eustace* (1847) satirize evangelical religion and warn of its peril to women. Besides religious fanaticism, in "A Serious Epidemic: Frances Trollope and the Evangelical Movement," Douglas Murray sees Trollope's works, especially *Vicar*, as purveyors of Tory/High-Church objections to Evangelicalism. Her three works uniquely historicize and criticize the Evangelical Movement, warning against its irrevocable effects on British and American perspectives, effects that would continue into the twentieth century and the next through fundamentalism.

The next two chapters focus on Trollope's depiction of women and aging. In the first, "Marriageable at Midlife," Kay Heath praises Trollope for breaking tradition by depicting widows as capable women who find opportunities and liberties in their unmarried state impossible for other women. Writing about the 1850s, W. R. Greg was alarmed at the over one million unmarried women in England. He called them "redundant women"; they were abnormalities because, in their unmarried states, they did not "sweeten[ ] and embellish[ ] the existence of others" (276). Frances Trollope, constantly thrown into financial crises because of her husband, perceived life for the unmarried woman in quite a different manner. Her widows' novels celebrate the capacity of the woman, especially when she is free from performing the demands of males. Heath detects the influence of Frances Trollope's *The Widow Barnaby* (1839) on Anthony Trollope's *Can You Forgive Her?* (1864). She emphasizes the former's defiance of social strictures on women and identifies the inheritance of that same defiance in the son's work.

The second chapter on aging, "Figuring Age and Race: Frances Trollope's Matronalia" by Mary Wilson Carpenter, recognizes Trollope as a woman who combined anti-agism with feminism and anti-racism. The true heroine of *The Life and Adventures of Jonathan Jefferson Whitlaw* (1836) is Juno, a black woman of more than seventy years of age. Juno's owner and vicious overseer (Whitlaw) live in terror of her and constantly yield to her commanding presence. Trollope values the power of not only the older woman, but also the power of a woman of color, thereby expressing a feminist and anti-racist view that was way ahead of other writings of the time.

After these considerations, two chapters survey Trollope's literary style and influence. The first is by Constance Harsh, well known for her *Subversive Heroines: Feminist Resolutions of Social Crisis in the Condition-of-England Novel*. "Putting Idiosyncrasy in Its Place: *Michael Armstrong* in Light of Trollope's Early Fiction" evaluates the novel's unique contribution to the condition-of-England novel through Trollope's mixing of concerns that had already emerged in her earliest fiction: her fascination with baroque horrors (*Jonathan Jefferson Whitlaw*), her penchant for

social comedy (*The Widow Barnaby*), her critique of patriarchal authority (*The Abbess*), and her focus on bands of like-minded people rather than
alienated individuals (*The Refugee in America*). This mixture is partly
responsible for the outré character that in its own time made *Michael
Armstrong* the most notorious member of its genre.

The last chapter on style and influence recognizes Trollope's innovative contribution to the early crime fiction. Predating those detective
novels by Edgar Allan Poe, Wilkie Collins, Charles Dickens, and of course,
Arthur Conan Doyle, *Hargrave* premiers a delightful detective, M. Collet,
who has to prove that an elusive Parisian jewel thief is none other than a
gentleman by the name of Hargrave. This, however, is not the only quan-
dary to be resolved. To Linde Katritzky the most engaging mystery of
the novel is whether two young women can marry the men they love
when their father stands between them and happiness. Besides situating
Hargrave in literary history, Katritzky's appreciates the multiple layers,
social satire, and inventive narrative style in her chapter, "The Intriguing
Case of *Hargrave*: A Tragi-Comedy of Manners."

Frances Trollope and the Novel of Social Change closes with two chapters that add two more compelling reasons as to why contemporary readers would want to read Trollope. The first is written by Linda Abess Ellis,
author of *Frances Trollope's America*. In a personable, self-revelatory style,
one that blurs the lines between fiction and nonfiction in perfectly typical Trollopian fashion, "Fanny Who?" asserts the value of reprinting
Trollope's novels and travel books. Linda Ellis takes an excursion to the
New York Public Library where she meets up with Frances Trollope. The
authoress instantly introduces herself as Fanny, not Frances, not Mrs.
Trollope, and definitely not Anthony's mother. Before Linda knows what's
what, Fanny, at age seventy-four, is crawling on all fours through some
ruins in Germany or tying her to a donkey in a gale while crossing the
Alps or giving her the mum at some soiree or excoriating America for its
false advertisements of freedom. Fanny proves an indefatigable travel companion who has something witty and wise to say about everything, and
lives life as an adventure inside a book.

The second chapter is written by Susan S. Kissel Adams, author of *In
Common Cause: The "Conservative" Frances Trollope and the "Radical"
Frances Wright*. "Frances Trollope's 'Modern' Influence: Creating New
Fictions, New Readers, a New World" measures Fanny's literary legacy—
the way in which she affected the writing style, content, and characterization of some of the writers who were her contemporaries as well as her
successors. Because of her moral courage, her willingness to take risks as
well as to create new types of heroines, encourage reform, and be frank
with her readers, Frances Trollope helped to modernize the fiction of her
times and open up new possibilities for the world's literary future.

The purpose of this collection, then, is to increase awareness of the contributions that Frances Trollope has made to literature with the hope that her works will return to print and that this nearly extinct species can be saved. If there had not been a Frances Trollope, there would not have been an Anthony, obviously, but would there have been a Dickens and a few other notable Victorian authors? One might wonder what works, perspectives, narrative styles, and social commentaries would not have developed in the Victorian canon if not for the effect Trollope had on the literary world and the world's perspectives concerning such crucial issues as slavery, rights of the poor and the working classes, and the political position of women. Most assuredly much social reform would have taken longer to bring about or would not have happened at all without someone like Trollope making injustice a moral outcry. The literati might continue in its neglect, failing to give credit where credit is due to Frances Trollope, as literary history has unfortunately done, but if one erases Trollope from the equation, one simply does not have the same British literature or British history as it is known today. Likewise one must want to consider what will be lost if Trollope continues to be ignored, as well as what can be gained if her works are revived, made readily available to a contemporary and future readership, and reappraised for their literary, cultural, and historical values. Plenty of Trollopian life and adventure lie in store that should no longer be denied to readers who love Victorian literature.

NOTES

1. The full statement follows: "The tourist was satisfied with the city, and all that it inhabit; and honey is less pungent than gall, especially when produced from the *apis Trollopiana*" (*Spectator* 11 [1838]: 210). With Trollope's literary reputation of being sardonic, this reviewer found it remarkable that her travels through Austria proved to her liking, and the country was spared her usual assault.

2. Qtd. in F. E. Trollope 1895: 4.

1

The Life and Adventures of a Clever Woman

Pamela Neville-Sington

In the back parking lot of the University of London Library there is a plaque that reads:

> FRANCES TROLLOPE (1780–1863)[1]
> Author, lived at 16 Keppel Street
> Near this site. Her sons, the authors
> THOMAS ADOLPHUS TROLLOPE
> (1810–1892) and
> ANTHONY TROLLOPE
> (1815–1882)
> were born there.

At the unveiling, which took place on June 15, 2000, the master of Birkbeck College remarked that the plaque was the University's way of saying "sorry" for tearing down, seventy years earlier, the Trollopes' family home—and most everything else in Keppel Street—to make way for the Stalinesque monolith that is Senate House.

Frances Trollope's name nearly did not appear on the plaque; it was originally intended to commemorate only one Trollope family member, her more famous son Anthony. For more than a century, Frances Trollope has been overshadowed by her youngest son's renown. Yet, during his lifetime, it was Anthony who had to struggle to come out from under his mother's shadow, so great was her fame. Frances' influence on her son was enormous: not only did he adopt her good working habits (rising between 4:00 and 5:00 A.M. to write before breakfast), but he also adapted many of her best plots and characters. Anthony, however, never acknowledged his mother's importance, and the disparaging remarks about her books that he made in his autobiography helped to bury her literary reputation. But recently critics and readers have begun to restore the balance, as this collection of essays and the Keppel Street plaque—where Frances Trollope receives top billing above her son—testify.

The master of Birkbeck might also have mentioned the other literary figures associated with Keppel Street. Jane Austen visited her brother Charles when he stayed with his in-laws at No. 22, and Charles Dickens' father breathed his last in a room on Keppel Street, with his son by his side. As far as we know, Jane Austen never met the Trollopes in Keppel Street, and the death of Charles Dickens' father occurred many years after the Trollope family had left the area. Nevertheless, their lives did intersect in significant ways. Jane Austen and Frances Trollope, born in 1775 and 1779 respectively, were almost exact contemporaries, and they both grew up, daughters of clergymen, in the West Country—a fact that informs their fiction. However, Jane Austen had been long dead and her novels somewhat out of fashion when Frances Trollope published her first book. As far as her life as an author was concerned, Mrs. Trollope was a contemporary of Charles Dickens. Old enough to be Dickens' mother, she was his literary rival in the late 1830s and early 1840s when both authors were moved to expose the evils of rapid industrialization and urbanization.

At one time or another during her life, Frances Trollope's popularity matched, and even exceeded, that of Jane Austen, Charles Dickens, and her son Anthony—despite what he would have had us believe. Mrs. Trollope was far more than the mother of a famous novelist, and, as I hope to show in this brief biographical essay, she deserves to take her rightful place alongside these other writers whose paths crossed (figuratively speaking) on Keppel Street.

DAYS OF THE REGENCY

Frances Milton Trollope was born in Bristol on March 10, 1779, the middle child of William Milton, vicar of Heckfield, Hampshire; and of his first wife, Mary, daughter of Francis Gresley of Bristol and his wife Cecily. Her maternal grandfather, a respected apothecary who lived in Bristol's fashionable Queen Square, could boast Norman ancestry. Her paternal grandfather, however, was in trade, variously described as a "distiller" and "saddler" of Bristol.

The Rev. William Milton took up the living of Heckfield in 1774, but after only a year he installed a curate and moved, first to Bristol, then to the nearby village of Stapleton, and eventually to Clifton, a fashionable spa town overlooking the city. He was one of that breed of nineteenth-century clergymen who dabbled in the new sciences and engineering, and his most important idea was the creation of a tidal bypass to control the water levels of the Avon, thus allowing ships to sail in and out of Bristol more freely. Of his three children, Frances—or "Fanny," as she was known to her friends and family—resembled her father most. Like him, she was incapable of sitting still and doing nothing if there was a problem to be solved or a situation to be improved. Her mother died when Fanny was only five or six years old, and she had to learn to be self-reliant. Together, these traits—initiative, tenacity, and independence of mind—were to give her the courage, strength, and ability to overcome the many crises that she would have to face in her lifetime; but they also made her sometimes act rashly, without thinking, and thus court disaster.

In 1800 William Milton remarried. His second wife was Sarah Partington of Clifton. The following year, after a twenty-seven-year absence, he returned to the quiet Hampshire village of Heckfield with his family to resume his duties as vicar. Fanny was twenty-two years old.

To imagine the world in which the young Fanny Milton lived, one need go no further than the novels of Jane Austen. Jane was only four years Fanny's senior. Jane's father was, like William Milton, a clergyman; their parishes were both situated in the Hampshire deanery of Basingstoke. Jane and Fanny would thus have admired the same red coats of the local militia, visited the same milliners' shops, worn the same fashions, subscribed to the same circulating libraries, and danced in the same assembly rooms above Basingstoke's town hall. They enjoyed the same pastimes: dancing, country walks, amateur theatricals, and reading. They would also have shared similar dreams of marriage and children. They were both to discover, however, that women who had too little money and too much learning did not find husbands easily. Extraordinarily, it seems that the two young women never met. In the same year, 1801, that Rev. Milton and his family returned to Heckfield, the Austens moved from Steventon to Bath.

THE LOTTERY OF MARRIAGE

The relationship between Fanny and her stepmother was never very close. Within three years of her father's marriage, she and her sister Mary, twenty-four and twenty-seven years old respectively, moved to London to keep house, at No. 27 Keppel Street, for their younger brother Henry, a clerk in the War Office. Fanny had a petite figure, a pleasant face, and "the neatest foot and ankle" on the dance floor (F. E. Trollope 1895: 2: 286). But she was also intelligent, well read, and outspoken—in a word, "blue"—and she was still a spinster when at twenty-nine she met the shy, sober barrister, Thomas Anthony Trollope. He was five years her senior and a neighbor in Keppel Street.

After a year's courtship, on May 23, 1809, Fanny and Thomas Anthony married and settled into conventional domesticity at No. 16 Keppel Street. Fanny loved to entertain and tended toward what we might call today "champagne socialism." Her friend Mary Russell Mitford later recalled that Mrs. Trollope "used to be such a Radical that her house in London was a perfect emporium of escaped criminals" (L'Estrange 3: 241)—that is, political refugees. Over the next nine years Fanny gave birth to seven children: Thomas Adolphus, Henry, Arthur, Anthony (the last to be born in the Keppel Street house), Cecilia, and Emily. The Trollopes' first-born daughter, another Emily, survived only long enough to be privately baptized.

Fanny adored her children, and her oldest son, Tom, had happy memories of the nursery: "My mother's disposition . . . was of the most genial, cheerful, happy, *enjoué* nature imaginable . . . and to any one of us a *tête-à-tête* with her was preferable to any other disposal of a holiday hour" (T. A. Trollope 1887: 1: 59). Fanny had the knack of making almost anything fun, even learning. By contrast, Thomas Anthony, whose great ambition was that his sons should follow in his footsteps to Winchester and New College, meted out punishment with a pull of the hair for any blunder made in reciting their lessons.

The Trollopes' secure world eventually began to fall apart. As the years passed, Thomas Anthony became ever more argumentative and erratic, almost certainly owing to the effects of calomel, a mercury-based drug that he took for chronic migraines. Although he had no experience farming, Thomas Anthony leased some 160 acres in Harrow from John, Lord Northwick, in 1816. The Trollopes moved to Julian Hill (Anthony Trollope's model for Orley Farm) and set about improving the property. Two years later they built a large house, christened Julians after the Hertfordshire estate of his uncle Adolphus Meetkerke, which Thomas Anthony expected to inherit. His prospects were dashed when the old man married and produced an heir in 1819. The Trollopes' finances went from bad to worse during the agricultural depression of the 1820s, and in 1824 their twelve-year-old son Arthur died of tuberculosis.

THE REFUGEE IN AMERICA

When Henry Trollope, fun-loving but idle, left Winchester in 1826 before completing his studies, his father was furious: he could not afford to support an indolent son. Within a year Thomas Anthony announced that financial pressures made it necessary to move yet again, this time to a run-down farmhouse. In an almost desperate act Fanny, Henry, and her two young daughters set sail for America on November 4, 1827, to join the charismatic reformer Frances Wright at Nashoba, a community in the backwoods of Tennessee dedicated to the education and emancipation of slaves. Frances Wright, one of the Trollopes' radical friends, had been a frequent guest at Harrow. Fanny thought the New World was Henry's best chance to find a good prospect in life; she also hoped to ease the family's financial burdens back home while escaping her husband's dreadful temper. She left her two remaining sons, Tom and Anthony, at home to continue their education. When her friend's utopian dream turned out to be a malaria-ridden swamp, Fanny decamped and headed up the Mississippi to Cincinnati, Ohio, then a booming frontier town dubbed the "Athens of the West."

Fanny's life in Cincinnati was a tragicomedy of failed business ventures, scandal, and illness. In an early effort to make money she devised the "Infernal Regions," a Dantesque spectacle featuring waxworks and electric currents. But Fanny's most ambitious undertaking was the Cincinnati Bazaar, which might arguably be deemed America's first shopping mall. The townspeople failed to patronize it, and Fanny ended up bankrupt and deathly ill with malaria. Cincinnati society never accepted Fanny. She had arrived in the city penniless, without references, and in the company, not of her husband, but of a young French artist, Auguste Hervieu, who despite the gossip was in fact nothing more than a devoted friend without whose help the Trollopes would have starved. After two miserable years in Cincinnati, Fanny admitted defeat and retreated to the East Coast, where she traveled for a year before returning to England in August 1831.

Fanny turned her experiences to good effect in her *Domestic Manners of the Americans*, published in March 1832, just three days before the final reading of the Reform Bill in the House of Commons. Since well before Fanny's homecoming, the entire country had been obsessed with the Reform Bill, an attempt to introduce democratic reforms to the parliamentary system by extending the franchise and abolishing the "Rotten Boroughs." The Bill's supporters held up America as a beacon of democracy and an example to be followed. The United States had long been regarded as the great democratic experiment, and every travel book about America was received as if it were a "party pamphlet," as John Stuart Mill remarked (qtd. in Mullen 2). It was in this politically charged atmosphere that Fanny wrote the final version of her preface to *Domestic Manners of the Americans*:

> Although much has already been written on the great experiment, as it has been called, now making in government, on the other side of the Atlantic, there appears to be still room for many interesting details on the influence

which the political system of the country has produced on the principles, tastes, and manners, of its domestic life. . . . By describing faithfully, the daily aspect of ordinary life, she [Fanny writes in the third person] has endeavoured to shew how greatly the advantage is on the side of those who are governed by the few, instead of the many. The chief object she has had in view is to encourage her countrymen to hold fast by a constitution that ensures all the blessings which flow from established habits and solid principles. (1997: 11)

Mrs. Trollope, who left England something of a liberal, had returned home very much a conservative. After her experience of the frontier, she felt strongly that American democracy was seriously flawed and should not be hailed as a paradigm of government. As far as she was concerned, that sacred American phrase "All men are created equal" was merely "mischievous sophistry." Fanny was clear-sighted enough to perceive that true equality was an impossibility in the United States of the 1820s: deep-seated prejudice barred racial equality, and economic equality was simply nonsense. Thus, she was happy to lend her support to the Tory cause in Britain. But, more importantly, she needed this first publication, which was, after all, from the pen of an unknown woman writer, to be a financial success. With all this in mind, Fanny cannily threw her controversial book into the political fray, hoping that the ensuing hubbub would make it a bestseller.

Her strategy worked. *Domestic Manners of the Americans* "sold like wildfire" (F. E. Trollope 1895: 1: 151), as the publisher John Murray noted, going through four English editions in the first year. To "trollopize," that is "to abuse the American nation," became a recognized verb in the English language. But, of course, the outcry was loudest in America. The English traveler E. T. Coke, residing in New York when the first American editions of the book appeared in the summer of 1832, wrote: "the commotion it created amongst the good citizens is truly inconceivable . . . and the tug of war was hard, whether the 'Domestic Manners,' or cholera, which burst upon them simultaneously, should be the more engrossing topic of conversation. . . . At every table d'hôte, on board of every steam-boat, in every stage-coach, and in all societies, the first question was, 'Have you read Mrs Trollope?'" (167–68). *Domestic Manners of the Americans* became the touchstone against which subsequent accounts of the United States were judged, and its publication launched Fanny's career as a writer.

FASHIONABLE LIFE

The earnings from *Domestic Manners* allowed the Trollopes to move back to their old home, Julian Hill, and live in relative comfort while

Fanny continued to write. Her husband had long since given up his law practice, and Fanny was now the sole breadwinner. However, despite three more books from her pen in two years, the debts incurred by the Harrow farm and Cincinnati Bazaar proved too great, and the Trollopes were forced to flee to Bruges to escape debtors' prison. Within a year both Fanny's beloved twenty-three-year-old son Henry and her husband were dead: the former from tuberculosis, the latter from the effects of mercury poisoning. Thomas Anthony's death came almost as a relief. Anthony later remarked that the touch of his father's hand "seemed to create failure. . . . But the worse [*sic*] curse to him of all was a temper so irritable that even those he loved the best could not endure it. We were all estranged from him, and yet I believed he would have given his heart's blood for any of us. His life as I knew it was one long tragedy" (A. Trollope, *Autobiography* 1987: 26).

Fanny was free to return to England after her husband's death, but she did not settle in any one spot for long. From 1836 she lived in Monken Hadley, a village north of London, until her eldest daughter Cecilia announced her engagement to John Tilley, one of Anthony's Post Office colleagues. After a brief period in London at 20 York Street, Portman Square, Fanny undertook to build a house in Penrith, Cumbria, christened Carlton Hill, to be near Cecilia and her husband, who was by this time (1841) surveyor of the north of England. But within a year Fanny had made up her mind to leave Carlton Hill: she found both the neighbors and the weather too dull. In 1843 she fulfilled her lifelong dream of visiting Italy, and there she remained for the rest of her life. From 1850 she shared the Villino Trollope, in the Piazza dell'Indipendenza, with her son Thomas Adolphus, and his wife Theodosia, also writers.

In 1849 Cecilia, thirty-three years old and the mother of five, died from tuberculosis. Consumption had been the family curse: as well as her two sons Arthur and Henry, Fanny had also lost eighteen-year-old Emily to the disease in 1836. Throughout it all Fanny supported her family with her writing: six travel books and thirty-five novels over a period of twenty-five years. Anthony Trollope recalled that "the doctor's vials and the ink-bottle held equal places in my mother's rooms. . . . Her power of dividing herself into two parts, and keeping her intellect by itself clear from the world, and fit for the duty it had to do, I never saw equalled" (A. Trollope, *Autobiography* 1987: 24).

As her son Tom testified, Fanny had the remarkable ability to "throw sorrow off when the cause of it had passed" (T. A. Trollope 1887: 1: 299). Fanny seemed to have boundless energy to host at-homes, devise charades, stage amateur theatricals, and organize picnics for family and friends. Yet she was invariably at her desk between 4:00 and 5:00 the following morning to write the allotted number of pages before breakfast. Anthony's wife

Rose said of her: "There was nothing conventional about her, and yet she was perfectly free from the vice of affectation. . . . She was lavishly generous as regards money; full of impulse; not free from prejudice—but more often in *favour* of people than otherwise,—but once in her good books, she was certain to be true to you. She could say a sarcastic word, but never an ill-natured one" (F. E. Trollope 1895: 2: 244). Over the years her circle of friends encompassed such diverse characters as the actors Edmund Kean and William Charles Macready; the political figures Ugo Foscolo, General Lafayette, and Prince Metternich; the reformer Frances Wright; the artists George Hayter and Hiram Powers; and the authors Mary Russell Mitford, Charles Dickens, and Elizabeth Barrett Browning.

TRAVELS AND TRAVELERS

The author of *Domestic Manners of the Americans* thought of herself first and foremost as a travel writer. Mrs. Trollope was writing during a period of great social upheaval, and not only in England but across Europe there was demand for political reform. European regimes were toppled and constitutions drafted. Her later travel books chart the often-subtle shifts in the volatile political climate as well as in her own attitude toward democratic reform.

In 1833 Fanny had set off for northern Europe with a view to "discover the real state of political feeling in the countries through which we travelled." Her experiences and observations of American society still dominated her political outlook. In *Belgium and Western Germany* (1834) Fanny insists that the "revolution" in Germany had been largely exaggerated by the radical British press. However, there was no room for such partiality in *Paris and the Parisians* (1836). Louis-Philippe's chaotic regime forced Fanny to realize that to give a coherent narrative of events was next to impossible and nothing could be taken for granted. "I found good where I looked for mischief," she confessed in the Preface to *Paris and the Parisians*, "strength where I anticipated weakness."

Vienna and the Austrians (1837) represents the real turning point in Mrs. Trollope's political outlook. For Fanny, the conservative Prince Metternich and the country he governed stood for those old-fashioned virtues, political stability, and social refinement, which were then under threat in the rest of Europe. However, her confidence in the old order was seriously undermined by the absurd and reactionary rules of exclusion—"cabalistic little vagaries" Fanny calls them—practiced by *la crème* of Viennese society. (Mrs. Trollope was the first English author to use the phrase "*la crème de la crème*.")

Her last travel book, *A Visit to Italy* (1842), suggests that Fanny had never wholly abandoned her radical sympathies. Since the early days of her marriage, when she welcomed Italian patriots such as Ugo Foscolo to her home in Keppel Street, Fanny had taken an interest in the struggle for Italian independence. Neither her disillusionment with American democracy nor her admiration for one of Italy's main oppressors, Metternich's Austria, had altered her view that Italy was a nation of heroes.

Despite her renown as a travel writer, Fanny calculated that traveling costs were outstripping her earnings. After the publication of *Vienna and the Austrians*, she decided to concentrate on writing novels.

"TICHOLAS TICKLEBY": FANNY TROLLOPE AND CHARLES DICKENS

Fanny's fiction was hugely popular in its day. Thackeray once confessed, "I do not care to read ladies' novels, except those of Mesdames Gore and Trollope."[2] "Certainly no other author has been so much read, so much admired, and so much abused," declared one critic.[3] Mrs. Trollope astutely aimed to hit the somewhat lowbrow taste of the circulating library, and this, as another critic noted, she did "remarkably well."[4] Jane Austen had once declared that, even for the sake of "Profit or Popularity," she "could not sit seriously down to write a serious Romance under any other motive than to save my Life."[5] Fanny had no choice: the lives of her children depended on the income from her novels. By 1839 she could command the huge sum of £800 per manuscript.

Early on Fanny experimented with several different genres, including the gothic novel (*The Abbess*, 1833). In her later novels, whether set in a cathedral town, a country estate, or London's West End, Fanny combined witty social commentary with strong and often melodramatic plots. At its best, her writing is subtle and well observed and, even in the most farfetched romance, she is able to convey with great skill the foibles and follies of human nature—and of English manners in particular.

But, above all, Mrs. Trollope excelled in biting satire and broad humor. Two of her best novels are *The Vicar of Wrexhill* (1837), which ridicules evangelicalism, and *The Widow Barnaby* (1839), whose "heroine" is a female rogue, struggling to make something of herself without the advantages of youth or a large income. In *The Widow Barnaby*, set in the West Country of their youth, Fanny gives a nod and a wink to Jane Austen's fiction. The heroine's sister is carried off, at age fifteen, by a redcoated officer, as was the young Lydia Bennet in *Pride and Prejudice*—the scoundrel's name is Willoughby, the name of the man who steals Marianne Dashwood's affections in *Sense and Sensibility*. Fanny turned her popular *Widow Barnaby* into a fictional series, an innovation in the English novel, with two sequels, *The Widow Married* (1840) and *The Barnabys in America* (1843).

Mrs. Trollope also wrote novels that dealt with social themes, such as the Poor Law. Her powerful anti-slavery novel *Jonathan Jefferson Whitlaw* (1836) preceded *Uncle Tom's Cabin* by more than fifteen years. For a time, Dickens saw her as a serious rival. In March 1839, at the height of her popularity, Mrs. Trollope produced the first monthly number of her latest novel, *The Life and Adventures of Michael Armstrong*. Her publisher, the unscrupulous Henry Colburn, announced that *Michael Armstrong* was to be "printed and embellished uniformly" with *Pickwick Papers* and *Nicholas Nickleby*—neither of which he published.

Dickens, who was still churning out monthly installments of *Nicholas Nickleby*, was annoyed but not surprised by Colburn's crude tactics. What did make him angry was the fact that Mrs. Trollope had scooped him. Dickens had intended to expose the inhuman working conditions in the Manchester cotton mills in *Nicholas Nickleby*. However, he abandoned his plans when he realized that Mrs. Trollope had beaten him to it in *Michael Armstrong*, set in Manchester and subtitled *The Factory Boy*. "If Mrs Trollope were even to adopt Ticholas Tickleby as being a better-sounding name than Michael Armstrong," Dickens wrote at the time, "I don't think it would cost me a wink of sleep, or impair my appetite in the smallest degree." "I will express no further opinion of Mrs Trollope," he added, "than that I think Mr Trollope must have been an old dog and chosen his wife from the same species."[6]

Dickens obviously had difficulty coming to terms with the fact that his main competitor was a woman, and one, moreover, who was old enough to be his mother. Both writers had a journalist's nose for a good story. They were equally at home with broad comedy and the "social novel." Fanny shared with Dickens the physical stamina and facility with the pen required to keep two books going simultaneously in monthly issues (she was the only female novelist at the time to do so). And Fanny excelled her young male rival in one thing: Dickens' female characters pale (literally) before her strong and vibrant women, of all ages, who think and act for themselves.

The rivalry continued. When, in 1840, Dickens set out for the United States, he was determined to like the new, burgeoning democracy—in defiance of the opposite view put forth by Fanny in *Domestic Manners of the Americans* a decade earlier. However, Dickens was as disappointed in the great democratic experiment as Fanny had been. His travel book, *American Notes*, was judged by the critics in terms of the *Domestic Manners*. Dickens was both praised and condemned for "Trollopizing" (Neville-Sington, *Fanny* 308). While writing *Martin Chuzzlewit* (1843–44), his first novel following his return to England, Dickens hoped to boost flagging sales by having his young hero set out on a ship bound for America to make his fortune. But the New World was not big enough for both Martin Chuzzlewit and Martha Barnaby, Fanny Trollope's larger-than-life creation whose adventures in *The Barnabys in America* had already been before the public for a year. Sales of *Martin Chuzzlewit* never really recovered (309).

Nevertheless, Dickens' sobering experience in the United States gave him a better understanding of Mrs. Trollope and the reputation that had been thrust upon her as the author of *Domestic Manners of the Americans*. His manners toward her became decidedly more gentle and respectful, and in December 1842 he confessed to her: "I am convinced that there is no Writer who has so well and accurately (I need not add, so entertainingly) described [America], in many of its aspects, as you have done."[7] The lives of these two literary lions would become inextricably linked when Dickens introduced Frances Ternan, the sister of his mistress, Nelly, to Mrs. Trollope in Florence. Miss Ternan eventually became the wife of Fanny Trollope's eldest son, Tom, and in 1895 she published the first biography of her mother-in-law.

THE ADVENTURES OF A YOUTH OF GENIUS: ANTHONY TROLLOPE AND HIS MOTHER

Fanny died on October 6, 1863, at age eighty-four, peacefully in her bed; she lies buried in the English Cemetery in Florence. She had retained her popularity to the end, despite the fact that her sharp satirical wit, and much of her subject matter, were considered increasingly "coarse" and "vulgar" as Victoria's reign progressed. In its review of her last novel, *Fashionable Life* (1856), *The Critic* deemed Mrs. Trollope "the *doyenne* of English authoresses."[8]

In 1855, the year before Fanny laid down her pen for the last time, Anthony's novel *The Warden* appeared. Though his fourth book, it was his first critical and commercial hit. His mother had helped him find a publisher for his first novel, *The Macdermots of Ballycloran* (1847). It was not a success. *The Athenaeum* suggested that Mr. A. Trollope find another name, for he "comes before the public with the disadvantage of not being the popular writer for whom careless readers might have mistaken him."[9] Anthony gave his second novel, *The Kellys and the O'Kellys* (1848), an Irish setting, like the first. It fared no better than the *Macdermots* and his publisher, Colburn (who was also his mother's publisher) told Anthony that Irish novels were not popular; moreover, he added, "it is impossible for me to give any encouragement to you to proceed in novel writing."[10] Undeterred, the young author set his next two works, *La Vendée* and a play, *The Noble Jilt*, in eighteenth-century Europe. It was almost as if

Anthony dared not venture into the sphere of contemporary English manners, which he knew so well, because he feared further comparisons with Fanny's writing. Anthony showed *The Noble Jilt* to his mother's old friend, the actor-manager George Bartley, who told him it was no good.[11] Despite his reservations, Colburn did bring out *La Vendée* in 1850, but historical subjects were about as fashionable as Irish ones. For his next literary venture, Anthony finally accepted his destiny and wrote *The Warden*, a novel set in the England of his day.

The publication of *The Warden* marks the moment when Anthony Trollope came into his inheritance, the Trollopian realm for which he would become famous but which was his mother's before him. As one critic noted, the English clergy, from the poor country curate to "haughty, dictatorial, heartless Bishops and preferment-seeking Rectors" had been considered Fanny Trollope's province since the publication of *The Vicar of Wrexhill* in 1837.[12] She set the scene for one of her later novels, *Petticoat Government* (1850), in a cathedral town "which we will distinguish by the name of Westhampton—chiefly because we know of no town so called." Just five years later, Anthony tells his readers that *The Warden* takes place in a cathedral town, "let us call it Barchester. Were we to name Wells or Salisbury, Exeter, Hereford, or Gloucester, it might be presumed that something personal was intended." Anthony later claimed that, when he wrote *The Warden*, he had "never lived in any cathedral city . . . never knew anything of any Close, and at that time had enjoyed no peculiar intimacy with any clergyman" (A. Trollope 1987: 71). This is somewhat disingenuous: he knew the clergy through his mother. Fanny's father had been a West Country clergyman; family holidays were often spent in the cathedral town of Exeter visiting her cousin; and Mrs. Trollope had famously clashed with their Harrow neighbor, the evangelical Reverend John Cunningham, over the godliness of charades (among other matters).

Anthony continued to draw on his mother's fictional world, a world filled not only with clergymen but also with strong-minded women. Some are high-spirited and warm-hearted like Kate Harrington in Fanny's *Uncle Walter* and Lady Mary Palliser in Anthony's *The Duke's Children*—both determined to marry the men they love in the face of parental opposition. There are also haughty, ambitious, and selfish women who have long since learned that they cannot afford to fall in love: such are Cassandra de Laurie in Fanny's *Lottery of Marriage* and Arabella Trefoil in Anthony's *American Senator*.

Central to the plots of both authors are an alarming number of motherless heroines and interfering aunts, such as Martha Barnaby and her niece Agnes Willoughby in Fanny's *The Widow Barnaby*. Martha's bumptious nature and amorous exploits reappear in the character of Arabella

Greenow in Anthony's *Can You Forgive Her?*, where they provide light relief to the main story of the motherless Alice Vavasor's dithering. Mrs. Greenow, like Martha Barnaby, marries late and well, and is widowed early. They both enjoy their newly acquired wealth by sporting luxurious widows' weeds, cambric handkerchiefs, and crocodile tears while carrying on flirtations with bogus military men, much to the embarrassment of their nieces who are traveling with them. Despite the fact that they are in mourning, Arabella Greenow and Martha Barnaby both insist on putting down their names for the assembly rooms in the resort towns where they are staying—ostensibly so as not to deprive the young girls of society.[13]

Anthony's books are often reminiscent of Fanny's because mother and son are drawing on experiences they shared and people they both knew. An unctuous evangelical clergyman, greedy for power and "accustomed in the course of his ministry to win young ladies . . . by means of a little propitiatory love-making," courts a rich widow and, in doing so, divides her family. The Vicar of Wrexhill, like Anthony's Obadiah Slope in *Barchester Towers*, was based on the Trollopes' Harrow neighbor, the Rev. Cunningham. Their much-loved Devonshire cousin, Fanny Bent, was the inspiration for Fanny's Miss Elizabeth Compton in *The Widow Barnaby* and Miss Jemima Stanbury in *He Knew He Was Right*: Devonshire-bred, old-fashioned, and outspoken spinsters. Both mother and son explored the tragic figure of Thomas Anthony Trollope in their fiction. Like Fanny's *One Fault*, Anthony's *He Knew He Was Right* is the study of a husband's obsessive attempt to control his wife.

The list of characters and plot lines that Anthony borrowed from his mother could go on and on. The plots of Fanny's *Mrs Mathews* and Anthony's *Mr Scarborough's Family* both hang upon the terms and conditions of a will. A young penniless orphan, greedy, selfish, and devious, connives to inherit a rich estate and runs away with the family diamonds: this describes both Sophy Martin in *The Ward of Thorpe Combe* and Lizzie Eustace in *The Eustace Diamonds*. A ruthless financier of dubious origins flaunts his wealth, is admitted to "the best society," and thus attracts investors in a high-risk speculation; the bubble bursts, the investors are ruined, and suicide follows. Monsieur Roche in *Fashionable Life* and Augustus Melmotte in *The Way We Live Now* are two such men.

Moreover, Anthony's strong narrative voice echoes that of his mother. Both authors create a certain rapport—even intimacy—with their readers. Just as Fanny interrupts her story to inform her readers on all sorts of matters, from the perfect number to have at a dinner party to the elusive nature of happiness, so Anthony gives his opinion on everything from women's fashions to liberal politics. Sometimes their views clash. Fanny often wrote on the delights of a picnic; Anthony—no doubt having been dragged along on too many family outings—hated them and said so in his novels. Both novelists occasionally leave their characters in suspended animation. In *Fashionable Life*, when Henry Hamilton proposes to Caroline Holmwood, Fanny explains at some length the heroine's feelings on the matter before declaring: "But I am leaving Henry Hamilton too long upon his knees." So, Anthony apologizes for having "kept the Greshamsbury tenantry waiting under the oak-trees by far too long" at Frank Gresham's twenty-first birthday party while he discusses the Gresham family background in *Dr Thorne*.

Finally, the creation of a fictional series was not an innovation that belongs to Anthony and the Barsetshire novels, as scholars have claimed, but to his mother and the Barnaby trilogy. Like the Barsetshire novels, the Barnaby series mimics reality: characters float in and out, they grow older, and sometimes wiser. However, when praised at a London literary dinner for this innovation in the English novel, Anthony did not take the opportunity to mention the precedent set by his mother (Hall, *Trollope* 302–3).

Fanny would not have minded the literary borrowings. Fiction had become the family business: two of her other children, Tom and Cecilia, were also published novelists. All of the Trollopes considered writing to be first and foremost a trade: Anthony famously compared himself to a shoemaker. Characters and plots were simply tools of that trade, to be shared freely between the various partners in the firm. Fanny would have considered Anthony's recycling of her plots as thrift rather than theft. After all, such borrowings were evident enough in *The Warden*, which she had read and enjoyed. Nevertheless, Anthony resented the fact that his ambition to become a novelist had so long been overshadowed by his mother's career. Anthony was an aspiring man of letters, and his mother's reputation as a "vulgar" authoress was a continual embarrassment, especially as her books, reprinted and reissued, were displayed alongside her son's in shops and circulating libraries.

Anthony used his autobiography, published the year following his death, as an opportunity to publicly distance himself from his mother. In it he criticizes her politics as merely "an affair of the heart" (1987: 18) and condemns her novels, claiming "in her attempts to describe morals, manners, and even facts, [she] was unable to avoid the pitfalls of exaggeration" (26). Tom was horrified at his brother's remarks: "there is hardly a word of this in which Anthony is not more or less mistaken" (T. A. Trollope 1887: 2: 332).

Anthony's criticisms seem to have hit their mark because, from the time his autobiography appeared in 1883, Fanny Trollope's novels suddenly ceased to be reprinted. Anthony had, in effect, buried his mother's literary reputation. Yet, he had publicly welcomed the renewed interest in Jane Austen inspired by James-Edward Austen-Leigh's memoir of his aunt, published in 1870. Anthony liked to be thought of as Jane Austen's literary successor; he was called such in an article by R. H. Hutton titled "From Miss Austen to Mr Trollope," published ten days after his death.[14] No one had ever accused the genteel Miss Austen of being vulgar. But Anthony was undeniably his mother's son, and that much-loved Trollopian world of scheming clergymen, bumptious country squires, and strong-minded women was the legacy that Fanny bequeathed to him— the last Trollope to be born on Keppel Street.

NOTES

The title of this chapter is the subtitle of my 1997 biography *Fanny Trollope* and is the title of one of Fanny's novels. Some excerpts were adapted from my chapter 13 of *Fanny Trollope: The Life and Adventures of a Clever Woman* and used with permission of Viking Penguin.

1. Unfortunately, the date of birth on the plaque is wrong. It should read 1779, not 1780.

2. *Fraser's Magazine* 18 (1843).

3. *New Monthly Magazine* 55 (1839).

4. *The Spectator* 6 (1833).

5. *Letters* 1 April 1816.

6. *Letters* 9 February 1839.

7. *Letters* 16 December 1842.

8. 1 September 1856.

9. 15 May 1847.

10. *Letters* 11 November 1848.

11. *The Noble Jilt* did not appear in print until 1923.

12. *The Critic* 15 April 1851.

13. The characters of Arabella Greenow and Alice Vavasor first appeared as Madame Brudo and Margaret de Wynter in Anthony's unpublished play, *The Noble Jilt*, written in 1850, only eleven years after the publication of *The Widow Barnaby*.

14. *Spectator* 16 December 1882.

2

Mrs. Frances Trollope: Triumphant Female Friendship in the Nineteenth Century

Helen Heineman

One of the first scholars to devote a sizable portion of a book to Mrs. Trollope was Michael Sadleir who, in the course of his analysis of her life and works, asked the rhetorical question, "Whence, then, Mrs. Trollope's power, fierce and undeniable, to infuriate contemporaries?" (1947: 113). A simple answer to that question lies in the power of her scathing assault on all aspects of American life, in her first book, *Domestic Manners of the Americans* (1832), as well as in the powerful social reform fiction she produced, attacking such inflammatory topics as the sexual abuses of evangelical fervor; child labor in the industrial factories in the north of England; the abuses of the New Poor Law, particularly in the case of unmarried mothers; and the first book to tackle the evils of American slavery, published fifteen years before *Uncle Tom's Cabin* and containing frank analyses of the sexual abuses of overseers on female slaves.[1] But perhaps her most provocative subject was the early creation of a new kind of strong and independent heroine for fiction.[2] Even more radical was her belief in the saving power of female friendships.

In her personal relationships, she was always a woman deeply committed to female friendships. In the early days at Harrow, and even when her own large family was plagued by illness or debt, she had the reputation of being "always a special friend of all the young girls" (T. A. Trollope 1888: 65). Across her lifetime she remained close to women, maintaining friendships with the clever and cultivated like Mary Russell Mitford, Madame Recamier, Madame de Chateaubriand, Princess Metternich, and

Rosina Bulwer, wife of the novelist. But the most important female friendships of her life were those with a trio of sisters, Harriet, Julia, and Fanny
Garnett, and with two other sisters, Frances and Camilla Wright. It was
in conjunction with these women that she first imagined the possibility
of a female community.[3]

Perhaps the idea originated in the way the men of their lives had failed
them. John Garnett had brought his daughters to America and in 1788
had created in their home at Whitehouse Farm in New Jersey a kind of
domestic utopian settlement. But he had died prematurely and left poor
financial arrangements behind him, so his wife and daughters were forced
to retreat to the continent where they lived in genteel poverty. Mrs.
Trollope's husband had squandered their family's resources in a bad
housing scheme, had offended his legal clients, and left his wife as the
sole support of the large and ailing family. Frances Wright, a wealthy
young Scottish heiress, orphaned at an early age, was the catalyst for a
plan to establish residency in the United States. She had bought land in
America in western Tennessee, where by means of a radical and innovative educational plan, she hoped to found a colony that would deliver a
solution to the blight of American slavery.[4]

But the letters her sister Camilla sent back to Europe, to the Garnetts
and Mrs. Trollope, spoke most glowingly, instead, of hopes for "a female
haven of affectionate companionship" (28). Frances Wright, for her part,
rang the theme of occupation, "useful, if strenuous," for women (28–
29). As she prepared for the journey to America, Frances Wright tried to
convince Mary Shelley, widow of the poet Percy Bysshe Shelley, to join
the Nashoba colony. In her fervent invitation, she spoke not of the eventual emancipation of slaves, but rather of her longing for sisterhood: "I do
want one of my own sisters to commune with and sometimes to lean upon
in all the confidence and equality of friendship" (48).

Indeed, her letter to Mrs. Shelley reads like a love letter to a woman
she had never met. Instead, Mrs. Trollope answered the call and sailed
for America to join her eloquent new friend. In the end, the colony failed
and all the women eventually rejected utopian socialism. In a fundamental
way, reform issues had conflicted with "their personal desires for freedom
and expanded destinies" (34).

The departure of Frances Wright for America came at a transitional
point in the fates of the circle of friends. Harriet Garnett, her mother and
sister, stayed behind in Paris, and extended their close circle of female
friends. Julia married Pertz and left for Hanover to settle in a foreign land
with men as her closest companions, a husband, and eventually three sons.
Her sisters often spoke of Julia's need for a daughter. Julia did become a
friend to women in trouble, like Clara Ranke and Madame Fauche, and

she had many female friends like Julia Smith, Mary Clarke, and Helen Martineau. Mrs. Trollope left for America with her new friend. Frances Wright was poised on the brink of a life of political achievement and Mrs. Trollope about to mine her rigorous experiences as a writer. From this point on, their sisterhood rooted itself in the letters that bound them together, in a massive correspondence of which over four hundred remain, "a priceless record of shared inner lives" (65).

The peripatetic Mrs. Trollope, unfortunately, kept none of the letters, but in her many novels she gradually began to depict the power of women and the importance of sisterhood. She had moved gradually in this direction. First, in her travel books, she described the role of women in the countries she had visited. In *Domestic Manners of the Americans*, she had documented "the lamentable insignificance of the American woman" (1949). In *Belgium and Western Germany in 1833*, she included vignettes of women, visited a convent of Belgian sisters, and included the journal of a Belgian lady. In *Paris and the Parisians in 1835*, she recorded dialogues that focused on the concerns of women and concluded that women there "have more power and more important influence than the women in England."[5] The plight of women had been her focus throughout.

Next, in her social reform fiction, she used women as the vehicles of social change, and this during a period when real women had no political influence or no right even to vote. Between 1833–43 she experimented with a new genre, the feminine picaresque, and created the Widow Barnaby, a middle-aged woman boldly in search of her fortunes on the road. In this comic mode, and in an earlier experiment with the Gothic, she could afford to have her heroines deviate from feminine norms of behavior. An Abbess, after all, can easily surround herself with female "friends" and engage in the task of saving defenseless young women, recalcitrant daughters, and a pregnant noblewoman in disguise. Later she created a host of predatory fortune hunters who viewed men frankly in terms of money, and without any pretense about feelings.[6]

Petticoat Government: a Novel (1850), whose title expresses this developing focus, is the first of a series of novels featuring heroines who realize their truest identities aside from marriage and in the company of other women. *Mrs Matthews* (1851) celebrates the happiness of the single female, as does *The Life and Adventures of a Clever Woman* (1854) and *Gertrude: or Family Pride* (1855). But the finale to these came in her last novel, *Fashionable Life: or Paris and London* (1856). There the main focus of her book is the importance of female friendship and the development of the female community.

Fashionable Life: or Paris and London opens with the men in young Clara Holmwood's life in power. Between her father, a wealthy corn merchant, and the manipulative Dr. Brixbourg, they make all the decisions about the management of Clara's fate and her soon-to-be considerable fortune, and without any consultation with her. After her father's death, Clara is to remain with the Brixbourgs until she comes of age. The arrangement is clearly a bondage she detests. To make the ensuing years tolerable, Clara and her Aunt Sarah put their meager allowances together to pay for a tutor to educate themselves (1: 3–4).

Of course, given the literary preferences of the time, Clara must have a prospective suitor, but Mrs. Trollope makes quick work of dispatching the conventional love interest, at least until the novel's third volume. To get the business over with quickly, strong-willed heroine that she is, Clara proposes to Henry Hamilton. Because of her wealth and his poverty, he conveniently refuses her offer and sails for Australia, leaving an opening for Clara to seek and find a supportive female community. In this last novel, which she composed before her death, Mrs. Trollope explores the subject that had long interested her, female friendships. The reader forgets Henry Hamilton easily, a fact Mrs. Trollope makes no attempt to conceal. Indeed, she ironically remarks of Clara: "As a heroine, she would have lost all claim to the sentimental interest of my readers, could they know how very few minutes during the 24 hours which then passed over her, were bestowed in meditations upon her aristocratic lover" (1: 86–87).

As soon as Henry is safely gone, Clara finds herself a little surprised "to feel how far she was from being miserable" (1: 192). Thus freed from a conventional life, she sets out to see the world, deploring how much "the happiness of English women seems to depend . . . upon the *accident* of being married, or not married." Mrs. Trollope had explored this theme earlier, in *Mrs Matthews* and *The Life and Adventures of a Clever Woman*. Here, she uses it to develop the related subject of female friendship.

Like her creator before her, with a brief regret that her education "had not been more *special*" (1: 199), Clara Holmwood decides to travel, fixing on Paris as a desirable destination. It is here that the book concentrates on its unique subject: the joys and satisfactions of the female community. Clara meets an aristocratic friend, Lady Amelia Wharton, who suggests "entering into a partnership together," the ingredients of which forged many a Victorian-style marriage. Lady Amelia agrees to provide the necessary social ingredient of aristocratic rank, while Clara, the rich heiress, will supply the money. The author intrudes with a pointed comment: "If all people set about carrying out their own arrangements and their own intentions, in as business-like and rational a manner as did the female co-partnership I am describing, there would be much fewer disappointments in life" (1: 242). Knowing their goal, these women worked persistently and cooperatively to achieve it.

Their friendly arrangement consisted of four females in different states of life. Lady Amelia is a widow; Annie, her young daughter, is a woman of marriageable age; Aunt Sarah is an elderly spinster; and Clara is a young heiress whose chosen suitor has conveniently rejected her. Each had different backgrounds, each had different present needs, but, as the author comments, "It would have been difficult . . . to find any other group of four females who, while each was so essentially different from the others, could, nevertheless, constitute a society in which each should so delightfully contribute to the enjoyment of the rest" (1: 247). This "society" is a version of what Nina Auerbach, in her analysis of such relationships in fiction, has called "communities of women." As the novel's second volume progresses, the women face a dilemma. Young Annie Wharton meets an ineffective and poor young man named Victor Dormont, with whom she quickly falls in love. Their "courtship" is never described nor given any scenic attention by the author. Instead the book focuses on the way the women friends rally around to help Annie and Victor through a number of increasingly melodramatic trials. As the "love interest" between Annie and Victor proceeds, the reader *never* sees them together. Rather, the author concentrates on the loving helpfulness and expressiveness of the circle of friends. To clear up Victor's financial woes, Clara settles some money—ten thousand pounds—on Annie and her eventual children. In a carefully stipulated provision, Victor cannot touch this money, an arrangement similar to Mrs. Trollope's own marriage settlement, which for a while had preserved her from the bankruptcy of her husband. When Clara tells Lady Amelia of her decision, the scene abounds in heavy sentiment, culminating with Lady Amelia's dramatic declaration: "The happiness that I have tasted since, I owe to you" (2: 175). Obviously, Mrs. Trollope's artistic heart is more focused on describing the affectionate effusions of female friendship than in detailing the sweet nothings of the young lovers.

Clara herself is excessively grateful for "the blessing of having found very precious friends," where she had only hoped for agreeable companions, and finds herself "a far happier being than she had ever hoped to be" (2: 176). As an actual character who appears in scenes and speaks dialogue, Victor Dormont appears for the first time at the end of the second volume, and he remains only a shadowy figure as the events of the novel's final volume unfold.

When Victor and Annie finally decide to marry, the reader is hardly surprised to find that their choice is to live within the female community of friends: "Why should Annie take any apartment at all? Why should they not live with us here?" (2: 265). Why not, indeed? And so they do.

In the third volume, a series of events provides the novel with more obligatory conflicts and troubles. Annie has a child (a baby girl, of course) and Victor begins a mysterious decline, both physical and mental, which culminates in his convenient suicide. The business he had entered, with a contribution from Clara, had failed. He had lost everything, including, it seems for a while, the rest of Clara's whole fortune. But she has no regrets, just thoughts about the future and how to continue the life of the once-again totally female community. Clara decides to rearrange their lives in England, musing happily as she does, that "the whole of our female conclave, baby Clara included, love one another truly" (3: 169).

In the end, Clara is reunited with Henry Hamilton, providing the novel with its conventional conclusion. But Mrs. Trollope's main artistic interest has been in celebrating the delights and benefits of female friendship.

Frances Trollope had begun her professional life with a stay at Frances Wright's Nashoba, and now ended it with this fictional rendition of a community of friends in Paris and London. After her death, her sons, Thomas and Anthony, only reserved some limited space for their mother's accomplishments in their own autobiographical works. It remained for a daughter-in-law whom she never knew, Thomas Adolphus' second wife, Frances Eleanor Trollope, to give Frances Trollope her first full-scale biography with its comprehensive portrait of a valiant and accomplished woman and author.

Indeed, her closest and most enduring friends had always been women. At Harrow there were aunts, friends, and neighbors. Throughout her life she took up the cause of women, of Madame Fauche, the consul's wife at Bruges, of Rosina Bulwer, trapped in an unhappy marriage, of the Okey sisters, exploited by Dr. Elliotson as subjects of his fraudulent experiments with mesmerism. She had sustained close friendships with a host of successful women and a lifelong relationship with the Garnetts.

In her last novel, she dared to depict a female community that was a last look at the saving power of female friendships. All through her long writing career, women had saved the day. Time and again they were the strong characters who achieved success in a world controlled by men. Men owned the factories, dominated the church, and controlled the finances in marriage and in the realms of politics and government. Yet time and again, they failed to wield their power for the common good. In Mrs. Trollope's novels women arranged for the assassination of the evil overseer in *Jonathan Jefferson Whitlaw*, they exposed the abuses in Sir Michael Dowling's factory, they foiled the seductions of the Vicar of Wrexhill, and they regularly disrupted all attempts to control them in marriage. In the end, in her last novel, they settled down to a comfortable life in Paris and London, living with one another in comfort, trust, and support, in a communal female arrangement whose happiness far exceeded any achieved by the more conventional heroines of the day.

NOTES

1. *The Vicar of Wrexhill; The Life and Adventures of Michael Armstrong, the Factory Boy; Jessie Phillips: a Tale of the New Poor Law;* and *The Life and Adventures of Jonathan Jefferson Whitlaw: or Scenes on the Mississippi,* respectively.

2. See my book titled *Frances Trollope,* chap. 4, "Novels of Feminine Consciousness: The Strong Woman," 82–99; chap. 5, "Novels of Feminine Consciousness: The Marital Imperative," 100–122; and chap. 6, "Novels of Feminine Consciousness: The Independent Woman," 123–33.

3. See my *Restless Angels: The Friendship of Six Victorian Women,* passim.

4. See *Angels,* chap. 2, "Frances Wright and the Second Utopia, 1825–1827," 23–62.

5. See chap. 2, "The Travel Books," 24–57.

6. See *Frances Trollope,* chaps. 4, 5, and 6.

3

Michael Armstrong:
Rereading the Industrial Plot

Priti Joshi

Since Catherine Gallagher's *The Industrial Reformation of English Fiction* (1985), "social-problem novels"[1] have enjoyed a measure of academic and scholarly interest. Elizabeth Gaskell's once obscure *Mary Barton* is today routinely assigned in undergraduate and graduate courses on the Victorian novel alongside *Vanity Fair* and *Bleak House*. Yet, not all industrial novels have fared equally well in this resurgence. Frances Trollope's *The Life and Adventures of Michael Armstrong, The Factory Boy* (1839–1840) continues to attract few scholars: the *MLA Bibliography*, for instance, contains only two citations for it, one from 1982, the other from 1977.[2] (Trollope's travel writings have drawn greater attention.) In fact, Gallagher herself mentions *Michael Armstrong* only in passing in a chapter on seamstresses and other exploited women workers, merely pointing out that the novel's protagonist "is an unusual fictional factory child" as he is a boy, not a girl (127).

One reason for this novel's continued obscurity is that it does not fit neatly into the category of the "social-problem novel." But the problem lies less with the novel itself than with the category that has been too narrowly defined. Scholars of Victorian fiction expect the industrial novel to be "about" conditions of labor or factory life. *Michael Armstrong* is indeed an exposé of industrial conditions. However, its most engaging plot line concerns not industrial conditions, but the emerging class-consciousness of its upper-middle-class female protagonist, and its sharpest revelation is of the interdependence of class and gender hierarchies in

England. But because industrial or social-problem novels have been read largely for their veracity or fidelity to "facts," few critics have attended to the alternative stories they may be telling, and instead *Michael Armstrong* has earned the distinction of being "unusual."

Trollope's novel is indeed an "unusual" text, but not in the way Gallagher means. It is an industrial exposé that is more about social exchange across class lines; a novel that is, in fact, about an heiress, rather than about a factory boy; a critique of England's class structure that nevertheless insists on nationalist exclusivity; an indictment of women's disempowerment and enforced ignorance that simultaneously demonstrates their complicity in structures of oppression. This intertwining of gender, class, and nation makes *Michael Armstrong* a rich text that deserves renewed attention.

Condemned at the time of its publication as an "exaggeration," *Michael Armstrong* is today considered by many critics to be an accurate and acute rendering of the horrors of early-industrial work conditions. Joseph Kestner writes that the novel captured "situations" well and borrowed closely from Parliamentary reports (*Protest* 52–55), and Helen Heineman writes that "contemporary documents bear out the truth of [Trollope's] descriptions" (*Frances Trollope* 67). Despite the opposing judgments of nineteenth- and twentieth-century critics, both operate from within the same set of assumptions about factuality or "realism." But to read industrial novels merely for their adherence to "actual" conditions assumes that their purpose was simply to "reveal" industrial abuses to a wide audience in the more palatable form of a novel rather than the dry Parliamentary reports or journalism. While this was certainly a component of their authors' intentions—Trollope stated in the Preface that she wrote the novel to "place before the eyes of Englishmen, the hideous mass of injustice and suffering to which thousands of infant labourers are subjected, who toil in our monstrous spinning-mills"—I suggest that "revelation" or exposé was only *part* of the work these novelists attempted to accomplish.

Charles Kingsley's *Alton Locke* (1850) demonstrates this point explicitly. During the eponymous, working-class hero's travels from London to the countryside as a Chartist delegate, a fellow delegate describes factory conditions to him. Alton, always indignant about industrial ills and usually eager to condemn the abuses of the rich, does not repeat or narrate the man's words. Instead, he describes his "rural cousin" launching into "a rambling bitter diatribe on the wrong [*sic*] and sufferings of the labourers; which went on till late at night, and which I shall spare my readers: for if they have either brains or heart, *they ought to know more than I can tell them, from the public prints*" (255; emphasis added).

Kingsley's rather offhand dismissal of the details of working conditions suggests that industrial novels were not exclusively focused upon revealing narratives of hardship, injustice, or misery. Indeed, Kingsley's distinction between journalism and fiction, and his assumption that his readers would already know the worst, alerts us to the alternative work industrial novels were attempting to accomplish and that has seldom been noticed.

Industrial novels were engaged in the more innovative and radical project of imagining a new set of social relations. The contours of this project were defined by Thomas Carlyle's vision of social relations, although the details were dictated by the generic constraints within which the novelists operated. In the epoch-defining "Signs of the Times" (1829), Carlyle bemoaned "the increas[ed] distance between rich and poor" (35). A decade later, after the betrayals of the 1832 Reform Bill led to increasingly tense relations between the working and upper classes,[3] Carlyle wrote that the solution to class warfare was "a genuine understanding by the upper classes of society what it is that the under classes intrinsically mean" ("Chartism" 122). In order to discover what "torments these wild inarticulate souls," he proposed fellowship between the classes because "all battle is misunderstanding; did the parties know one another, the battle would cease."

Carlyle's paternalist vision, yearning for a utopian past, nevertheless struck a cord among his contemporaries: the distance or lack of engagement between the upper classes and poor became a matter of grave concern for many essayists, politicians, clergy, and social commentators. The period between 1832 and 1850 saw a proliferation of essays on the "condition of England"; an astronomical rise in philanthropic giving and activities; Parliamentary investigations that led inspectors and reformers into mines, factories, and slums; myriad reform groups such as the Manchester Statistical Society and the Health of Towns Association; and, of course, novels. These efforts spanned the political spectrum (Lord Shaftesbury was a Tory, Edwin Chadwick was a Whig), arenas (political bills, social reforms, administrative restructuring, philanthropy, and individual charity), and gender (Charles Dickens, Elizabeth Gaskell, James Kay-Shuttleworth, and Harriet Martineau). The institutions they spawned were a legal and political infrastructure to legislate and enforce laws regarding labor, health, and housing conditions; building projects; and philanthropic schemes to initiate or increase contact between classes.[4] Whether they emerged from religious or civic institutions, advocated state intervention, or were adamantly opposed to it, all these efforts were anxious to reestablish relations between classes that were severed by urbanism and industrialism.

While many institutions and individuals attempted to suture the gulf between classes and promote greater social cohesion, only in fiction did the effort to *establish* cross-class relations find a narrative voice. This is hardly surprising; the novel as a form narrates social encounters. Furthermore, as Frederic Jameson has argued, narrative form serves to "invent imaginary or formal 'solutions' to irresolvable social contradictions" (79). Michael McKeon has drawn upon this insight to demonstrate that the English novel in particular emerged precisely to mediate intractable social problems (20–21). From its very origins in Richardson and Fielding, the novel imagined or invented resolutions to sticky social problems or contradictions, such as the status inconsistency of status of a woman like Pamela who was of low birth but high principles. That these resolutions were imaginary or "unrealistic" (such as Pamela's marriage to Mr. B) seemed to matter little because the form in which they were told was persuasive. As Ian Watt has pointed out, the new representational techniques of the novel were so innovative that many of Richardson's readers forgot to attend to his content, which was as "improbable" as any romance (204–5). These narratives were popular not because they provided "believable" solutions, but because they provided readers with handy fictions to understand their new world—increasingly urban, based on kinship rather than merit—and morality.

Therefore, early nineteenth-century novelists were working within a generic tradition that focused on narrating social relations and providing resolutions to social conflicts. As a result they took up Carlyle's challenge to effect increased relations across class lines in the way they knew best: they imagined and narrated the actual encounters between men and women from different classes. Social-problem novels explored the problem of establishing and creating relationships between rich and poor. Because these novels have been read only with an eye to their historical accuracy, factual fidelity, or political positions, their emphases on the journeys of discovery that characters make to cross class boundaries have been neglected. A reading of *Michael Armstrong* that focuses on the "industrial-exposé" theme neglects the more socially radical narratives the novel develops—the story of crossing class lines, of engaging with the Other, and of building cross-class relations—and its critique of England's class and gender hierarchies.

The plot of *Michael Armstrong* can be briefly summarized. Sir Matthew Dowling, the cruel and boorish owner of one of the harshest cotton mills in Lancashire, "adopts" one of his factory workers, Michael Armstrong, in an effort to impress Lady Clarissa Shrimpton, a titled, pretentious, and penniless Scot who encourages Dowling's flirtations. The nine-year-old Michael is made to leave home—where he lives with his sick mother and crippled brother—and move into the Dowling mansion, where he is treated poorly by all the Dowlings except the plain daughter, Martha. Mary Brotherton, a wealthy young neighbor whose fortune is based upon her dead father's mill, witnesses Dowling's cruelty to Michael and begins to ask questions about mills and the lives of workers. The bulk of the next two hundred pages is given over to her investigations into and slow discovery of the horrors of factories and their impact on children.

Meanwhile, Dowling secretly "apprentices" Michael to the remote Deep Valley mill where parishes send pauper children, ostensibly to learn a trade, but where they are put to work for the profit of the mill's owner. Most of the children die within a year or two, but the owner does not mind because, as he explains, he has studied the population returns and knows "the rate at which pauper children are multiplied" (217). After much trouble, Mary finally discovers Michael's location, and travels unescorted to Deep Valley to rescue him. Once there, she is erroneously informed that he died in a fever epidemic. Disappointed, she instead rescues Michael's patient, long-suffering companion, Fanny Fletcher. Horrified by the inhumanity of Deep Valley and disheartened about the possibility of introducing better work conditions, Mary adopts Michael's crippled and now-orphaned brother Edward, and with her two charges leaves England for the Continent.

The narrative reverts to Michael who, despite five years of harsh work, poor living conditions, and a meager diet at Deep Valley, has grown to be a strong lad who manages to escape. Back in Lancashire, he learns that Fanny and his brother are alive and living in Germany with Mary Brotherton. After some qualms about the potential class differences between him and his brother, and hesitation at the thought of being dependent on Mary, he eventually sets off for the Continent. Before Michael leaves, however, he hears that the now bankrupt Dowling has died, and he generously offers to pay for his former tormentor's burial. In Germany, Michael finds that Mary has brought up Fanny and Edward to be a young lady and gentleman. She insists that Michael join their family.

Michael Armstrong is both one of the harshest critiques of industrial labor conditions and one of the most despairing about the possibilities of change. The novel raises a number of solutions to the problem of child labor, from private charity to organized philanthropy to mills run on Owenite principles. It systematically rejects each in favor of the Ten Hours Bill. Yet, while the novel's *rhetoric* advocates government regulation, its protagonist Mary *enacts* change on a small scale through private charity. Critics have seen this contradiction as a sign of Trollope's weakness as a writer or her confused politics. On the contrary, it reproduces a fairly common position in Victorian debates about poverty: the most effective response to social conditions was two-pronged, including *simultaneous* state intervention and "personal" contact. Trollope's emphasis on Mary's nongovernmental actions and solutions, then, emerges not from confusion, but from an acceptance of the mutually supportive relation between the political and social. Furthermore, Mary's actions allow Trollope to develop the novel's alternative plot line: a narrative of cross-class relations rather than an industrial exposé and abstract solutions to it.

In fact, what I am calling the "alternative" narrative occupies more pages than the industrial one. Despite the novel's title, Michael, the factory boy, plays a very small part in the novel: he appears on and off in the early pages, is a rather uninteresting character, disappears almost entirely during a lengthy middle section, and only reemerges in the last one hundred pages, a strapping eighteen-year-old, to reclaim his narrative. Trollope could as well have named this novel *The Trials and Travels of Mary Brotherton, The Concerned Heiress, In Search of Truth*. Most of the novel belongs to Mary—whose surname invokes the Carlylian desire for brotherhood—her encounters with the poor, and her process of discovering their lives. Her growing consciousness of industrial conditions through her engagement with Michael and other factory workers is the only developed narrative in the novel and the one that most absorbs our attention and sympathy.

Indeed the very language of the text reflects this split between the industrial narrative and the cross-class narrative. The language used to describe Mary's travails contrasts markedly with the abstract language condemning industrial ills. The descriptions of industrialism are harrowing, yet also distant and labored. The narrator describes Dowling's mill thus: "a monstrous chamber, redolent of all the various impurities that 'by the perfection of our manufacturing system,' are converted into 'gales of Araby' for the rich, after passing in the shape of certain poison, through the lungs of the poor" (80). The language is academic and stilted. Its use of well-worn phrases of praise (in quotes) for England's manufactories is intended as sarcasm, but reads instead like the work of a writer who has only recently been introduced to an idea, but who has not yet absorbed it and is not able to use it for dramatic purposes. The notion that the bodies of the poor act as a purification system for the evils of industrialism, obscuring the relationship between product and process, could be powerful were it not buried so deep in the metaphor that it does not quite emerge. The novel abounds with clumsy passages when it describes mills or work conditions.

By contrast, Mary's developing consciousness, her conversations with Michael or Martha, her strategizing, anger, and despair, her attempts to forge relationships with the poor, and the frequent misunderstandings that ensue are all skillfully developed. For instance, watching Dowling's cruel treatment of Michael, the narrator remarks:

> Mary made up her mind as to the best way of rescuing the pale trembling child, whose voice and form haunted her, from the horrible bondage of Sir Matthew Dowling's charity. The question was not altogether an easy one. She could hardly doubt that very strong indignation would follow any open effort on her part to interfere with a child publicly held up as the favoured object of Sir Matthew's loudly-vaunted benevolence, and moreover, privately marked out by his vindictive nature as a victim to his hatred. (113)

Bordering on the melodramatic, the passage is not, however, clichéd. Mary's consciousness of the politics of her location, her comprehension of Dowling's machinations, and her understanding of the response any action on her part would evoke indicate Trollope's sensitivity and insight into women's vulnerability in a largely male economic and social world. Rather than stilted language that shouts indignation, this passage is quieter and more effective for that. Its critique of Dowling as well as those in the community who effectively serve to prop him up through their silence is pointed and meets its mark in a way that the awkward language of the industrial passages does not.

Trollope's sharpest writing, however, surfaces in her satiric descriptions of her villainous characters. The novel begins with Dowling, who, much to the distress of his wife, is courting the attention of Lady Clarissa. The latter "drove only one pony instead of four horses . . . [and] was neither young, handsome, nor rich, but . . . was Lady Clarissa, and this was enough" (5). Dowling, whose "estimate of the outward advantages of his extensive person was indeed not a low one," follows the lady in her "daring escapade" from the drawing room because he is "not insensible to the charm of getting talked of in the neighbourhood about his devotion to Lady Clarissa any body" (7). In the garden, anxious to prevent her from taking the path toward his mill, Dowling provokes a "fight" between a tired old cow and his dog that succeeds in frightening Lady Clarissa into his arms and draws the attention of two small boys walking by. Dowling calls out to one of them to chase back "that devil of a beast" (14), which the boy obediently does, upon which Lady Clarissa thanks her "deliverer" and promises him that he will be "comfortably clothed and fed for the rest of [his] life" at Dowling Lodge (14–17). Galled at the thought of "being thus entrapped, and forced to adopt '*a bag of rags out of his own factory*' (for it was thus he inwardly designated little Michael)" (17), Dowling nevertheless agrees, remembering rumors of a strike and his manager's hint that an act of charity on his part would settle the workers

(6). The characters' inflated sense of self-importance and their insistence on casting themselves in a hyperbolic melodrama is relentlessly and bitingly mocked in passages such as these.

But the scene's elaborate architecture with Dowling's thwarted desires, his fawning, and the Lady's class pretensions also carries a pointed critique. Their adulterous flirtation enacts and sexualizes a powerful sociological drama played out throughout the nation: the tense but necessary alliance between the old nobility and a newly minted one. In the early nineteenth century, the anxieties and desire for status and wealth, legitimacy and relevance, power and acceptance were the two sides of an elaborate interplay that shaped the relations between the titled and the moneyed. In locating the novel within the context of this negotiation of relations between industrialists and aristocrats, Trollope located her contribution to industrial conditions within a broader framework of changing class relations in England. As a result, she demonstrates that the working class was not the only class seeking acceptance and a voice; the recently wealthy upper middle class was too. Dowling and Mary Brotherton—one looking to emulate the corrupt nobility, the other seeking to fashion a positive relation to the lower classes—are the two sides of this emerging identity.

The clearest indication that *Michael Armstrong* is concerned less with exposé than social exchange is that much of the novel's action occurs not in a factory but inside the homes of two upper-class characters. Michael, the *factory* boy, is adopted into Dowling's household, and it is his *displacement* from the factory and a working life that begins this story. Thus, it is not factory work—brutal conditions or long hours—*per se,* but the *end* of work that is the catalyst of this novel. At Dowling's house, despite its proximity to the mill, no one has ever seen a factory worker. While the family and guests mock and disdain Michael, Mary Brotherton is moved to ask about the people to "whose labours all the people in this neighbourhood own their wealth . . . myself including the rest" (44). The focus here is not on Michael, but on Mary. Her first encounter with a worker lifts the veil off her eyes and transforms her from a lonely young woman into a purposeful investigator.[5] Thus, although Michael's adoption is precipitated by an act of hypocritical and self-promoting "charity" that Trollope sharply satirizes, it also initiates the critical interaction between classes. Trollope, extending Carlyle, emphasizes the importance of face-to-face interactions for breaking down the isolation of classes. These interactions, ironically, occur in the homes of the upper classes.

From the moment of this encounter the novel becomes Mary Brotherton's, who acts as our guide into the horrors of factory life. She does not, however, simply learn about industrial conditions, but must *uncover* them through a tedious and difficult process that Trollope narrates in excruciating detail. We learn of Mary's discoveries but also journey with her down the wrong turns, dead ends, and blind alleys she takes on the road to learning the "truth." She is presented with a number of falsehoods about the poor that she must gradually expose and discard. For instance, she is told that they have no "family feeling and attachment" (94), are vicious and desolate (96), idle, ignorant, and extravagant of their plentiful wages (107), filthy, fraudulent, and infectious (126), and prostitutes and drunks (130). These "descriptions" come from men and women, mill owners and overseers, friends and governesses. Each interlocutor provides ample "evidence" for his or her views, and Mary is persuaded by each for a time until she poses the critical question: Why should an entire class of people be so reviled and avoided by their betters? That Trollope narrates in such detail all the falsehoods Mary must painfully unmask, as well as her slow process of doing so, underscores that the narrative of Mary's enlightenment and awakening consciousness is central to the text.

The process of discovery that Trollope narrates both relies upon observation and offers a critique of it. Initially, Mary's only source of information on factory conditions is Dowling himself, whom she dislikes. She decides that it would be better "to *see* and judge for [myself], instead of taking Sir Matthew Dowling's word for it" (151; emphasis added). After *watching* Michael for several weeks, Mary approaches a factory girl who tells her about mill conditions, common punishments inflicted on workers such as the stick and strap, and the mill children's illiteracy and hunger (153–57). But Mary's visit to Michael's home is the turning point. As she enters the hovel he shares with his mother and brother, the narrator writes: "The misery around her was no longer a matter of doubtful speculation, but of most frightful certainty. Neither was it any vice in little Edward Armstrong [Michael's brother], which drove him to offer up his sickly suffering frame to ceaseless labour at the rate of threepence for each long, painful day. She felt oppressed, overwhelmed, and almost hopeless" (169). What finally allows her to break through the veil of stereotypes is her own observations, her conversations with the poor, and her visits to their homes. Thus, only physical contact with the poor allows Mary to experience a moment of identification and finally break the cordon of lies that was all that was available to her thus far.[6]

Yet, even as Trollope thematizes the transformative power of direct observation, she recognizes that the act of "seeing" is never straightforward, but always obscured by social and economic factors. As Mary prepares to enter a worker's cottage, Dowling tries to stop her by calling out, "You know not to what you are exposing yourself—fraud, filth, infection, drunkenness!" (126). When she ignores his warning and enters nevertheless, the narrator writes:

> Her first idea on looking round her was that perhaps Sir Matthew was in the right. Filth she saw; infection might lurk under it; and who could tell if fraud and drunkenness might not enter the moment after, to complete the group?
>
> But there was so little of selfishness and much of courage in the heart of Mary Brotherton, so *she presently forgot every notion of personal danger, and was thus enabled to see things as they really were.* (126–27; emphasis added)

Linking Mary's ability to "see" to her ability to *relinquish* her class protections and sense of self ("forgot every notion of personal danger"), the passage suggests that class position determines how or what one sees. In doing this, it explodes the basic assumption of investigative reports—the transparency of observation—and draws attention to the subjectivity of the observer.

Yet, in *Michael Armstrong*, gender and duty, more than class, complicate the act of seeing. Trollope probes the relation of gender to acquiring knowledge in the parallel narratives of Mary and Martha. While Martha observes the same unhappiness in and cruelty to Michael as Mary does and is as pained by it, she comes to entirely different conclusions about the *meaning* of these observations. For instance, when Michael's mother complains that she wishes she didn't have to see her children "care-worn," Martha concludes, "How true is what my dear father says about the factory people . . . how wonderfully they do all hate work" (147). Mary has been fed the same lines about the workers' laziness, but she quickly "sees" that the culprit is not laziness but fourteen- to eighteen-hour workdays. Martha never "sees" beyond the cordon of lies; her conclusions are tinged by her position within her family, a point underscored by her invocation of her "dear" father.

What makes it difficult for Martha to "simply observe" is that, although sensitive and kind-hearted, she is, unlike Mary, attached, both in the sense of having a family and in her loyalty and love for her hard father. He, in turn, unabashedly exploits this loyalty, as when he uses her to persuade Mrs. Armstrong to sign the form releasing Michael into "apprenticeship" (160–62). Martha's difficult position in loving her father, in ignoring or trying to put the best light on his greed and poor treatment of workers, and in being asked to "spy" on him to discover where he has sent Michael (227–28) are sympathetically explored by Trollope, who uses this subplot to complicate the too-easy call to observation. Martha's actions—or refusal to act—undermine Carlyle's rational certainty that if the upper classes could "see," they would act. When ultimately her "eyes had been . . . opened to the hard and avaricious nature of her father's character" (292), she withdraws into silence rather than violate familial bonds. Thus, even as Trollope explores Martha's pain and confusion within the context of her disempowerment, she also suggests that Martha's silence makes her complicit in Michael's oppression.

Martha's refusal to act as an investigator in her home threatens to bring the narrative to an abrupt end. Only Mary's decision to leave *her* home and embark on an investigation renews the novel's narrative energy. Significantly, as Martha invokes filial duty to explain her inaction, Mary invokes another equally solemn duty to justify her unorthodox actions. When the Rev. Bell, a proponent of the Ten Hours Bill and the only other character concerned about the plight of workers, attempts to dissuade Mary from embarking on her search for Michael, she replies:

> Do not set me down in your judgements as a hot-headed girl, indifferent to the opinions of society, and anxious only to follow the whim of the moment. Did I belong to any one, I think I should willingly yield to their guidance. But I am alone in the world; *I have no responsibilities but to God and my own conscience*, and the only way I know of, by which I can make this desolate sort of freedom endurable, is by fearlessly, and *without respect to any prejudices or opinions whatever*, employing my preposterous wealth in assisting the miserable race from whose labours it has been extracted. If you can aid me in doing this, you will do me good; but you will do me none, Mr Bell, by pointing out to me *the etiquettes by which the movements of other young ladies are regulate*. . . . [T]o check any possible usefulness by a constant reference to the usages of persons with whom I have little or nothing in common, would be putting on *a very heavy harness*. (232; emphases added)

While initially respectful of social conventions ("do not set me down . . . as indifferent to the opinions of society"), Mary quickly supplants them with God and conscience. These give her the authority to call the "opinions of society" first "prejudices," then "etiquettes," and finally a "harness." The end point of the continuum—harness, a term that alludes to domesticated animals—tarnishes those who are narrow-minded ("prejudiced") and those who allow themselves to be limited by social constraints ("etiquette"). Such constraints are supplanted by Mary's allegiance to a different standard, her conscience. The passage also underscores that Mary must remain single. Were she attached, she would, like Martha, be restrained by loyalty and duty. Insofar as these restraints keep Martha from knowledge, indeed make her an unwitting collaborator and accomplice in the persecution of Michael, Mary's freedom from familial ties is necessary because it allows her to escape from the expectations of her gender role and become a *social actor*.

But once again, Trollope does not rest here. Even as she develops the possibilities that Mary's freedom from family allows her, Trollope also explores the limits this freedom imposes on Mary. Convinced by the Rev. Bell that the schooling and clothes for local children her money could buy would only salve her conscience but not address the larger problem (208–9, 296), Mary acts on a plan that she initially describes as "too much out of the usual course to be safely indulged in": that of "making a man of learning of Edward, and a woman of fortune of Fanny" (295). Sensing that her "romantic and absurd" idea of educating the two orphans "would bring down upon her criticisms, and probably the reprobation, of the whole neighborhood" (295), Mary leaves England. Thus, while freedom from familial constraints allowed her to become an investigator, her gender location did not allow her to intervene and enact change. A woman with no political voice, in a novel that takes the rhetorical position that the only solution is a nationally legislated one, Mary can only escape the country.

Trollope's choice of a woman protagonist for a novel that endorses political action and a legislative solution may appear ill conceived. After all, would not a wealthy, male protagonist who enters politics and enacts new laws serve Trollope's purpose better? If Trollope's project was not to narrate change, but rather to detail the *process* of discovering the Other and building bridges across class boundaries, then her choice of a woman protagonist is exact. As a woman in a culture that imposed ignorance on the majority of women, Mary is the perfect vehicle to explore the journey of discovering and engaging the Other. A woman protagonist also allowed Trollope to explore and redefine the constraints under which women operated—family as imposing silence and ignorance, not a rosy-tinted, sentimental place of refuge—as well as their own complicity in structures of dominance.

The generic form of the novel allowed Trollope to imagine and narrate what so many Victorians anxiously desired after Carlyle's alarm about the "condition of England." But the novel form also imposed constraints. The expected outcome of the social interactions Trollope imagined was matrimony. Having escaped convention and propriety, Mary and her entourage were now in that space in novel-land that ends in marriage. But outside the world of the novel in 1840s England, a marriage that transgressed class lines was a scandal. Nine years after her flight from England, in a letter to the Rev. Bell about Fanny's and Edward's marriage prospects, Mary articulates her fears of this scandal:

> I can hardly hope to find a continental wife or husband for my adopted children, sufficiently English in habits and character, to permit my inviting them to make a part of my family. Yet marry abroad they must, I think, if they marry at all—for I will never by my own free will expose them to

the mortification likely to ensue upon such an explanation respecting their origin, as must be the consequence of any matrimonial negotiation in England. (330)

The extraordinary contradiction in this passage between Mary's nativist desire for an English family and her simultaneous recognition and rejection of the nation's rigid class-consciousness and hierarchies, between her patriotism and egalitarianism, reveals the novel's difficulty in producing a resolution to the social contradiction of class relations without simultaneously reflecting some aspect of that contradiction. By making Edward and Fanny gentlefolk, Mary's intervention in the problem of class relations goes beyond philanthropic projects or legislation. It aims at the very heart of class relations by literally bringing the poor home, thereby reshaping the meaning of "family." Yet precisely because her actions undermine one set of deeply held convictions, Mary cleaves to another—national exclusivity. Hence, one notion of particularity—class—is struck down only to be replaced by another—nation.

Mary's distance—both literal and figurative—from England is the outcome of her distaste for England's class system with its rigid boundaries. The narrator tells us that "circumstances over which . . . [Mary] had no control, for truly they had preceded her birth, had rendered her own country less dear to her than it is to most others; and she therefore . . . determined to plant herself elsewhere" (386). Yet, the contradiction she articulates in the letter to Bell underscores the contingent nature of her solution: Although she has physically escaped England's class hierarchy, she can never fully escape its ideological underpinnings in a myth of national superiority.

While her wealth allowed her the protection to erase class boundaries and associate with the poor in the most intimate way, it also exacted a price: the "family" she creates is so isolated and self-reflexive that it cannot hope for matrimonial closure. That is, until Michael joins them. This fortuitous event provides the novel with a happy ending: Fanny and Michael discover they have loved one another since their first meeting in Deep Valley and they marry. But what not only closes this narrative also *silences.*[7] It is another marriage. In the final paragraphs, the narrator tells us that a "tourist" to the Rhine residence of Mary "will probably observe two very loving and happy pairs, to whom it serves as a common yet, in some sort, a separate home. . . . But however much a gossiping inclination might lead to a more explicit detail, there is really no room left to enter upon it." The narrator follows this enigmatic passage with a metacommentary on methodology: "There are some facts which no wise historian will ever venture to dilate upon, lest their strangeness should provoke incredulity; and great wisdom is shown by such forbearance; for it is infinitely better that an enlightened public should be driven to exclaim, '*How very obscure this passage is!*' than '*How very improbable!*' " (386). The protest, of course, only draws attention to the enigmatic "improbable" that is clearly the marriage of Mary Brotherton and Edward Armstrong. Their marriage is literally the unspoken event of the novel that Trollope could not bring herself to name, let alone narrate.

Trollope's evident discomfort in naming—her choice of "obscurity" over "improbability"—and effort at silence paradoxically draws attention to the marriage and raises two questions: Why is this marriage necessary? Why is it the unspeakable event of the novel? The answer to the first question lies in generic conventions; the answer to the second, in social conventions.

With a handful of exceptions, most eighteenth- and nineteenth-century novels end with a marriage, no matter how improbable. Pamela, the servant girl, and Jane Eyre, the governess, each marries her master. Marriage was the protagonist's "reward" for enduring and growing and, despite Fielding's ridicule of Pamela for reaping the material rewards of marriage for her supposed morality, all of *his* protagonists are similarly rewarded. By tradition if not plausibility, the plot of the novel propelled its protagonist toward marriage. Thus, the easy answer to the first question is that convention demanded a marriage.

Michael Armstrong does, however, end with one marriage. Why did Trollope require a second? The answer to this question requires consideration of the work that marriage accomplishes in a novel. Joseph Boone has argued that the marriage plot is a "restrictive convention" (17) that exerts a "potentially repressive power . . . over authorial intention and textual production" (13) and inhibits the genre from developing (134). Moreover, he argues, the marital ideal played an ideological role as a metonym for social order that "disguise[d] the asymmetries encompassed within the trope of 'balanced' order" (7). By contrast, some feminist critics have argued that the marriage plot does not just support hegemonic ideologies such as domesticity, but also contains a subversive potential. Ruth Yeazell suggests that while the courtship plot may have constrained the heroine, it also allowed novelists to make these heroines the subjective center of the novel. She argues that "to represent [the heroine] as a subject was also to represent, however obliquely, her energies and desires" (237). The marriage resolution allows women's erotic desires to assume a narrative form (Yeazell 190; Green 2).

While Boone's reading is too schematic (marriage = bad; no marriage = good), Yeazell's does not explicate this novel as Trollope's silence erases Mary's subjectivity or desires. Jameson's notion that the ideological position a text propounds can be "an *imaginary resolution* of the objective contradictions to which it thus constitutes an active response" (118; emphasis added) can better help explain this marriage. While resolutions such as marriage may be "false," they can have an important function in responding to "objective contradictions." In the case of *Michael Armstrong*, the contradiction of English class relations—the contradiction between rhetoric of caring for the poor and a reality of extreme exploitation—could only be resolved in an "imaginary" way, through a marriage that was not realistic, but was generically permitted.

The answer to the first question, then—why is Mary and Edward's marriage necessary? —is twofold. First, generic convention required marriage for the protagonist. To deny Mary marriage would be to punish her for asking questions and investigating, for leaving home, for overstepping her gender role, for challenging industrialists, and for creating an alternative "family" that rivaled both the nuclear family and England's class structure. By having her marry, Trollope rewards and condones these "violations." Second, the convention allowed Trollope to narrate a perhaps fanciful response to the social constraints of English class relations—constraints that spoke of the poor as "brothers," but denied them access to the "family." Thus, the novel's "happy ending" is not a sign of Trollope's exaggeration or domesticity, but rather an imaginary resolution of the objective contradictions of England's class system. With this marriage Trollope imagines an alternative to England's rigidly stratified and hierarchical class structure. Moreover, the marriage serves not as a metaphor that masks the asymmetries of social relations, as Boone's argument would have it, but as a solution that by its very "improbability" *highlights* the social inequalities inherent in England's class relations.

Yet while Trollope clearly needed the marriage, she was unable to name it. Why? Her silence that is not complete is an indication of her discomfort with this marriage. Needing and wanting Mary's marriage, Trollope nevertheless feels the scandal of this union. As indicated earlier, cross-class marriages were not new to the English novel. But, although Pamela eventually marries Mr. B., she first proves herself his "equal" by displaying a *moral* superiority that balances if not surpasses his greater wealth and physical power. Similarly, Jane Eyre marries Rochester only after proving her superior morality—she will starve before she violates religion and law—and after Rochester is emasculated, thus "equalizing" their status difference. *Michael Armstrong*, however, does not achieve or strive for this "balance." Mary and Edward's union violates not only class differences, but also assumptions about proper gender roles: Mary is wealthier, older, healthier, and more active than the poor, passive, crippled, sickly Edward. Moreover, she is also his guardian, and the balance of positive attributes she holds is not "righted" by a long-lost merchant-uncle or a miraculous cure for Edward's infirmities. Perhaps all too aware of the disbelief, skepticism, or worse, mockery this violation of "proper" gender hierarchy would evoke in the more staid readers she set out to persuade with the publication of this novel, Trollope achieves closure by hinting at the union but refusing to name or narrate it. For us, her caution signals some of the anxiety that lay behind the discourse of cross-class encounters: that these could become cross-class *romances*, turning the metaphor of "brotherhood" into the reality of a "family."

Rising to Carlyle's challenge, Trollope used the possibilities of the novel form to imagine an alternative to the class disparities of the day. But she could do so only at a price: by having her protagonist escape geographically and generically. In terms of plot, the protagonist must leave England, and as a writer, the narrator must violate novelistic convention by refusing to name or narrate her heroine's "deserved" closure of a marriage. In attempting to erase or blur one set of boundaries—class—Trollope, whether she supports them or not, finds herself trapped in another set of rigid boundaries—gender and nation. The solidly English family on the banks of the Rhine, whose story is marred by the nonnarratability of one union because it violated class as well as proper gender hierarchies, indicates that the disparities of nineteenth-century class relations could be overcome only if other social disparities—national exclusivity and gender hierarchies—were firmly maintained.

NOTES

1. Kathleen Tillotson calls them "social" novels; Raymond Williams, "industrial" novels; Arnold Kettle, "social problem" novels on the grounds that not all of them dealt with industrial conditions and that the English novel has been "social" from its very inception; and Constance Harsh calls them "Condition of England" novels. For a brief review of the names for these novels, see Josephine Guy, 26–32. The novels included in this category vary depending on a critic's definition, but the common ones are: *Alton Locke, Felix Holt, Hard Times, Mary Barton, North and South,* and *Sybil.* While there are good reasons for the varying names, for the purposes of this chapter, I use the terms "industrial" and "social-problem" novel interchangeably.

2. Kestner's "Men in Female Condition of England Novels" and Wallins' "Mrs. Trollope's Artistic Dilemma in *Michael Armstrong.*" There have also been books, notably Helen Heineman's *Frances Trollope* (1984) and Kestner's *Protest and Reform* (1985). Two recent biographies of Trollope (Pamela Neville-Sington's 1997 *Fanny Trollope: The Life and Adventures of a Clever Woman* and Teresa Ransom's 1995 *Fanny Trollope: A Remarkable Life*) indicate a renewed interest in her life, but more recent critical work is still lacking.

3. I use the term "upper classes" here to include the old ruling aristocracy, landowners, and the rural squirearchy, the newer industrialists, manufacturers, bankers, and merchants, as well as the emerging middle class of professionals, lawyers, inspectors, doctors, surveyors, and writers. In using this collective for such a diverse grouping, however, I do not mean to suggest that they were homogenous in status, outlook, occupation, income, political position, or manners.

4. For programs of state intervention, see Corrigan and Sayer, Cullen, Dyos and Wolff, and Poovey; for a variety of philanthropic projects including state-sponsored ones, see Finlayson, Harrison, Hollis, and McCord; for private charity, see Morris, Owen, and Prochaska.

5. Heineman compares Mary's investigative methods to the question-and-answer sessions of Parliamentary reports (*Frances Trollope* 69).

6. Mary also learns from the Rev. George Bell, a clergyman active in legislative reforms, who discusses workers' ages, hours, and wages, as well as philanthropy, the Ten Hours Bill, and political economy. He is, however, the final stage in her process of discovery. Her own observations and conversations initially convince her of an injustice. Bell merely corroborates what she saw, informs her of its extent, and assures her that what she has observed is systemic, not isolated.

7. The notion of "silencing" used here is loosely borrowed from D. A. Miller's *Narrative and Its Discontents* (1981). He uses the term "nonnarratable" to describe events that cannot generate a story and that bring a narrative to closure (4–5).

4

"Fair, Fat and Forty": Social Redress and Fanny Trollope's Literary Activism

Ann-Barbara Graff

On me dit que pourvu que je ne parle ni de l'autorité, ni du culte, ni de la politique, ni de la morale, ni des gens en place, ni de l'opéra, ni des autres spectacles, ni de personne qui tienne à quelque chose, je puis tout imprimer librement.

[I have been told that as long as I do not talk about the powers that be, or religion, or politics, or morals, or people in high places, or the opera or other entertainment, or about people devoted to a cause, then I am free to print whatever I please.]

Le Mariage de Figaro
(Epigraph, *Domestic Manners of the Americans*).

From the beginning of her career as a writer, Trollope wrote as a social satirist distinguishing herself as a champion of women, children, and the laboring poor, addressing such themes as political injustice, moral hypocrisy, and sexual inequality in a variety of genres, including the novel, verse satire, gothic romance, detective story, and travelogue. Having experienced financial hardship herself (brought on by her husband's mismanagement of their affairs and by legal prerogatives that denied her access to her own funds) and having witnessed and documented the ill-treatment of women, children, and slaves in the United States, Britain, and Europe, Trollope wrote with a passion and authority that were difficult to challenge. Moreover, at a time when it was unusual for women to write about topical political issues, Trollope wrote purposefully to influence the consciousness of her readers, to enhance the social roles of women, and, in novels like *The Life and Times of Michael Armstrong, the Factory Boy* (1840) and *Jessie Phillips: a Tale of the Present Day* (1844), to affect the legislative agenda of the House of Commons. As a consequence, her critics routinely maligned her as unfeminine, coarse, vulgar, and bitter. Undaunted, she persisted, subverting generic conventions and popular expectations to inscribe a feminist alternative in her work.[1]

In light of the contemporary custom-driven restrictions placed on women's engagement in public debate, an ethos that authorized and encouraged critics such as Thackeray to write in a review of *The Vicar of Wrexhill*, "Oh! . . . that ladies would make puddings and mend stockings!" (79),[2] or an anonymous critic to write in an article titled "Gallery of Literary Characters" in *Fraser's Magazine* (1833):

> Is she [Trollope] to write of politics, or political economy, or pugilism, or punch? Certainly not. We feel a determined dislike of women who wander into these unfeminine paths; they should immediately hoist a mustache— and, to do them justice, they in general do exhibit no inconsiderable specimen of the hair lip. (qtd. in Heineman, *Mrs. Trollope* 183–84)

Trollope's willingness to address thorny political questions, like child labor practices in *Michael Armstrong* and Poor Law reform in *Jessie Phillips*, and the strategies she employed to do so, raise interesting questions about the nature of women's authorship and activism, as well as the relationship of politics, feminism, morality, and art. Certainly, it is well known that Trollope wrote for reasons of financial expediency and, it might be argued, that she selected controversial topics to gain notoriety. She was a professional writer who wanted to know about payment (and scrupulously educated her son, Anthony, about the relationship of publishers, authors, and profit). She also made shrewd guesses about the marketplace: if it was bawdiness the public wanted—and would pay for—then it was bawdiness she would provide; for instance, in *The Widow Barnaby* (1839), Trollope pens a comic novel about a recent widow "fair, fat and forty" who unabashedly seeks her fortune and sexual gratification. If this cost her her reputation as a lady, it had the compensation of providing her family with a livelihood. However, Trollope's choice of subject matter, more importantly, reveals a great deal about her sense of moral purpose, her aims, and her conception of (political) reform and literary activism, and, more generally, highlights the terms and tenor of contemporary cultural and political contests that are enacted in her work. What she wrote about reflects a growing awareness of the needs and problems in the society surrounding her, coupled with a growing dissatisfaction with the constraints of women's prescribed role.

In her novels, Trollope, like Brontë and Gaskell after her, sets out to identify and mitigate the evil intrinsic to the new social order—a systemic evil (rooted, as she saw it, in hypocrisy) that resulted from the dehumanizing consequences of laissez-faire economics and industrialization—typified by the isolation of morality and economics as well as by the disruption of older paternalistic notions of hierarchy and deference. Relying on strong-minded, independent, middle-class women to drive the action and prosecute offenses, Trollope details in her fictions a process of education whereby her heroines try (admirably but unsuccessfully) to re-animate a sense of duty and kinship among the classes as an antidote to contemporary social ills (Bodenheimer 22–23). Trollope's decision to focus on women is dependent on her characterization of the sources of social problems as a function of a failing sense of community.

Trollope subscribes to a theory of gender espoused by Wollstonecraft, what modern scholars label "maternal feminism." Goodness is what women bring to the human enterprise and women come by that goodness through maternal instinct. For Trollope, women's goodness—their moral astuteness—not only authorizes but in fact requires the enlargement of women's traditional sphere of activity to include a public role. Her position is an extension of the Victorian belief that it was a woman's calling and responsibility, through the offices of wife and domestic companion, to guide and uplift her more worldly and intellectual mate. Where some read this highly nuanced ideology as another ruse to keep women locked away in the private sphere, Trollope sees it as justification for women's liberation from that sphere, for nurturing qualities and moral arbitration were what the public sphere urgently needed. In fact, these are what she contracted to provide and what her "female knights," those heroines who present "a moral counterpoint to the apparently agentless system . . . free from the taint of male power or social dominance," embody (Bodenheimer 25; 23).

However, beyond her desire to privilege bourgeois women's experience and moral authority, her social critique is decidedly limited—even conservative—in nature. She is satisfied with a hierarchical distribution of power among the classes; she is not seeking to redress the political disenfranchisement of the laboring poor or women through legal or bureaucratic remedies; she is not asking Parliament to get involved in the negotiation of wages, but she presupposes that the property holders, factory owners, and parliamentarians have a moral responsibility to those whom they employ and govern not to exploit them. When that sense of obligation is upset, the whole nation is set at odds, the social contract is breached, and anarchy inevitably follows. In essence, what Trollope offers in rebuttal to contemporary ills is a potentially paradoxical program of reform-minded paternalism. And while the "dramatically staged female subversions finally fail to engage with the novels' emphatically male structures of power" (Bodenheimer 35), Trollope has thrown down the gauntlet to her reader (to continue the metaphor of the questing knight) to redress the abuses that her heroines have exposed and that exist, more problematically, in the real world than in her fictions. Take Jessie Phillips as a case in point.

Four years after *Michael Armstrong*, in *Jessie Phillips*, Trollope continued to focus on the systemic weaknesses and inequity of British society. Whereas in the former she ostensibly argues for legislation redressing the exploitation of the laboring poor, in the latter novel she confronts the insensitivity and obduracy of new but existing legislation that redefined the welfare system to the particular disadvantage of women. Dealing with politically inflected themes like illegitimacy, poverty, and the discontinuity between law and justice, and focusing on unconventional female archetypes like the elderly pensioner (Margaret Greenhill), the widow (Mrs. Buckhurst), the single young woman with spunk (Ellen Dalton and Martha Maxwell), and the innocent maid of simple honesty (Jessie Phillips), Trollope extends the range of subject matter available to women writers and acts as a witness to a silenced/silent subject. Subtitled *a Tale of the Present Day*, but set ten years before it was written and published, *Jessie Phillips* is an indictment of the 1834 Poor Law reforms, specifically the *relief reforms*, which placed greater emphasis on the workhouse or "union" (and the fact of confinement) rather than on outdoor relief and the *bastardy provisions* that were revised to prevent unwed mothers from demanding support from the fathers of their children. To reify her dual focus in this novel, which is narratologically more complex than her earlier works, Trollope uses two competing and intersecting plot lines that focus on two female knights errant, Martha Maxwell and Ellen Dalton, who independently "unmask the guilty secrets of the patriarchs, set out to rescue the victimized poor, and reap their rewards in the conventional form of marriage" (Bodenheimer 25), while acting according to their role as moral beacons to identify the hypocrisy at the root of the social evils perpetrated in Deepbrook.

In the eponymous Jessie–Martha Maxwell plot, this early "fallen woman" novel recapitulates the basic story line of Elizabeth Inchbald's *Nature and Art* (1794) and forecasts Elizabeth Gaskell's *Ruth* (1853), George Eliot's *Adam Bede* (1859), Thomas Hardy's *Tess of the D'Urbervilles* (1891), and George Moore's *Esther Waters* (1894), all of which adopt with few alterations the same basic predicament of an innocent young girl who believes the promise of marriage from a squire's son and submits to his advances, only to become pregnant and then ostracized by the community upon the birth of her baby. In each of these novels, the plot is resolved uniquely, as each novelist chooses to address different aspects of law, justice, sexuality, and morality. In Trollope's novel, Jessie is taken to the workhouse but escapes with her child and the help of a fellow inmate. Exhausted from the delivery of the baby and her own "delivery" from the workhouse, Jessie falls asleep in a barn, where the child's father (coincidentally nearby) kicks the baby to death in an obviously and self-consciously parodic inversion of the biblical story of Jesus' birth in a manger. Of course, Jessie is charged with the crime. Eventually, the truth about the baby's paternity and murder is discovered by Martha Maxwell (a typical Trollopian heroine, a middle-class woman with boundless energy and an inquiring mind who attempts to blackmail the father into either marrying Jessie or providing for the child and, when that fails, hires Jessie's legal counsel to defend her during her trial), but it is too late; Jessie has died of grief and (on the same day) the baby's father—motivated by guilt, fear, sorrow, or the desire to avoid prosecution (his reasons remain ambiguous)—has accidentally killed himself, "plung[ing] headlong" into a stream where "he was sucked down into a hole . . . and, from some cause or other, rose not again till long after life was extinct" (345).

In the second less programmatic plot, Trollope interweaves the concurrent stories of a proliferation of male characters (Poor Law administrators, clergymen, and landowners) to paint a landscape of life in a provincial town at a moment of great social change as they struggle to implement the Poor Law reforms and, by virtue of a complicated structure of parallels and contrasts, to offer readers a wide variety of viewpoints, changing perspectives, and penetrating analysis of human nature, which demand that readers constantly revise their judgments, alter the balance of their feelings for every character, and enlarge their understanding both of the fictional world and of the real one.[3] In truth, the second plot is dominated by Ellen Dalton and her efforts to expose the insufficiency of the Poor Law as exemplified by the treatment of Mrs. Greenhill by the Poor Law administrators.

The plots converge in the final section of the novel when Martha Maxwell and Ellen Dalton team up during the trial to rescue Jessie, when circumstantial evidence is marshaled against her, when she herself has come to believe her accusers, who offer no alternative theory of the crime. Ellen and Martha have indefatigable energy, but they cannot move the system. Though Jessie is declared not guilty by reason of temporary insanity, she cannot be restored or redeemed; she dies a fallen woman (not a murderer), victimized by Frederick and the system of laws that ought to have protected her. The system also makes Ellen and Martha complicit, as they feel compelled not to identify Frederick as the father/murderer for fear of damaging the reputation of the Dalton family and destabilizing the entire community of Deepbrook, which looks to the Daltons for leadership.

At the time the novel begins, a new assistant-commissioner of the workhouse is being installed in the idyllic community of Deepbrook. The installation of Mr. Mortimer—even his name distinguishes him as an agent of death—reflects a new attitude to the poor sparked by the passage of Poor Law reform. Where once outdoor relief was offered and charity was regarded as a moral duty, now all petitions for assistance are met with dehumanizing scorn, sarcasm, and insult from administrators (a new class of bureaucrats) who preen and practice their rebukes, trying to outwit each other, insulting the character of the poor who appear before them, in a setting that closely mimics but ultimately mocks the solemnity of a courtroom. An early incident in the novel clearly sets the tone. Mrs. Greenhill, a well-respected pensioner, is forced to petition the board for assistance for her grandchildren. Her son has borrowed money using her name as collateral; he cannot pay his creditors and is jailed. At once, she is "shewn into the room," where:

> a particularly active-spirited guardian . . . newly appointed, and really liking the employment, addressed her from his place at the bottom of the table round which they were sitting, with the concise question, rather loudly articulated,—
> "Who are you?"
> "My name, sir, is Margaret Greenhill."
> "What do you want?" was the next demand.
> "Assistance, sir, for—"
> "Yes, yes; you need not go in that direction, we all know that. Of course, that is the cuckoo cry, from first to last,—'Assistance, sir.' I wish, to my soul, that we could have a little variety, and that some of you would have the exceeding kindness to want something else." (23)

In this exchange, the commissioner's failure to recognize Mrs. Greenhill, who has lived in this community all her life, as well as his unwillingness to listen, his rudeness, abruptness, and impudence, suggest an antagonism rooted solely in Mrs. Greenhill's newfound state of poverty. Her social identity and worth are now literally dependent on her (son's) financial solvency. Another commissioner continues the interview,

> "Shame! shame! shame! " cried the indignant Mr. Huttonworth, all propensity of mirth being for the moment conquered and subdued by his virtuous abhorrence of the profligate maternity, thus openly avowed. "Are

you not ashamed,—a woman of decent appearance like you are, to come and ask the active, honest, intelligent, thrifty part of the population to rob themselves and their own children (honestly brought into the world, with the consciousness that there was power to maintain them),—are you ashamed, old woman, to come here to take their money out of their pockets, in order to feed this litter of brats, that you know in your own heart and conscience ought never to have been born at all?" (25)

What seems to be at issue for the commissioner are female profligacy and the fecundity of the poor; this is ironic given Mrs. Greenhill's character and age, the fact that the children in question are not her own but her son Tom's, that her family has not been poor very long (so that it would be difficult to argue that the children were the product of the imprudent sexual practices associated with the poor as opposed to prudent planning on the part of the bourgeoisie), and that the family has been thrown into poverty because of Tom's admirable, if misguided, ambition to advance in the world of business from the position of lowly carpenter to esteemed rank of boss and builder—but it is in the disproportionality, incongruity, and disrespectfulness of Huttonworth's response to Mrs. Greenhill's plea for assistance where lies Trollope's implicit rebuke of the new system of relief. Huttonworth is clearly echoing Malthusian fears about population growth in light of what was perceived to be a growing competition for resources in his indictment of the lower classes for producing more off-spring than they could support, suggested in his parenthesis: "(honestly brought into the world, with the consciousness that there was power to maintain them)." His remarks reveal his anxiety about the nature and causes of poverty, his belief that poverty is a moral not an economic con-dition and, concomitantly, that his role as a relief commissioner involves providing moral judgment rather than financial assistance.

Over the course of her petition, Mrs. Greenhill's penury is seamlessly metamorphosed into an outward sign of her debased moral nature. Huttonworth impugns her moral character and the legitimacy of her grandchildren—asking her if she feels no "shame," contrasting her to the "active, honest, intelligent, thrifty part of the population" who presum-ably would prefer to starve than ask for assistance, comparing her grand-children to those "honestly brought into the world," and implicitly ac-cusing her of dissembling by suggesting that her "decent appearance" belies a flawed nature. He can do this simply because he takes his cue from the new law and disavows any personal responsibility for Mrs. Greenhill's condition. Dramatizing an individual case before the commission, Trollope reflects how (quickly) poverty has become a moral indictment and how the social/moral dynamic has changed as a result of Poor Law reform: no longer do the charitable "give"; instead, the poor "take." As a consequence, the administrator feels no qualms about dismissing the children as a "litter of brats" that should have been culled at birth, the implicit suggestion of his remark that they "ought never to have been born at all," prefiguring and problematizing the subsequent death of Jessie's child. After all, if Huttonworth believes that poor children ought not to have been born, that they can be compared to animals and are worth less than other children, he ought to hold the murderer of Jessie's baby to a different standard than that of a common criminal; to follow the logic of his position through to its natural conclusion, he might even be grateful that one more child is not going to be presented to the administrators for care. Additionally, Mrs. Greenhill's case provides Trollope with the opportunity to examine women's particular disadvantage. The New Poor Law affects women disproportionately: women have fewer legitimate sources of income than men, women are more dependent on others for their physical and financial security, women are primarily responsible for the care of children, yet the law is blind to these realities.

Mrs. Greenhill's son's recklessness is virtually ignored by the commissioners. Tom borrowed money and overextended himself; more importantly, he traded on his mother's reputation and income to secure loans that would enable him to expand his business, only to end up in debtor's prison, thus throwing his children onto the helpless shoulders of a woman who could not earn a living. This older woman (three-fold vulnerable by virtue of her age, gender, and class) is asked to carry the burden of raising children who are not her own and of finding money (without any real sources of employment) to rescue her son from his own mismanaged affairs, with the workhouse and ignominy looming in the offing. Trollope is clearly indicating an injustice not only in the law but also in the way it is enacted. The law and its prosecution exacts its "pound of flesh" from the most vulnerable members of society, those least responsible for their predicament and those least likely to reclaim their lives by force of will. In the way in which the Greenhill case is resolved, Trollope also illustrates an alternative model of charity. Ellen, the eldest daughter of the village squire, unsentimental, intelligent, independent-minded, secretly donates a personal legacy and puts the widow on a temporary allowance during Tom's imprisonment for debt, which allows the widow Greenhill and her grandchildren to resist the workhouse. Ellen's generosity, an example of an older tradition of giving, challenges the value, inevitability, and modernity of the new public and bureaucratic system, which provides little comfort and exacts great punishment.

The way in which a society treats the poor reveals a great deal about its ideological foundations. According to Samuel Johnson, "A decent provision for the poor is the true test of civilization. . . . The condition of the lower orders, the poor especially, [is] the true mark of national discrimination" (qtd. in Boswell 182). By setting the novel in 1834, Trollope allows her characters to debate the New Poor Law (at the time it was passed) and speculate how it might evolve over the next ten years (when she is actually writing), assuming for herself the benefit of hindsight. From the beginning, the administrators admit to a general discomfort over the new law and are forced to confront their own ideological presumptions about the poor and about laws generally as instruments of statecraft and social policy. The newly appointed administrators (who are not lawyers but landowners) are placed in the difficult position of interpreting, evaluating, and implementing the law, from a position of ignorance or naiveté. One question that is tacitly raised and debated early on concerns the nature of law itself: is a law a dynamic document that reflects social realities and the conscience of the community, or is it an unforgiving edict that its administrators are meant to blindly enforce? This question is difficult to answer, in part, because of the nature of the political federation: while local governments may be best able to respond to local contingencies, there is an argument to be made for the establishment of national standards; concomitantly, though the national government, fettered as it is by bureaucracy and precedent and removed from local realities, may engineer ill-fitting solutions in each case (brandishing a sword when a teaspoon would do), it can be argued that it compensates for its arbitrariness by the seemingly impartial and uniform character of justice it offers. Of course, this discussion begs the question, Where does mercy fit into the equation? The administrators must confront the fact that the New Poor Law was drafted in distant London, a place they imagine to be antiseptic and disinterested, but must be administered in a bucolic, closely bound community like Deepbrook—a complication that is manifest in the transplantation and acclimatization of Mr. Mortimer from London to Deepbrook. Not surprisingly, each commissioner articulates a different point of view. For instance, Mr. Wilson, the rector of Hortonthorpe, argues that the legislators in London could not have imagined or intended the consequences of the law:

> If all that has been done towards rendering the labouring poor of England helpless, hopeless, destitute, and desperate, was *intended* by the framers of the New Poor-Law, they would stand before us in colours that it would be libellous to assign them. We are, therefore, bound not only by Christian charity, but by social discretion, to nourish a belief in their having so far blundered in their most difficult task as to have done much which they had no intention of doing. . . . I am perfectly convinced that this is the case, and that by far the best and wisest mode of assisting the legislation in saving

the country from absolute and inevitable destruction that must have en-
sued from the continuance of the old law, is by NOT following to the letter
the enactments of the new one. (53)

Alternatively, Huttonworth worries, "that the bill can[not] work as it
ought to work, as long as local acquaintance and neighbourly feelings have
any opportunity of interfering" (30). For Huttonworth, the administration of the law is undermined by human feeling; what is needed for ultimate utilitarian efficiency, he argues, is a more mechanical and disinterested approach to sentencing. However, given his abrasive character and
the stridency of his opinions, Trollope is clearly rebuking the implication
that the law ought to be anything but the codification of reason tempered
by feeling or mercy. Nevertheless, despite Huttonworth's discreditable
view, he seems to be winning the debate: petitioners, no matter what their
circumstance or character, inevitably are sent to the Deepbrook Union,
an informal prison, which has "the faculty of obliterating from the minds
of all without, the remembrance, even of the names, and the existence,
of those within it" (40). In essence, this is what the New Poor Law demands and the commissioners are following the letter of the law.

The New Poor Law requires that the administrators incarcerate the in-
digent; in effect, depriving the poor of their freedom and self-respect, de-
basing and humiliating them by inscribing their names on public rolls,
alleviating only the worst of their poverty by providing the most meager
sustenance (feeding the inmates gruel, for instance, to insure that the poor
would not want to stay in the workhouse) while, at the same time, exposing them to diseases bred in the close confines of the workhouse. The
poor are demoralized and dehumanized by the public and legal status of
dependency codified by the new law. The rich and bourgeoisie, on the
other hand, resentful of the demands the poor, are now required to make
on the public purse, rather than on individual charity. As a result of the
law, the social order is upset. Where once the "haves" shared with the
"have-nots" and the social order was maintained through the act or, at
least, the perception of caring, Mr. Rimmington worries that the thread
that ties rich and poor may have been irreparably cut by an act designed
to ameliorate the problem of poverty. He asks,

> The cruel part of the business is the [*sic*] having cut the tie that, through-
> out the whole country, bound the rich and the poor together by interests
> that were reciprocal, and which could not be loosened on either side, with-
> out injury to both. What is the connexion between them now? (55)

In effect, the new law jeopardizes not only the paternalistic structure of
society but also the legitimacy of the social order, the ethos that binds

rich and poor together. Benjamin Disraeli, in *Sybil* (1845), written one year after *Jessie Phillips*, uses the potent metaphor of "two nations" to characterize the schism between rich and poor, suggesting an internecine conflict fed by mutual distrust, fear, and loathing:

> Two nations; between whom there is no intercourse and no sympathy; who are as ignorant of each other's habits, thoughts, and feelings, as if they were dwellers in different zones, or inhabitants of different planets; who are formed by different breeding, are fed by a different food, are ordered by different manners, and are not governed by the same laws. (1980: 96)

Significantly, from the beginning, agitation against the New Poor Law merged with a variety of other issues: child labor, women's labor, taxes, Corn Laws, national debt, temperance, education, emigration, private property, even the family. Thus, the controversies of the 1830s and 1840s went beyond the New Poor Law or the issue of poverty narrowly defined, and raised the largest questions about property and equality, natural law and social contract, the rights and duties of individuals, as well as the obligations of the society and the state. What gives the question of poverty its urgency is not, as Engels thought, the fear of social revolution, but the sense of moral inversion and social disarray. In this context, it is easy to demonstrate a schematic affinity between *Jessie Phillips* and *Michael Armstrong*; moreover, in *Jessie Phillips*, as in *Michael Armstrong*, it is again the women in the community, particularly Mrs. Buckhurst and Ellen Dalton, who are most troubled by recent changes, most active in seeking redress and provide most starkly a counterpoint to the arguments of the male coterie of bureaucrats. Mrs. Buckhurst, in conversation with Ellen, says,

> "I sometimes fear . . . that I am too apt to encourage the propensity of disliking new laws and lamenting old ones, which is attributed to the aged on all occasions. . . . And yet, " she added, "not all the candour I can school myself into expressing, can . . . make me approve the erection of that bare-faced monster of a Union Poor-house, which seems to glare upon us with its hundred eyes from what used to be the prettiest meadow in the parish. I wish I had not seen [it] . . . —I wish . . . I had not seen old Simon Rose, with his granddaughter, poor soul! and her three little ones, standing before that dreadful Richard Dempster, the governor, looking as if they thought that life and death depended on his will. I have never got the group out of my head since. All the fearful change in the treatment of the poor, which has followed the erection of this prison-like place, *may* be very useful. . . . But even the new commissioner himself might be inclined to make some allowance for the poor blundering old people of the district, if he did but know the contrast between what they see now and what they

4.1: "The DeepBrook Union" by John Leech in Frances Trollope, *Jessie Phillips: a Tale of the Present Day*. 3 vols. London: Colburn, 1844: 16.

looked on formerly. We have a worse name to our house of refuge there . . . than the new folks have given theirs. We called it the workhouse, which bears a sort of threatening in its name; and it was not, nor was it intended to be, a dwelling to be desired or sought for. But oh! the heavy change! Deepbrook Workhouse was to Deepbrook Union what a free state is to a slave state in America. But this will never do . . . !" (16)

Mrs. Buckhurst acts as the collective memory of the community, dispensing an oral history and a sense of moral rectitude that puts the new law in context. Is the care of the poor a legal or a moral question? How can we avert our eyes to the sorrow and circumstances of our friends, those whom we have lived along side for generations, especially in a time of genuine need? Memory and mercy work hand in hand for Mrs. Buckhurst, a fact revealed in her tortured recollection of the Rose family at the Union door and emphasized by the same scene illustrated by John Leech. The combined text and illustration put the reader in the comparable and privileged position of recalling the family in their misery (Illustration 4.1). Moreover, the twin ironies of changing the name of the workhouse to Deepbrook Union and of locating the Union on "the prettiest meadow," do not escape her watchful eye either. Mrs. Buckhurst is attuned to the past and wary of the future. She is aware that there are new statutes that redefine the poor and set out protocols for the administration of relief which reflect the changing attitudes of the time; however, there is nothing inviolable about statutes and protocols. The law reflects its ideological foundations: it is only possible to incarcerate the poor in a workhouse when they are allotted fewer rights and a lesser status than those citizens with property and the good luck to keep it. While a new Poor Law may be necessary, a point which both Mrs. Buckhurst and Trollope herself are willing to concede, the law exceeds its warrant when it confuses poverty with crime or character, abrogating the Constitution as well as Christian doctrine by denying individuals their dignity. For Trollope, the law, like art, is about morality: each should be humane, personal and function to regulate the lesser human passions. There is no "practical wisdom" nor "morality" in a law that is exacting, unforgiving, and arbitrary; there is nothing inherently modern or Enlightened about the New Poor Law; instead, it is a monument to "expediency" (352): it conceals the poor behind the walls of the workhouse and attempts to obliterate them from communal memory, but fails to address the underlying causes of poverty or recognize the common humanity of people, animated by Mrs. Buckhurst and Ellen Dalton who refuse to abide the indignities of the system.

Another aspect of Poor Law reform involved the redrafting of the bastardy provisions; these reforms provide the context for the Jessie plot in

Jessie Phillips. Whereas the relief reforms strained the structure of society that bound rich and poor, the bastardy reforms compromised the ethos that bound men and women. Where once the financial responsibility for children sired out of wedlock was the obligation of the father, bowing to pressure, the law was changed. Women alone assumed financial responsibility for their children. In 1834, "all laws enabling a woman or a Local Authority to charge a man with being the father of an illegitimate child, and enabling a magistrate to levy maintenance upon him, arrest him, or attach his goods and chattels, were repealed" (Henriques 113). Men no longer had to pay support. In *Jessie Phillips*, Frederick Dalton, the scion of the Dalton family, a rogue who fashions himself a Byronic hero, is keenly aware of this legal reform and his timely good fortune:

> The terror that formerly kept so many libertines of all classes in check was no longer before him, the legislature having, in its collective wisdom, deemed it "discreetest, best," that the male part of the population should be guarded, protected, sheltered, and insured from all the pains and penalties arising from the crime he contemplated. "No, No," thought Mr. Frederick Dalton, "thanks to our noble lawgivers, there is no more wearing away a gentleman's incognito now. It is just one of my little bits of good luck that this blessed law should be passed. (67)

Frederick typifies the decadent aspects of English society; he is the epitome of the aristocratically decadent world. In genealogical terms, he is the end of the line, epitomizing and fulfilling all that had gone before—the end, it should be stressed, of descent through the male line. With a new provision in place that exempts him from financial responsibility, Frederick believes he is at liberty to seduce women without fear of the consequences. Without the protection of the law, the virginal and gullible Jessie, who Frederick seduces after a protracted courtship, becomes:

> poor wretch! . . . the victim of the short-sighted policy of her country, which, while hoping (vainly) to save a few yearly shillings from the poor-rates, has decreed that a weak woman (that is to say a weak *poor* woman) who has committed this sin shall atone for it by being trampled in the dust, imprisoned in a workhouse with her wretched offspring till driven from it to seek food for both by labour, that the most respectable part of her own sex refuse her upon principle! . . . Why, he, being of the sex which make the laws, is so snugly sheltered by them that there is no earthly reason whatsoever why he should not go on in the course he has begun, and thank the gods that he is not a woman. (204)

As the narrator makes clear, Jessie is not Frederick's victim nor is she the victim of her own sexual passion. Rather, she is her nation's "help-

less scape-goat" (204); she is the "victim of . . . her country," of an econo-
mizing strategy, forsaken and then "trampled in the dust" because, unlike her male counterpart, she is without political influence or identity. If
the law were just, she would have recourse to Frederick's support, to the
promise of anything but moral and physical degradation, and Frederick
would not be protected from opprobrium. However, because the law is
written by men, who presumably see some advantage in exempting themselves from financial responsibility for their illegitimate children, Frederick
in theory can rest easy "snugly sheltered" by the laws, while Jessie is exposed to the scorn of the community. Of course, this presupposes that
the law is the final arbiter. In practice, Frederick cannot free himself from
his conscience (a force more powerful than any other earthly agent). Al-
ternately, he is wracked with guilt over abandoning Jessie, with fear as
he expects his relationship with her to be revealed and his prospects for
the future, his title, inheritance, and marriage to a more suitable lady, to
be jeopardized, and with false almost hysterical confidence or presumption as he tries to persuade Ellen that her accusations/suspicions of him
are proof of her delirium. Believing that the baby alone is the evidence
of his indiscretion, Frederick kicks it to death, but this only compounds
his guilt and fear, especially when Jessie is charged with the crime. Jessie's
conscience works in contradistinction to Frederick's. Jessie assumes full
responsibility for her baby's death, even though she is unconscious when
the child is murdered; she believes that a good mother ought to have been
able to protect her baby and a bad mother was just as likely to kill her
own child as allow it to be killed. She patiently awaits her execution, with
a demure and quiet resilience that affirms her true worth, signaling, as
well more sadly, that the Poor Law has killed her spirit and her baby, with
the law being personified by Frederick himself; Frederick dies a coward
and an egotist who cannot admit guilt, culpability, or contrition. The tragedy of this ending is a portentous warning about the danger and deca-
dence of illegitimate progeny, as well as a stunning indictment of the intellectual and moral poverty of the dominant culture, the regressive
tendencies, and the inverted logic, which could not imagine Frederick's
guilt and speculated wildly about Jessie's.

Jessie's case history provides proof that the real source of tribulation is
simply the dependent status of women. She is, we are told,

> Too weak, too erring, to be remembered with respect, yet not so bad but
> that some may feel it a thing to wonder at that she, and the terribly tempted
> class of which she is the type, should seem so very decidedly to be selected
> by the Solons of the day as a sacrifice for all the sins of all their sex. Why
> one class of human beings should be sedulously protected by a special law
> from the consequences of their own voluntary indiscretions, it is not very

easy to comprehend; but it is more difficult still to assign any satisfactory
reason why another class should be in like manner selected as the subject
of special law, for the express purpose of making them subject to all the
pains and penalties, naturally consequent upon the faults committed by the
protected class above mentioned. . . . I will not venture any protest against
this seemingly one-sided justice, beyond the expression of a wish that the
unhappy class, thus selected for victims, were not so very decidedly, and
so very inevitably, the weakest, and in all ways the least protected portion
of society. There is no chivalry in the selection, and, to the eyes of ignorance like mine, there is no justice. (349)

Jessie has been "selected . . . as a sacrifice" not to propitiate the gods but
to "sedulously protect" men from the consequences of "their own vol-
untary indiscretions." *John Bull* was shocked: "Mrs Trollope has sinned
grievously against good taste and decorum. The particular cause of the
Act which she has selected for reprobation is the *bastardy clause*—not
perhaps the very best subject for a female pen" (qtd. in Ransom, *Fanny
Trollope* 152). In 1844, however, in part as a result of the novel's popularity, the bastardy clause was amended, restoring to unwed mothers the
rights that had been taken from them with the Poor Law reforms; namely,
that fathers of illegitimate children be compelled to assume financial responsibility for their offspring. But again, as in *Michael Armstrong*,
Trollope's willingness to engage in this debate, one in which the rules of
propriety are so decidedly and obviously upset, has less to do with bastardy itself than with the outrageousness of the laws devised to address
it.[4] As the passage makes clear, the bastardy provision codified "special"
laws to prosecute one class of people (women, poor women) who were
least able to defend themselves. There is "no chivalry," "no justice" in
exploiting people made vulnerable by their class, gender, and circumstance; in fact, society exploits women repeatedly: initially, by failing to
protect them from the sexual whims of men, by not educating them appropriately about the ways of the world, by not discouraging men from
acts of sexual adventurism, and subsequently by freeing men from the consequences of their actions while demanding that women assume sole responsibility for their illegitimate children. Jessie's example challenges an
ideology of separate spheres that encourages women to remain in the
domestic sphere, pretty, petted, and ignorant, all the while unsafe and
unprotected by the institutions that purport to represent reason, morality, and justice. At the same time, Ellen Dalton and Martha Maxwell provide counterpoints to this model of female conduct and acquiescence.
Though they are unable to affect "the system," they are able to check
the prohibitions of the bastardy clause, expose the moral failings of the
Poor Law reforms, see through male stratagems to provide Jessie with

counsel, and gain comfort in the knowledge that they were right to have faith in an innocent girl. All laws, Poor Law, bastardy provisions, factory acts, and marriage and divorce laws, need to protect the weakest members of society. For women, children, and the laboring poor this means that the law must grant either equality or protection; if the law cannot guarantee individual liberty, dignity, and virtue, then responsibility for them ought to be granted to the individuals concerned.

In her work, Trollope disrupts the convenient binarisms of private/ public, domestic/political, virtue/vice, female/male, mass fiction/social criticism; however, she is not an iconoclast. What Trollope found shocking and distressing was immorality whether it existed in the closeted sexual practices in Deepbrook or in the exploitation of children in the northern textile mills. Her critics attacked her on the basis of her gender and on a presumption that she violated a code of decorum that prevented women from engaging in political discussions, but, as for most reformers in this period, her religious faith provided a context and an underpinning for her activism; her goal is clearly to contribute to the restructuring of society on moral principles. However, by submerging her moral vision into the texture of life, vividly imagined and dramatically presented, Trollope helped to define an important tradition in English fiction, the popular novel infused with social protest. In her fiction and travel writing, she provides ample evidence of her political interest: she drew complex female characters; wrote sexually frank, realistic social fictions; and expanded the conventions of female authorship. As Katherine Tillotson remarks, Trollope played a crucial role in extending the parameters of Victorian fiction to include the sociopolitical by moving it away from making "love and marriage seem the main business of life" (122). In truth, Trollope does not so much move away from the marriage plot as expand the possibilities of political discussion around the implications of the domestic, imploding some of the popular misconceptions about domesticity, woman's sphere, and the role of women in society, providing a counterpoint to the entrenched ideology of separate spheres.

NOTES

1. Trollope saw gender politics at work in the home as well as on the public stage, and she was equally critical of injustice in both spheres. Mocking her critics, who insisted she write "domestic" fictions, that is, novels about submissive women, Trollope wrote *The Widow Barnaby* (1839) and *One Fault* (1840), one of the first novels (along with Wollstonecraft's *Mary*) to dramatize an unhappy marriage in which the fault (as indicated in its title) lies in the jealous character of the husband. In *One Fault* Trollope provides a new model of female conduct; as the narrator explains, if the long-suffering heroine had been "a high-spirited

violent woman . . . her liberal, gentlemanlike, and honourable husband might have been cured, after a few years . . . of those pampered vices of temper which now neutralized or smothered all his good qualities" (2: 153).

2. This sentiment as expressed by Thackeray was commonplace enough to be ironically echoed in *Jane Eyre*: as Jane muses, "It is narrow-minded in their more privileged fellow-creatures to say that they ought to confine themselves to making puddings and knitting stockings, to playing on the piano and embroidering bags. It is thoughtless to condemn them, or laugh at them, if they seek to do more or learn more than custom has pronounced necessary for their sex" (Brontë 141).

3. There is a great deal to be said about the possible influence of Trollope on George Eliot, or, if not influence, then about the comparable approaches each author took. For instance, the intersecting plots of *Jessie Phillips* anticipate the pattern of *Daniel Deronda*. As well, the focus and trajectory of what I have called the second plot, that is, the social documentary plot of *Jessie Phillips*, is comparable to that in Eliot's *Middlemarch*, itself a novel set in the recent past about a momentous time of political turmoil in the idyllic regions of England.

4. It is my contention that while critics were disturbed by the explicit political content of *Michael Armstrong*, that the passing of a Factory Act was peripheral to Trollope's goals. Despite the fact that her critics chose to focus on the political content of Michael Armstrong, more interestingly and importantly, the more fundamental question that Trollope addresses in the novel is, how did the system of child labor come about originally? How depraved is the attitude of people that they allowed the system to be created in the first place and then perpetuated it, even after an outcry from the mills and mill towns, and from people of unblemished character like her own Mr. Bell?

5

A "Serious Epidemic": Frances Trollope and the Evangelical Movement

Douglas Murray

It is unfortunate that Jane Austen, talented daughter of a late-eighteenth-century high-church rectory, never clarified her views on Evangelicalism, that movement in the Church of England whose effects on Anglo-Saxon religion and character have never sufficiently been acknowledged.[1]

On the one hand, Austen writes the following to her favorite niece Fanny Austen Knight, who found herself strangely attracted to the very serious Rev. Mr. John-Pemberton Plumptre: "As to there being any objection from his *Goodness*, from the danger of his becoming Evangelical, I cannot admit *that*. I am by no means convinced that we ought not all to be Evangelicals, & am at least persuaded that they who are so from Reason & Feeling, must be happiest & safest."[2] Austen shrouds her statement in ambiguity, as if she does not wish to be too committal with a favorite niece. But two years later, writing to her sister Cassandra, she could be more frank: she writes of her Evangelical cousin, the Rev. Edward Cooper, "We do not much like Mr Cooper's new Sermons;—they are more full of Regeneration & Conversion than ever—with the addition of his zeal in the cause of the Bible Society."[3] Austen's comment is astute, observing as it does both the distinguishing doctrine of the Evangelicals—their assertion that each believer must be able to cite experiential evidence for his or her salvation—and a distinguishing policy of the Evangelical party: its support of the British and Foreign Bible Society, which preferred distributing Bibles to prayer books.[4] However, her letters never mention William Wilberforce, the virtual leader of the movement, though she does express occasional disapproval of Hannah More, the Evangelical party's writer-in-residence. And Evangelicalism does not surface at all in her novels—unless, that is, one argues that the Rev. Edmund Bertram's (and his future wife Fanny Price's) dour displeasure, evident throughout *Mansfield Park*, presage an Evangelical future.

The attitude of another talented daughter of a late-eighteenth-century high-church rectory was fortunately much clarified: Frances Trollope's *The Vicar of Wrexhill* (1837) is a key document in understanding Tory/High-Church objections to Evangelicalism, expressing dismay at the new movement, which was greatly altering the church into which she had been baptized.

Trollope's biographers all find the origin of this novel in her acquaintance with the Rev. John William Cunningham, the Evangelical rector of St. Mary's, Harrow and the author of *The Velvet Cushion* (1814), a work much reprinted on both sides of the Atlantic. As is well known, Frances disliked Cunningham for his handling of the death in 1822 of Lord Byron's illegitimate daughter Allegra, born to Byron and Claire Claremont. Cunningham would not allow the funeral service to be read in St. Mary's, and refused the father's request for a memorial monument, on the grounds that such a plaque would teach young Harovians to "get bastards " (Neville-Sington, *Fanny Trollope* 69)—yet, at the same time, praising Byron's work and sending unctuous compliments to the mourning poet. Cunningham was later to move into Julians, the house that the Trollopes occupied in Harrow before financial difficulties forced them to leave. During these Harrow years, the Trollopes primarily socialized with opponents of Cunningham and Frances wrote "Signs of the Times. The Righteous Rout," a brief comic play in rhyming couplets satirizing the dullness of an Evangelical evening: a rout was "A fashionable gathering or assembly, a large evening party or reception" (OED), but in Trollope's play the fictional Rev. Mr. Fripp serves "The not inebriating, but cheering tea" rather than wine (1), and conversation turns upon such subjects as children's contribution to the "branch missionary child's committee":

'tis so sweetly pretty

To see each saintly little angel come

Holding between its' finger and its' [*sic*] thumb

The halfpenny that once was spent in sin. (4)

Frances Trollope undoubtedly had reason to satirize and dislike Cunningham—but ample reason for such savagery as in the fictional portrait of William Cartwright, who is not just a killjoy but a scheming villain?

Cunningham's writings do not, at first reading, provide justification for such savagery. *The Velvet Cushion* is a surprisingly mild, nonvenomous document, in fact, one whose Evangelical positions reveal themselves only slowly. *The Cushion* is an imaginative account of the history of the English Church, from pre-Reformation times to the early nineteenth century, told from the point of view of a velvet cushion, the sort of pulpit cushion upon which an eighteenth-century preacher would rest his notes, as in the well-known engraving *The Sleepy Congregation* by William Hogarth (October 1736).[5] In its combination of imaginative point of view and allegory, *The Velvet Cushion* recalls Swift's *A Tale of a Tub*, which reimagines the history of the Western church as an account of the argument among brothers Peter, Martin, and John over a coat inherited from their father. *The Cushion* is, for an Evangelical work, on occasion surprisingly generous to the Church of Rome, the cushion reminding "good Protestants, that you owe to Popery almost every good thing that deserves to be called by the name of a Church. Popery is the religion of Cathedrals—Protestantism of houses—Dissenterism of barns" (17).[6]

Most commentators suggest that Frances Trollope's portrait of the Rev. Cartwright derives from a combination of her dismay over Cunningham's hypocrisy at the time of the Byron burial, from her fear that Cunningham's kisses of peace could turn into less innocent caresses, and from her class-based perspectives that the Evangelicals were low class. No one grants her any interest in religion or insight into ecclesiastical history. The general tenor of commentary is that Frances and her household were "only nominally religious" (Hall, *Trollope* 1991: 15). Some of this attitude derives from the Trollopes' eldest son Thomas Adolphus (1810–1892), who wrote in his memoirs, "I think there was a perfunctory saying of some portions of the catechism on a Sunday morning. . . . But . . . in our own minds, and apparently in those of all concerned, the vastly superior importance of the Virgil lesson admitted of no doubt."[7] Scholarship can never hope to gauge the depth of Frances Trollope's religious life, but the more one examines her portrait of W. J. Cartwright, the more astute a commentator on religion and the Evangelical movement she becomes. The novel *The Vicar of Wrexhill* is, in fact, a well-argued Anglican refutation of the Evangelical position, an astute commentary upon its typical methods, and an almost prophetic analysis of its effects.

The mild tone of *The Velvet Cushion* only gradually reveals its tendentious Evangelicalism. Significantly, Frances Trollope noted exactly what makes it an Evangelical tract and refuted that insinuation in *The Vicar of Wrexhill*. What is most original about *The Cushion* is its account of the Restoration and eighteenth-century church. It claimed that the Enlightenment saw the institution of a new sort of Roman Catholicism without the Pope: in that era, Cunningham writes, "the genius of Popery, I mean—the form without the spirit of religion presided in the pulpit, and at the altar, almost as much as ever" (60). After the Restoration of Charles II, the pulpit cushion "heard little more of Christ, and faith, and conversion. . . . Pomp grew, and devotion languished. Violent assaults were made on the sanctity of the Sabbath" (58–60). The Enlightenment church—which would include the church of Frances Trollope's father—was simply "Popery in a mask" (60), presumably awaiting a second reformation in the form of the Evangelicals, represented by the author, J. W. Cunningham.

Trollope begins *The Vicar of Wrexhill* by refuting Cunningham's claim that the Enlightenment had marked a lapse or lacuna in the history of the church. She opens with an idyllic sketch of the region of Wrexhill in the early 1830s, before the arrival of the Evangelical clergy. Wrexhill is made up of village, manor house, an "antique church" of "grey and mellow beauty," and a "pretty Vicarage, as if placed expressly to keep watch and ward over the safety and repose of its sacred neighbor" (1). The church's age suggests an unbroken religious continuity—it is an outward and visible sign of apostolic succession—and the Vicarage's role "to keep watch and ward" over the church is emphasized; there is no hint that any previous generations have allowed any dilapidation of the building or witnessed any falling off of the vicar's activity and care.

The other chief characteristic of the church and vicarage is the "luxurience" of "immortal and unfading" ivy that freely proliferates. Some, the narrator notes, would trim the vine, but the former rector, now dead, representative of the pre-Evangelical English church, would not allow "those graceful pendants" (1) to be shorn. Here, the ivy serves in fact as the first indication of the anti-Evangelical theme of the novel and as an indication of the profoundly Anglican theology of Frances Trollope. This ivy is not a symptom of a romantic taste for greenery but rather an image that, for Trollope and the Anglicans, nature and her works are not distrusted.

A brief historical-theological digression is in order. The first great apologist for the new Church of England had been Richard Hooker (c. 1554–1600), whose *Laws of Ecclesiastical Polity* defined Anglican approach to Grace, natural reason, and secular culture. Hooker, writing to defend the Church of England against Calvinism, rejects the Calvinists' view that Nature and Grace are completely opposing forces. For Calvin, for the Elizabethan Puritans, and later for their ideological descendants the Evangelicals, nature, natural reason, the secular are so fallen that they must be eradicated; the world is to be divided into the clean and the unclean, and it is the task of the religious to eradicate the unclean. But for Hooker, all things that exist still partake in God's original goodness (1: 164): he writes "Wisdom and reason—even wisdom and reason which are not directly heaven-inspired—are good: The bounds of wisdom are large, and within them much is contained" (1: 236). Even if a man does not constantly focus upon God, his actions are not any less devout:

> We move, we sleep, we take the cup at the hand of our friend, a number of things we oftentimes do, only to satisfy some natural desire, without present, express, and actual reference unto any commandment of God. Unto this glory even these things are done which we naturally perform, and not only that which morally and spiritually we do. For by every effect proceeding from the most concealed instincts of nature His power is made manifest. But it doth not therefore follow that of necessity we shall sin, unless we expressly intend this in every such particular. (1: 238)

Hooker is hesitant to separate human motivations and the world into clean and unclean: "The Gospel, by not making many things unclean, as the Law did, hath sanctified those things generally to all, which particularly every man unto himself must sanctify by a reverend and holy use" (1: 240).[8]

Such were not the views of Richard Hooker's most striking sixteenth-century opponent, whose mission was to divide the universe and all human acts into the godly—which were to be cultivated—and the ungodly—which were to be zealously eradicated. This opponent argued, for example, that because unsanctified pans and brooms had not been allowed in the Temple at Jerusalem, the Apocrypha and the Elizabethan *Book of Homilies* were not to be read in churches (1: 157; qtd. in Lewis 446). The name of this opponent—a name withheld until this moment—was Thomas Cartwright (1535–1603). The representative of this Elizabethan in Frances Trollope's *Wrexhill* is, well, the Rev. Cartwright.

Among Frances Trollope's chief charges against W. J. Cartwright is that he is a ruthless, un-Anglican eradicator. He does not promote neo-medieval fêtes, such as that which had celebrated the coming of age of Charles Mowbray, and instead institutes fundraisers for foreign missions. He institutes a fashion among the women for hair carefully pulled back. He is distrustful of high and ornate human art, exiling even Handel's oratorios and Haydn's *Creation* on the grounds that "a simpler style is preferable" (113). He rids Wrexhill of its schoolmaster and publican. Under his tutelage, Italian songs are banished (120); English secular songs are discarded and old tunes are provided with new words. A popular ballad

> Fly not yet[;] 'tis just the hour,
>
> When nature like the midnight flour,

That scorns the eye of vulgar light,

Begins to bloom. . . .[9]

becomes

Fly not yet! 'Tis just the hour

When prayerful Christians own the power

That, inly beaming with new light,

Begins to sanctify. . . . (114)

Note the characteristic distrust of nature and its bloom (a distrust to which Hooker had alerted us) and the substitution of the new light of grace and sanctity.[10]

Cartwright's real masterpiece of remaking is the Mowbray family, whose name is almost obliterated from Wrexhill. Cartwright marries the recently bereaved widow Clara Mowbray, and old Mowbray Manor is renamed Cartwright Manor. The "bright waving locks" of Fanny Mowbray, youngest child of the manor house, once as luxuriant as the ivy around the church and rectory, are now tamed: "All her beautiful curls had been carefully straightened by the application of a wet sponge; and her hair was now entirely removed from her forehead, and plastered down behind her poor little distorted ears as closely as possible" (123). Cartwright so communicates his distrust of the fallen world to his future bride, Clara, that she worries about the morality of sharing stagecoach transportation with the unregenerate. As she argues, "It must be an abomination in the eyes of the Lord . . . that [the saved] should be seen travelling on earth by the same vehicles as those which convey the wretched beings who are on their sure and certain road to eternal destruction!" (145–46). Episodes such as these indicate that Trollope's dislike of the Vicar is not a class-based dislike of the restive and ignorant lower orders but rather a theologically informed position.

The Vicar of Wrexhill demonstrates Trollope's knowledge of the history of the evangelical movement and its methods. The career and behavior of Cartwright serve as an allegory of the movement. First, Evangelicals believed that the earlier Wesleyan revival had been a failure because of Wesley's insufficient cultivation of (in the eighteenth-century phrase) "the people who matter. " As Ford K. Brown wrote, "Wesley had relied on simplicity and godly sincerity" (57). In contrast, William Wilberforce consciously determined to walk with and thus influence the great: he, in his words, wanted an Evangelical leader to "raise his voice in the high places of the land; and do within the church, and near the throne, what Wesley had accomplished in the meeting, and amongst the multitude" (qtd. in Brown 76). This is Cartwright's procedure in Trollope's novel. Despite his supposed distrust of the world, he determines that he can, chameleon-like, appear a man of the world in order to influence the opinion of the fashionable world: in the evenings at Mowbray Hall, "His language and manners became completely those of an accomplished man of the world; his topics were drawn from the day's paper and the last review: he ventured a jest upon Don Carlos, and a *bon mot* upon the Duke of Wellington" (135).

One of the Evangelical Movement's most successful ploys was gaining influence through causes, most notably its public zeal for the abolition of slavery and for foreign missions. Many commentators have wondered why Evangelicalism, in general not concerned with political rights and social issues, should have so interested itself in abolition.[11] Historians of the movement have sometimes argued that Evangelicals were less interested in the abolition of slaves than in a popular movement that would galvanize potential Evangelicals and bring them into the fold. This argument is made even by those who are sympathetic to the movement, as Ford K. Brown, who writes that "the young Evangelical Party needed a great by-end, a subsidiary or instrumental cause that could be made into a crusade, inspiring large numbers of moral and earnest men and women to share in an emotional and spiritual undertaking identified with Evangelical leadership" (114). By the time of Trollope's novel, slavery had already been ended in British territories, but the need for a great by-end continued. The great causes for Cartwright are foreign missions and the production of religious tracts. There is never any evidence in the novel that tracts, mission money, or missionaries ever reach the lost, but Cartwright turns the parish into a beehive of fruitless feminine activity: there were to be "missionary meetings, branch-missionary meetings' reports, child's missionary branch committees, London Lord's-day's societies, and the like" (142).

Despite the success of Cartwright's schemes through much of the novel, *The Vicar of Wrexhill* allegorizes one problem the Evangelical movement faced and never completely surmounted: the problem of succession. Cartwright's son Jacob is a mere hapless puppet, last heard of as a member of a "troop of strolling players" (358). His daughter, Henrietta—far worse—is an atheist. Henrietta's atheism is the novel's great secret, hinted at in the manner Victorian novels of sensation usually reserved for revelations about criminal pasts, illegitimate children, and bigamous marriages. Henrietta's secret is at last revealed in its full horror. Frances Trollope's sensationalism is prescient about Evangelicalism, for a history of the movement in nineteenth-century Britain demonstrates that its fervor was difficult to maintain from one generation to another. An impressive list of Victorian notables were *former* Evangelicals, adherents in their youth but later critical of the movement: Charlotte and Emily Brontë and Samuel Butler, for example. Some former Evangelicals became skeptics, such as Mary Ann Evans and Benjamin Jowett. Many children of prominent Evangelical households became the ecclesiastical opposites of their fathers: Samuel and Robert Wilberforce and Edward Pusey joined the Oxford Movement; Henry Edward Manning and John Henry Newman became Roman Catholic. Sir Leslie Stephen, skeptic and father of Virginia Woolf, was grandson of one of the Evangelical high command, and E. M. Forster was descended from the most financially savvy of the Evangelical Clapham Sect, the Russian merchant John Thornton, who had devoted much of his fortune to buying advowsons, that is, the right to name clergymen to Church of England parishes.

Though *The Vicar of Wrexhill* concerns itself with the British church and was addressed to a British audience, Frances Trollope was more cosmopolitan than most British novelists of her era, a true woman of the world. Her *Domestic Manners of the Americans* demonstrates that she saw Evangelicalism as a worldwide phenomenon. Her visit to west Tennessee and Cincinnati in 1828–29 came less than three decades after the famous Cane Ridge (Kentucky) revival of August 1801, a week-long event, as defining for its century and country as Woodstock was to be 160 years later. Mainstream religious historians now read Cane Ridge as one of the key moments of American religion. Less traditional commentators on the American scene concur: Harold Bloom, in *The American Religion: The Emergence of the Post-Christian Nation* (1992) interprets Cane Ridge as the beginning of a central American belief system that has permeated American life ever since, a system seemingly Christian but, according to Bloom, "scarcely Christian in any traditional way" (37).[12] Bloom considers the "American Religion" to be a form of the early Christian heresy Gnosticism, relying as it does on private knowledge directly communicated to the believer at a single point in time—that is, at the moment of conversion. Bloom's theological analysis may be maverick, but he is certainly correct that something new was in the air. Frances Trollope, too, observed the aftermath of Cane Ridge, fully aware that a religious sea-change had taken place, that a new force had become, in her words, the "un-national church of America" (*Domestic Manners* 1969: 58).

In *Domestic Manners* Trollope particularly interests herself in the new movement's power over women. On the one hand, Evangelicalism as Trollope described it was a feminized movement, with far more female than male adherents. In Cincinnati, every evening "brings throngs of the young and beautiful to the chapels and meetinghouses. . . . The pro-

portion of gentlemen attending these evening meetings is very small . . . "
(57); "I never saw, or read of any country where religion had so strong
a hold upon the women, or a slighter hold upon the men" (58). In New
York City, the women attend church while the men travel to a pleasure
garden across the river in Hoboken (272–73).

Yet, as Trollope is quick to note, increased manipulation of and predation upon females accompanies this increased female interest in religion.
She writes that "The influence which the ministers . . . have on the females
of their respective congregations, approaches very nearly to what we read
of in Spain, or in other strictly Roman Catholic countries" (58). This
control was exercised by inciting religious hysteria. Some of the most
memorable pages of the *Domestic Manners* describe revivals in post-Cane-
Creek America; Trollope provides one of religious historians' best sources
for religious practices such as the "anxious bench," where young women
waited trembling for the sort of religious experience would reveal to them
their salvation[13]: "It was a frightful sight to behold innocent young creatures, in the gay morning of existence, thus seized upon, horror-struck,
and rendered feeble and enervated for ever. One young girl, apparently
not more than fourteen, was supported in the arms of another, some years
older; her face was pale as death; her chin and bosom wet with slaver;
she had every appearance of idiotism" (63).

Such hysteria is bad enough, but Frances Trollope—the alert, satirical
product of the eighteenth century and the Regency—could easily see
where such excesses could lead: to sexual predation. In Cincinnati, "the
prostrate penitents continued to receive whispered [from clergymen]
comfortings, and from time to time a mystic caress. More than once I
saw a young neck encircled by a reverend arm" (62). In Philadelphia in
1830, she hears of an itinerant preacher, at first viewed with "a curious
mixture of spiritual awe and earthly affection" (217) who, upon leaving
town, left seven girls pregnant.

Even before her visit to the United States, Frances Trollope already
feared that Evangelicalism could lead to sexual license. Back in Harrow,
she had warned one of her neighbors that the Rev. Cunningham's kiss
of peace would "change its quality if repeated" (T. A. Trollope 1887: 1:
93). But her American experience intensified her detestation for such
behavior, a judgment that becomes a theme of *The Vicar of Wrexhill*.
Cartwright converts mostly women (along with a few tradesmen, who are
primarily interested in doing business with Evangelical households).
At least four women fall in love with Cartwright: Mrs. Mowbray, her
daughter Fanny, and the widows Richards and Simpson; the latter he gets
pregnant. These and other women's emotional and sexual jealousies lead
to dissension and disagreement; though Evangelicalism purports to bring

peace and love, its adherents in *The Vicar of Wrexhill* fill their time in disagreements. The control Cartwright exercises is not only emotional and sexual but is also financial. Early in the novel, the widow Clara Mowbray becomes a very wealthy woman because her late husband's will left her (rather than their eldest son, the twenty-one-year-old Charles) in control of his substantial estate and fortune. Clara, however, has no understanding of financial and legal matters, and Cartwright unscrupulously advises, and then marries her.

Cartwright exercises control in Wrexhill through additional means: through the careful use of spies. Trollope reports, "It may, I believe, be laid down as a pretty general rule, that those persons who conceive, or profess it to be their duty, to dive into the hearts and consciences of their fellow creatures, and to regulate the very thoughts and feelings of all the unfortunate people within their reach, are not very scrupulous as the methods used to obtain that *inward* knowledge" (287). Mrs. Clara Mowbray Cartwright becomes a willing conveyor of information: while she delivers tracts to the poor of the parish, she collects "scraps of gossip," which she jots down for the use of her interfering husband (214). But Cartwright possesses a more professional agent. He, "according to the usual custom of evangelical divines, had his village matron, ostensibly only a merchant of apples, gingerbread, and lollypops, but entrusted with as many secret missions of inquiry as the most jealous pontiff ever committed to a faithful and favoured nuncio on quitting the gates of Rome. . . . Sources of information such as these had never been overlooked or neglected by Mr Cartwright at any period of his ministry" (287–88).[14] Up until Trollope's time, the English had associated the Roman Catholic Church with espionage and counter-intelligence movements—a theme developed in *Father Eustace* (1847), in which an undercover priest schemes to convert the heroine Juliana for the purpose of gaining her wealth for the Church. Thus, *The Vicar of Wrexhill* ironically equates the Evangelicals with one of their historic enemies, the Church of Rome, since both groups plot for increased power.

Trollope's protest against religious tyranny helps elucidate her contribution to her era's discussion of the Woman Question. Tory women—such as Frances Trollope—are notoriously difficult to place ideologically. For example, the seventeenth-century Aphra Behn, now generally seen as a proto-feminist figure, was staunchly Tory and pro-Stuart. Trollope can look quite conservative in rejecting a movement that has been hailed as liberating for women. Carroll Smith-Rosenberg has argued that Evangelical

> women pioneered in the creation of a range of new roles for religious women. Inspired by revival enthusiasm, they founded national religious

organizations, distributed Bibles and tracts, led Sunday schools, and raised money to send missionaries to the Sandwich Islands and to the new urban ghettos. They founded female seminaries intent on both asserting women's right to education and preparing women as missionaries for the United States and abroad. Those more worldly in their orientation followed the millennial enthusiasm into a host of reform movements: Garrisonian abolition, moral reform, temperance. These women wrote legislative petitions, edited national reform journals, and developed nondomestic skills and expertise as administrators, publicists, and lobbyists. (201)

However, as has been noted, *The Vicar of Wrexhill* is suspicious of feminine religious activities and presents them as mere busywork. And it suggests that Charles Mowbray, Senior, has been grievously mistaken to leave control of his estate to his wife: she is unprepared, ignorant, and open to every false suggestion. Patriarchal figures representing the old Toryism are generally praised in the novel, in particular the Mowbray's neighbor Sir Gilbert Harrington, named in Charles Mowbray's will as an executor of the estate. At the same time, the young Charles Mowbray is a patriarch-in-training. Trollope implies that all would have been well had such men remained firmly in control of womenfolk. She advocates a similar exercise of male power in the new world: in *Domestic Manners*, she blames American men for allowing the Evangelical movement to reduce their own power: "Did the men of America value their women as men ought to value their wives and daughters, would such scenes be permitted among them?" (63) How can the men of America allow their wives and daughters to attend church, "bound in the chains of a most tyrannical fanaticism . . . immured with hundreds of fellow victims, listening to the roaring vanities of a preacher, canonized by a college of old women? . . . Do they fear these self-elected, self-ordained priests, and offer up their wives and daughters to propitiate them?" (273–74)

Here, Trollope can *sound* like a reactionary proponent of increased male control. Yet she is not so dismissive of unsupervised female intellect as at first she appears, for the real heroine of The *Vicar of Wrexhill* is Rosalind Torrington, an heiress and orphan, whose education under an exemplary Church of Ireland clergyman has given her the ability to judge and reject Cartwright. She rejects his inelegant, ranting extemporaneous prayers. She is able to simultaneously maintain her religion *and* practice the fine arts. She deplores preachers who "believe there is righteousness in mixing the awful and majestic name of God with all the hourly petty occurrences of this mortal life" (116). She protests against the "paroxysms" that Cartwright is able to induce in young Fanny Mowbray (88). She—along with Lady Harrington, who energetically assists and advises her husband, Sir Gilbert—provides an image of the strength of mind that is available to women.

Yet, despite these positive figures, what readers remember is manipulative, destructive Evangelicalism. In light of Frances Trollope's prescience about the movement, it is hardly surprising that her reading of the ecclesiastical situation is gloomier than her son's. Anthony's Rev. Slope is a comic character, finally bested, humiliated, and exiled; he is never a serious threat. Readers are left to assume that the Grantleys and Arabins will continue to prosper in unchanging Barsetshire. Anthony is less interested in theology and ecclesiology than in how personalities and parties interplay in complex organizations. But for Frances Trollope, Evangelicalism is a "serious epidemic" (*Vicar* 358), and *The Vicar of Wrexhill* has deep roots in history; it is a more perceptive, more troubling document than her son's treatment of the same theme.

NOTES

1. A student could read the major anthologies of British literature—the Norton, Longman, and Oxford—and learn nothing of the movement or its impact. However, Harold Bloom's *The American Religion* makes important arguments that could spur literary critics to a new reassessment of the significance of Evangelicalism for American culture.

2. *Letters*, 18–20 November 1814: 280. That Austen is less than happy with Fanny's suitor is evident in the comment that precedes her discussion of Plumptre's Evangelicalism: "I have no doubt that he will get more lively & more like yourselves as he is more with you; —he will catch your ways if he belongs to you" (280). Austen concludes her qualified praise of Plumptre by advising caution and delay: "And now, my dear Fanny, having written so much on one side of the question, I shall turn round & entreat you not to commit yourself farther, & not to think of accepting him unless you really do like him" (280).

3. *Letters*, 8–9 September 1816: 322.

4. See Brown, *Fathers of the Victorians*, 244–50, for the history and significance of the Bible Society, founded in 1804. Early in its history, the Bible Society was opposed by the High Church party.

5. *Engravings by Hogarth* 36.

6. Lest any reader suspect Cunningham of a secret affinity to Roman Catholicism, *The Velvet Cushion* also contains the following: "Popery has, perhaps, too much affinity with the corruption of our nature to die a natural death, but, I begin to hope, it may be suffocated by the Bible" (26). Frances Trollope herself is very anti-Roman Catholic in *Father Eustace* (1847).

7. *What I Remember* 1887: 1: 13–14.

8. Recent attacks on modern and primarily Evangelical revivals of ancient cleanliness codes include L. William Countryman's *Dirt, Greed and Sex* and Bruce Bawer's *Stealing Jesus*. Commentators have sometimes traced current divisions among Anglicans worldwide to Evangelical insistence on perpetuating cleanliness codes. At the 1998 Lambeth Conference (a decennial meeting of Anglican bishops), the assembled leaders took what, from American and British

reactions, was a surprisingly hard line against homosexuality. Much of the harshest opposition to this "uncleanness" came from territories Christianized by evangelicals—for example, much of the third world and the archdiocese of Sydney, Australia, whose early Evangelical chaplain the Rev. Samuel Marsden, the "flogging chaplain," set the tone for the subsequent development of the archdiocese.

9. The text of this ballad, by John Andrew Stevenson (1761–1833), can be found in the Bodleian Ballads Catalogue Harding B 11 (4274).

10. The Evangelicals' attack on wit and pleasure had long been one of Trollope's satirical targets. In "Signs of the Times. The Righteous Rout," dating from her Harrow years, she describes the contents of an Evangelical young lady's album:

Saint Paul's head, sketched in pen and ink;

"Fly not yet" to words of grace;

The death bed talk of Master Blink;

Lines on a fallen virgin's case;

Sonnets upon heavenly love;

A pencil drawing of Saint Peter;

Emblems:—The pigeon and the dove;

Gray's odes turned to psalm tune metre:

A christian ode in praise of tea,

Freely translated upon Redi. (8)

Trollope reused these lines in *The Vicar of Wrexhill*, ascribing them in the novel to Charles Mowbray the younger (167). In the novel, Trollope makes one significant change from her earlier version: she substitutes "Here's the bower" (another popular song) for "Fly not yet" and, in the novel itself, provides a fully Christianized version of "Fly not yet." Here, it is clear that her experiences with Cunningham are being recycled into the portrait of Cartwright.

11. Calvin, Thomas Scott, and John Newton had all argued that Evangelical Christians should not concern themselves with politics.

12. Bloom writes, "There are indeed millions of Christians in the United States, but most Americans who think that they are Christian truly are something else, intensely religious but devout in the American Religion, a faith that is old among us, and that comes in many guises and disguises, and that overdetermines much of our national life" (37).

13. It is just this sort of self-validating mystical experience that causes Harold Bloom to label the "American Religion" a form of Gnosticism.

14. Another parish informant is the Rev. William Collins in Austen's *Pride and Prejudice*. Collins serves as the eyes and ears of Lady Catherine de Bourgh. See my "Gazing and Avoiding the Gaze" (45), which examines parish overseers in light of Michel Foucault's discussion of Enlightenment Panopticism.

6

Marriageable at Midlife: The Remarrying Widows of Frances Trollope and Anthony Trollope

Kay Heath

In 1863 Frances Trollope was eighty-four and living in Florence with her son, Thomas. The author of forty-two books, she had long since ceased writing and had been senile for two years. Back home in England, her other son Anthony, was producing his fifteenth novel, *Can You Forgive Her?* (1864–65), but he took a hiatus in September in order to accompany his oldest son, Harry, to Florence for tutoring. On that journey, Anthony made what would be his last visit to his mother. She died on October 6, after he had returned to England (Hall, *Trollope* 257). Anthony resumed work on the novel several days after Frances' death.

The relationship of literary influence between Frances and Anthony Trollope is curiously highlighted in the work he was doing at the time of her death. Perhaps the most popular of her characters was the roguish heroine of *The Widow Barnaby* (1839). A middle-aged woman scheming to remarry, her antics challenge stereotypes of female dependency even as they entertain. The novel was so successful it was followed by two sequels, *The Widow Married* (1840) and *The Barnabys in America* (1843). At the time of Frances Trollope's death, Anthony was creating Arabella Greenow, the remarrying widow of *Can You Forgive Her?* The correspondences between Martha and Arabella are so numerous, that it is hard to believe that Anthony did not realize he was rewriting a character first created by his mother. He does not mention the matter when discussing Arabella in his autobiography, though he does claim that he never knowingly adopted the work of any other author.[1]

Anthony would have been familiar with *The Widow Barnaby*—he comments that Frances' "best novels" were written in the 1830s (*Autobiography* 1996: 25), which indicates that he both read and approved of at least the first widow novel. He would have also been aware of *The Widow Barnaby* because the novel was lucrative, helping to save the floundering fortunes of the Trollope family.

Though the two widows are initially similar, Arabella's plot eventually begins to differ generically. Anthony's travels caused a break in the composition of *Can You Forgive Her?* at the end of the tenth chapter, just after the flirtatious Arabella's beach picnic. When her story resumes in chapter fourteen, written just after Frances' death, the widow's plot begins to undergo fundamental change. Anthony changes her story from a satire to a more serious tale of midlife affect.[2]

Though we can only speculate about the psychological impact of her death on Anthony, we can see in *Can You Forgive Her?* that after Fanny's life ended, his appropriation of her work takes on a form of its own, less akin to her satiric style. Her death seems to lead him away from her transgressive feminism expressed in comedy to a more gradualist version portrayed in a romance plot.

By examining the similarities between Martha and Arabella, I will demonstrate the pattern of influence at work between mother and son. Then in exploring the differences between the widows, especially those occasioned by the generic shift in Anthony's work, I will suggest political and historical reasons that may have occasioned the turn from comedy, which had been such a successful vehicle for Mrs. Trollope. I argue that Frances consistently uses the comic aspect of her widow to subvert restrictions under which women lived, challenging them with the hyperbolic intensity of Martha's behavior. While Arabella's plot in *Can You Forgive Her?* provides comedy, her story parallels the more realist plots of Alice and Glencora and takes its dignity from them. And in comparison to her initial Martha-like portrayal, Arabella's plot is much less comedic and she becomes more conventional and valorized. Despite this change, Arabella's fate is ultimately similar to Martha's. Both widows choose to marry a rogue for pleasure while maintaining their autonomy, using the experience and property afforded them by widowhood and midlife to overrule the restrictions of the marriage market. Though Anthony Trollope did not overtly share his mother's feminist aims, the influence of her agenda is evident in Arabella Greenow.[3]

Whether satiric or serious, Martha and Arabella suggest new possibilities for women "of a certain age" in Victorian England.

THE REMARRYING WIDOW IN NINETEENTH-CENTURY ENGLAND

Though widows had faced behavioral proscriptions before the Victorian era, they were in a unique position of restriction in the nineteenth century. Due to lower adult mortality rates, marriage duration began to increase in the eighteenth and nineteenth centuries. Lawrence Stone suggests that marriage lasted longer during the Victorian period than at any other time in history, because "declining mortality rates had not yet been offset by rising divorce rates" (*Family* 56).[4] While marriage duration was high in the Victorian era, remarriage became less common, especially for women.[5]

Longer marriages and fewer remarriages resulted in a large number of British widowed persons in the nineteenth century, the majority of which were women because mortality rates and incidence of remarriage were both higher for men than for women (Jalland 230).[6] Widowhood was looked at as "a final destiny, an involuntary commitment to a form of social exile," especially as women aged, while men who lost their wives were encouraged to remarry (231, 259). Widows often found themselves in a position of dependency and circumscription, forced to turn to their extended families for support. Mourning customs, much stricter for women than for men, served as tangible evidence of the limitations placed on widows in Victorian England. Though mourning strictures were lessened across the course of the century, suggesting that widows were slowly given more freedom, statistics show that widows remarried less and less as the century progressed.[7] Widows who did attempt to marry were depicted as undesirable buffoons in literary conventions that were well established by the nineteenth century. Satiric treatment of widows is evident in the earliest extant English play, Udall's *Ralph Roister-Doister* (1550s), in which the widow Constance Custance is made ridiculous by Ralph's amorous advances. This tradition continues in Restoration drama with the Widow Blackacre in Wycherley's *The Plain Dealer* and with Lady Wishfort in Congreve's *The Way of the World*, plays in which Barbara Todd argues "engendered an enduring stereotype of the early modern widow as a woman who anxiously sought a husband at *any cost*" (54–55). In the eighteenth century, characters like the Widow Wadman of Sterne's *Tristram Shandy* are incongruous objects of love. Martha Barnaby is identified with this comedic widow trope by nineteenth-century reviewers—for example, a critic in *The Athenaeum* (1839) writes of *The Widow Barnaby*:

> As a distinct personage in our fictitious literature, *The Widow* occupies a place . . . entirely apart and individual. . . . We know her points as well as

those of . . . the parasites whom the Elizabethan authors again and again presented on the stage . . . at all times, and in all places, The Widow remains one and unalterable; a blithe and self-seeking pursuer of every man who is marriageable and modest—an unsympathising ogress in the ranks of her own sex—audacious and experienced in planning—resolute in obtaining—turning off her deep designs, when threatened with discovery . . . making of her weeds a flower-bed under which lurks artifice and device—calling up the memories of a dead husband as a bait to ensnare a living one—loquacious—lynx-eyed-oily-tongued: something like this . . . with whose bereavements satirists, prose and verse, make merry, is the Widow in general. . . . (9)

While Martha Barnaby has many of the characteristics associated with the trope of the ridiculous remarrying widow, her autonomy and self-determination also place in the tradition of the picaresque hero, which, in the nineteenth century, usually featured only male rogues. Helen Heineman argues that "with the widow Barnaby, Mrs. Trollope created the feminine picaresque, a lady ready to pack her trunks of a moment's notice, one who enjoyed herself immensely while exploring and exploiting life's possibilities for a middle-aged woman" (*Mrs. Trollope* 157).[8]

A picaroon in several senses, Martha is a rogue who transgresses social convention and travels from location to location in a series of husband-hunting adventures that feature her creative exploitation of the boundaries of propriety. Twentieth-century critics interpret Martha as an expression of Frances Trollope's own independent spirit, in some ways a rewriting of the author's own life. Martha sails to the United States as a famous author and purports to write a book on her travels, parodying Frances' own journey to America, which produced perhaps her most famous book, *Domestic Manners of the Americans* (Ransom, *Fanny Trollope* 124; Heineman, *Mrs. Trollope* 165). Heineman argues that Martha is Frances' "first heroine to project clearly the author's own fortitude and autonomy, self-assertiveness and curiosity about the world and to embody the significance and drama of her own strenuously active life" (*Frances Trollope* 88). Heineman sees Frances' message in *The Widow Barnaby* as "uncomplicated and direct"—that "women could maintain their inner autonomy and gain the maximum of economic independence." When the novel's narrator comments that Martha is "a strange mixture of worldly wisdom and . . . female folly," according to Heineman the "folly was all for show, the worldly wisdom was the real woman" (*Frances Trollope* 90).[9] In seeking a husband, Martha yields to the convention that a woman must have a man, but she does so only on her own terms. Behind the satire on her behavior is Frances' earnest attempt to suggest an alternative self-determination for midlife women—the portrayal of a widow who retains control over her own life instead of giving in to the dictates of society or the demands of a husband.

SIMILARITIES: TWO TRANSGRESSIVE WIDOWS

That Arabella is an appropriation of Martha Barnaby is made quite clear by a comparison of their traits and behaviors. Martha and Arabella are demographically similar—Lord Mucklebury describes Martha as "a widow, fair, fat and forty" (252),[10] and she possesses an estate in excess of four hundred pounds a year. Arabella is widowed at age forty and possesses an estate of forty thousand pounds (49). The repetition of forty in Martha's age and fortune are taken to new heights when Anthony multiplies her four hundred pounds into Arabella's forty thousand. The re-iteration of forty is not only an artifact of the widows' similarity, but also stresses their middle-aged status in contrast to the typical young heroine.

Martha is a forthright husband-hunter from the start, made evident when she catechizes herself soon after her husband dies: "Q: What is it that I most wish for on earth? A: A rich and fashionable husband" (56).[11] Arabella is a bit more demure in stating her husband-hunting intentions. She repeatedly claims she is not looking for a new spouse, saying "My heart is desolate, and must remain so" (62), and "one husband is enough for any woman, and mine lies buried at Birmingham" (437). However, her actions belie her words, and she is obviously on a quest to remarry as she strategically flirts with her two suitors.

In order to attract husbands, Martha and Arabella capitalize on their widowed status by flaunting the fortunes they have gained from the pre-vious marriage. Upon her arrival at Clifton, Martha asks for the "best rooms in the house" (78), and Arabella makes a point of staying at the largest house in the row at Yarmouth (59), because she "desired that all the world should see that she had forty thousand pounds of her own" (60). The widows also try to look more prosperous by attempting a class rise through engineering a change in their maids, giving them elite-sounding names. Martha calls Betty Jacks "Jerningham" (75) and Arabella alters her maid Jenny's name to "Jeannette" (75), designations that con-form to the widows' notions of gentility.

The widows not only promote outer evidences of their financial solid-ity as widows, but they find great inner satisfaction in the autonomy af-forded them by their widowhood. The narrator describes Martha's feel-ings at her bereavement: "She certainly felt both proud and happy as she thought of her independence and her wealth. Of the first she unquestion-ably had as much as it was possible for a woman to possess, for no hu-man being existed who had any right whatever to control her" (53).

Arabella tells her niece Kate after her husband's death, "I'm not dependent on the world,—thanks to the care of that sainted lamb. I can hold
my own; and as long as I can do that the world won't hurt me," and the
narrator adds that "Mrs. Greenow was probably right in her appreciation
of the value of her independence" (63). Each woman appreciates the independence made possible by property and experience, even though they
make it a point to describe their great grief and cry ostentatiously in the
presence of others.

Martha and Arabella use duty to their nieces as an excuse for their early
resumption of social life, and their explanations to the younger women
are almost identical. Martha tells Agnes,

> be assured, my dear, that however much my own widowed feelings might
> lead me to prefer the tranquil consolations of retirement, I shall consider
> it my duty to live more for you than for myself; and I will indeed hasten,
> in spite of my feelings, to lay aside these sad weeds, that I may be able,
> with as little delay as possible, to give you such an introduction to the world
> as my niece has a right to expect. (54)

When Arabella puts her name down at the Assembly Room, she tells her
niece Kate:

> I know very well what I owe to you, and I shall do my duty . . . society
> can have no charms now for such a one as I am. All that social intercourse
> could ever do for me lies buried in my darling's grave. . . . But I'm not
> going to immolate you on the alters of my grief. I shall force myself to go
> out for your sake, Kate. . . . (62)

By making a claim to duty as they present their nieces on the marriage
market, both widows enable themselves to circulate in society. When they
say they sacrifice their own wishes to obey this duty, they infer an inner
inclination for the retirement of mourning, but their evident relish to
resume socializing satirizes their claims to grief.

In addition to the prevarication in their claims of sacrifice to assist their
nieces, both widows lie about how long their husbands have been dead
in order to circumvent the protracted mourning period required of widows. Martha Barnaby tells her landlady that she has been a widow for
"very nearly six months," while the narrator informs us that "Mr. Barnaby,
however, had been alive and well exactly three months after the period
named by his widow as that of his death" (83–84). Arabella Greenow,
too, doubles the time of her widowhood; when her husband has been
dead for six months, she tells Cheesacre "you don't know what it is to
have buried the pride of your youth hardly yet twelve months" (184).

When she has been a widow for nine months, she refers to the "melancholy circumstance" as having taken place fifteen and then eighteen months previously (363).

Martha and Arabella accelerate the chronology of their widowhood because, as midlife women, they are running out of time in the marriage plot. They do not want to waste time, and enter society with the express intention of finding a mate before they are buried alive for life in the social insignificance of permanent widowhood. By dissembling about the length of their widowhood, they create a time that is parallel to and triumphs over the mourning period. They are successful in controlling their money, and, as I will discuss, their bodily performance as widows. By lying about the length of their widowhood, they even manage to exert a certain amount of control over time—the most threatening element to their search for husbands in midlife.

The widows reenter society in the same types of public entertainment. When Mr. Barnaby has been dead about six months, Martha puts her name down for the Assembly rooms at Clifton, subscribes to the library (a center for gossip and meeting), and attends a ball. She does decide it may be impolitic to dance at the ball in front of her wealthy sister-in-law, but she plays cards, displaying much "vivacity" and "enjouement" (145). Arabella settles in Yarmouth when she has been a widow for four months and makes similar social advances, registering at the Assembly Room, receiving guests, all the while smiling "from beneath her widow's cap in a most bewitching way" (63), walking on the pier with her suitor Captain Bellfield and her niece Kate, and rowing with friends down the beach for a picnic on the sands (66).

Martha and Arabella also transgress mourning customs by using their widow's weeds in service of the marriage market. Victorian widows were held to exacting standards of mourning: two years of full black attire were required until late in the century. For a year and a day dresses of dull, nonreflective black paramatta and crepe were worn, followed by dullish black silk trimmed in crepe for nine months and three months of combined silk and wool or cotton paramatta. In the final six months widows could assume the colors of half mourning—grey, lavender, or black and white in their trimmings (Jalland 300; Cunnington and Lucas 268). Frances Douglas, an etiquette advisor, wrote that while excesses of mourning can be harmful, "almost worse than the woman who mourns too much is the woman who mourns too little. One can forgive her garments, but not her apologies" (114).

Martha challenges this conventional paradigm by finding her mourning weeds "so hatefully unbecoming in her estimation that she firmly believed the inventor of it must have been actuated by some feeling akin to that which instituted the horrible Hindoo rite of which she had heard, whereby living wives were sacrificed to their departed husbands" (57). In her defiance of mourning and her comparison of it to suttee, Martha charges the custom not only with being inappropriate, but unchristian or (perhaps even worse) un-British. In either case, by flouting propriety, she suggests that women's identities should not be subsumed by those of their dead husbands.

Martha begins to transgress mourning customs when she has been a widow only three months. During a short sojourn in Exeter she not only leaves black crepe for black satin and silk, but wears lavender half-mourning until soon "there was no colour of the rainbow that did not by degrees find its way amidst her trimmings and decorations" (84–6). Though she assumes deep mourning again six months into her bereavement when she reaches her sister-in-law's house at Clifton, she soon moderates black satin with bright colors, so that "although in mourning, her general appearance was exceedingly shewy and gay" (123). The widow's audacity is emphasized by her contrast with Agnes, who continues to wear mourning at her aunt's behest (ostensibly because Agnes looks well in black, but, the narrator tells us, really because it will save the widow money to have her serviceable mourning dresses made over for the younger girl). Agnes, true to the female mourning prescription, says that her veil makes her feel "more comfortable" in public (132). Though Martha's ploy to be free of mourning and outshine her niece is comically perfidious, it is also liberating, enabling her to circumvent the confines of mourning and husband-hunt to greater advantage.

Like Martha, Arabella transgresses standards of proper behavior about mourning, but instead of mourning too little she uses her weeds to her advantage. At the picnic in Yarmouth, we are told, "She had not mitigated her weeds by half an inch. She had scorned to make any compromise between the world of pleasure and the world of woe" (69). Instead of slighting mourning early, she wears her black dresses and widow's caps coquettishly, employing them to make her more attractive to her suitors. Her impropriety is not in gaudy colors but in the amount of attention she lavishes upon her gowns. Arabella shows her widow's weeds to Kate "with all the pride of a young bride when she shows the glories of her trousseau to the friend of her bosom" (61), obviously not the proper attitude for a grieving widow. She also wears her widow's cap "jauntily," so that it shows "just so much of her rich brown hair as to give her the appearance of youth which she desired" (362). By wearing her mourning as a flirtation device, she undercuts its intended purpose: "there was that of genius about Mrs. Greenow, that she had turned every seeming disadvantage to some special profit, and had so dressed herself that though she had obeyed the law to the letter, she had thrown the spirit of it to the winds" (362). She makes her mourning too attractive, and angles too obviously for another suitor to be grieving according to standards of propriety.

The widows' wiles are effective: six months after her husband's death, Martha has a proposal from Major Allen, and she decides to leave Clifton so that "her marriage, within seven months of her husband's death, might not take place under the immediate observation of his nearest relations" (183). Though this engagement is canceled, she becomes the bride of Mr. O'Donagough a few months later. Arabella receives a proposal from Cheesacre at the picnic when she has been a widow for about five months (82–83), but she takes it as an insult. She gives Bellfield "ground of hope" before she has been a widow a year (502), and he is accepted and kissed just a year from Greenow's death (723).

DIFFERENCES: WHEN COMEDY GOES STRAIGHT

The multiple similarities between the two widows make evident that Arabella Greenow is a direct literary descendent of Martha Barnaby.[12] As I have argued earlier, at the point in the manuscript that Anthony was writing when Frances died, he converted the comedic subplot of the re-marrying widow to a straight plot of serious midlife affect. The differences that occur in Arabella after the change make her more like the valorized, conventional heroine of most Victorian novels, and she begins to contrast in several ways with the hyperbolically inappropriate and funny widow Barnaby.

Anthony Trollope initially uses Arabella's plot as comic relief from the challenges of the marriage market that befuddle Alice and Glencora, the heroines of the other two plots. Why would he then lessen the satire of the widow subplot and present Arabella in a more serious mode? Improvement in the rights of women that occurred in the 1850s, the decade before Anthony wrote the novel, offered new ways of envisioning a middle-aged widow on the marriage market as more than just humorously inappropriate. Agitation for women's property rights was quite strong in the 1850s (eventually leading to the Married Women's Property Acts of 1870 and 1887), and the debate surrounding the Divorce and Matrimonial Causes Act of 1857 resulted in protection orders that guaranteed a woman's ability to hold property separate from her husband in the case of his desertion. These developments enabled women to be more independent and self-determined.

Another important factor is the Divorce Act, which changed ideas about remarriage by introducing a new and scandalous phenomenon—previously married but now single men and women who were not widowers and widows. After 1857, the number of divorces slowly increased, and by the early 1860s, stories of divorce were much in the press, while trials became such a spectator sport that seats were hard to obtain (Horstman 87). Some had speculated that women would be hesistant to seek divorces, shrinking from conflict and publicity, but in 1858, the first year the Divorce Act was enforced, 97 of the 253 divorce petitions were filed by women (Horstman 86), and in the period 1858 to 1868, women initiated 40 percent of divorce proceedings and 92 percent of judical separations (Savage 26).

With these events, a new specter arose—the possibility of remarriage by the divorced. The clergy had been in an uproar before the Act was passed, objecting to the possibility that they would be forced to remarry the adulterous party of a divorce. The Attorney General agreed that clergymen could refuse to perform such marriages on the basis of conscience but stipulated that the church could not be forbidden for use by such couples (Stone, *Road* 380–81). Initially, the number of remarriages was small: of the 4,000 divorces that were granted between 1861 and 1876, only 696 marriages involved one divorced partner, and only thirteen unions occurred between two divorced people. The number of remarriages increased steadily over the century, however. While only ten divorced people remarried in 1861, 390 remarried in 1900, indicating that the stigma of remarriage for the divorce continually waned (Horstman 156). The concept of remarriage among the divorced must have influenced the status of the remarrying widow even as early as the 1860s. Next to a remarrying divorcee, the remarrying widow would have seemed a paragon of virtue. As a result of the circulation of these unprecedented ideas about marriage, its dissolution, and remarriage, Anthony Trollope was writing in an era when he could envision a remarrying widow as less improper and therefore less comic than his initial Martha-like portrayal.

One example of the contrast between the two widows is in the portrayal of the emotional aspects of their mourning. Martha's grief is short-lived and based on practicality. She is "really very sorry" for her husband's death and weeps "with little or no effort" the week he dies. However, after the funeral and reading of the will "she very rationally began to meditate upon her position, and upon the best mode of enjoying the many good things which had fallen to her share" (1: 53). She continues to use her bereaved state as a convenient device for arousing sympathy, while also making the most of the freedoms and goods garnered from her widowed state.

Arabella's mourning begins like Martha's but is later taken out of the realm of comedy and developed as enduring and sincere. The narrator initially describes her lamentations as a "performance" in which she would "address the shade of the departed one in terms of most endearing affection" using ostentatious—and incorrect—Latin ("Peace be to his manes.") Though Kate "is surprised to see that real tears . . . were making their way down her aunt's cheeks" (61), she observes that the tears are checked by a fashionable mourning handkerchief, an image that draws attention to the performative quality of Arabella's grief, thereby questioning its sincerity.

After chapter ten, however, Arabella's mourning is presented as sincere, and as James Kincaid argues, her grief "is not entirely hypocritical" (47). Even after her engagement to Bellfield when prevarication about her grief would no longer be of service to her campaign on the marriage market, Arabella tells Kate that though she will remarry, she will never truly love again: "As for love, my dear, that's gone—clear gone! . . . Some women can love twice, but I am not one of them. I wish I could" (584). Kate notes later that even after her engagement her handkerchief "still bore the deepest hem of widowhood," and she knows Arabella will continue to use it until she is remarried (714). The handkerchief has become a symbol of sincerity instead of a marker of performance. Despite her engagement, Arabella's sorrow over Greenow's death has become believable by the end of the novel. Her presentation of grief is much more self-consciously performative than Martha's. Arabella is able to have it both ways—she uses her mourning to her advantage but still presents it as believable and transforms other characters' initial scorn to sympathy.

In both novels, a rivalry between the generations is set up as the texts call attention to the middle-aged widows' bodies in contrast to those of their nieces, especially in regard to their clothing. The two cases differ in that Agnes acts as a reverse foil for her aunt, revealing Martha's dowdiness, while Kate, in contrast, is overlooked in favor of her aunt. Arabella is allowed to be authentically attractive while Martha's charms remain overblown in the realm of comedy.

In *The Widow Barnaby*, Agnes' simple elegance acts as a foil to emphasize Martha's audacious showiness. When they attend church for the first time in Clifton, Agnes is wearing deep mourning for her uncle—all black except for a white collar—provided from Martha's cast-offs. The widow is the antithesis of Agnes, claiming many liberties of dress, and her excessive costume is described with comedic copiousness: "On this occasion she came forth in a new dress of light grey gros-de-Naples, with a gay bonnet of paille de riz, decorated with poppy blossoms both within and without, a 'lady-like' profusion of her own embroidery on cuffs, collar, and pocket-handkerchief, her well-oiled ringlets half hiding her large, coarse, handsome face, her eyes set off by a suffusion of carmine, and her whole person redolent of musk" (129).

The text comments that the two are "as strangely matched a pair in appearance as can well be imagined" (129). This juxtaposition continues throughout the novel, highlighting Agnes' upper class taste and looks with Martha's more ostentatious image. When Frederick Stephenson first sees Agnes, he proclaims, "In my life I never beheld so beautiful a creature . . . her form, her feet, her movement," while his companion, Colonel Hubert, is taken aback that she would appear with a companion who is "such a dame as that feather and furbelow lady" (133). Repeatedly in the novel, Martha's forthright showiness emphasizes how much liberty she allows herself to take, in contrast to her understated and refined niece.

Even before the shift from comedy to realism takes place in *Can You Forgive Her?* Arabella's physical presence eclipses that of her niece. Her clothing is not described in minute satiric detail as is Martha's. Instead, her genuine physical attractions switch the usual paradigm of an older woman giving way to the superior beauty and marriageability of a younger one. When Arabella goes to church on her first Sunday in Yarmouth in "all the glory of her widowhood," the niece knows she has been over-shadowed: "Kate Vavasor became immediately aware that a great sensation had been occasioned by their entrance, and equally aware that none of it was due to her. . . . How many ladies of forty go to church without attracting the least attention! But it is hardly too much to say that every person in that church had looked at Mrs. Greenow" (60–61). Arabella's attractions are remarkable not for their ostentatiousness, as are Martha's, but because of her age. She shows that a middle-aged woman can have authentic sexual appeal in a Victorian novel. She thereby becomes more like the conventional female ideal while also challenging the stereotype of the remarrying widow as too old to be taken seriously in a romantic and sexual plot.

Martha and Arabella also differ in regard to their selfishness and generosity toward their nieces and others. Martha always acts as an agent of the self. Autonomously intent on her own advantage, she never balks at the chance to use others to promote her schemes, but constantly challenges the convention of the shrinking, dependent widow. While Martha consistently uses Agnes for her own devices, Kate says of Arabella, "with all her faults, I believe she would go through fire and water to serve me" (284). Martha gives away her used clothes to her servant Jerningham as bribes to get her to spy on men and to Agnes as a way to save money, but Arabella's gift of cast-off clothes are presented as desirable acquisitions in their own right: "When Mrs. Greenow made a slight change in her mourning . . . Jeanette reaped a rich harvest in gifts of clothes" (172), and the narrator tells us that Arabella "would spare neither herself nor her purse on Kate's behalf" (64). Martha loudly attests to her sacrifices and generosity toward her niece while giving her only a closet to sleep in, cast-off mourning gowns to wear, and eventually threatening to turn her out "neck and heels into the street" if Agnes will not agree to be Martha's purveyor while she is in debtor's prison (306). Arabella's behavior, though not always entirely selfless, is represented by the text as motivated by genuine goodwill toward her beneficiaries. Though she is independent, her altruism hints at an angel-in-the-house spirit of service, an attribute of which Martha is completely devoid.

Arabella is also less comic than Martha because she does not attempt to cover up increasing signs of age with makeup. Perhaps the most scandalous of all Martha's personal habits is her propensity to wear rouge, a habit mentioned many times by other characters in the novel as a marker of her vulgarity and mendacity. Victorians thought rouging improper (though it became increasingly popular and more accepted over the course of the century), because it was considered not only vanity, but a visual lie. Mrs. Merrifield writes in 1854, "We violate the laws of nature when we seek to repair the ravages of time on our complexions by paint . . . it is not only bad taste, but it is a positive breach of sincerity" (2). Other characters in the novel disapprove of Martha's tendency to "paint." The narrator tells us that when she "touched up her bloom to the point she deemed to be the most advantageous," her sister-in-law concludes she looks "precisely like a clever caricature" of herself (104). Her brother-in-law decides that he will "feel more comfortable when the rouge pots were all gone" from his house, because they are a bad influence on his daughters (108), and even Martha's fiancé O'Donagough threatens to delay their marriage unless she stops rouging until their missionary appointment is secure (373). Martha does abate her use of makeup when such action serves her purposes, but though other characters disapprove of her cosmetics, she flouts their censure by continually returning to the "paint pot."

In contrast, *Can You Forgive Her?* specifically points out that Arabella does not use rouge. When Bellfield accuses her of giving way too much to grief, she cries and her tears "in their course [show] that she at any rate used no paint in producing that freshness of colour which was one of her great charms" (179). Despite the other wiles she may use to capture male hearts, Arabella's beauty is depicted as not in need of artificial enhancement, making her acceptable according to Victorian propriety.

Martha and Arabella both lie in the cause of husband-hunting, but Arabella is eventually forgiven for her mendacity. After the failure of her first flirtation with Major Allen because she has deceived him about the extent of her fortune (as he has her), Martha plans her "next campaign" at Cheltenham. The narrator tells us that "she knew that the exploits she contemplated were hazardous, as well as splendid; and that, although success was probable, failure might be possible . . . " (221). Her lies are presented as comic and daring, one of the skills by which she will attain her goal of entering into society and marrying a rich husband. *Can You Forgive Her?*, in contrast, downplays Arabella's dissimulation by presenting it as merely a foible. While other characters as well as Arabella herself acknowledge that she reconstructs the truth, her lies are presented as either unimportant or acceptable. Kate has been aware of Arabella's revisions in regard to the length of her widowhood, her intentions in regard to remarrying, and her pursuit of suitors, but this does not prevent her shift in attitude from vilifying to admiring her aunt. Near the end of the novel, Alice, hearing Arabella's version of events, realizes that her aunt is consciously reshaping what has happened, but that "she had a pleasure in telling her own story, and told it as though she believed every word that she spoke" (714). Arabella's prevarication is presented as charming, perhaps even a bit cute.

Despite the shift from the comedic to a romance mode, Arabella's plot is resolved in ways similar to Martha's. Both widows use a similar strategy of practical compromise to choose a flirtatious rake for pleasure, but one who will allow them a large measure of independence. This strategy hilariously challenges propriety when practiced by Martha, but is suggestively liberated in the romance plot of Arabella.

Martha decides to marry the would-be missionary Patrick O'Donagough after she has experienced several reverses—the failure of her plan to snag Lord Mucklebury, her arrest for debt, the refusal of the flirtatious lawyer Morrison to render legal help when he discovers her financial problems, and Agnes' resistance to obeying her commands from prison. These events cause her hopes and expectations to be lowered, vexing her (368). Thus humbled, she decides to make the best match she can with the possibilities open to her. She prudently looks into the affairs of O'Donagough, a penniless but well-connected man, the illegitimate son of a lord who provides him with financial bailouts. She decides that he will do quite nicely, because not only will " 'The reverend Mr. O'Donagough'. . . look very well in the paragraph which she was determined should record her marriage in the Exeter paper" (370), but he is handsome and a decade her junior (333). In addition, with O'Donagough she will be able to maintain autonomy by retaining control of her money. They immigrate to Australia and the charming scoundrel suits Martha until his excesses at the horse races lead to his death. Always dexterous in adapting her plans to suit her need of the moment, she manages quite easily on the last page of the novel to make a similar match with another rascal, her old lover, the Major Allen, who conveniently turns up in Sydney at the right moment. Martha manages to have it all her own way—obtaining a husband for her pleasure while also retaining her independence.

Arabella's husband hunt ends in a similar way. Though her forthright determination does seem to usher her through problems with disarming dexterity, she does not find the marriage market uncomplicated. She settles for Captain Bellfield as a husband who is problematic yet palatable. Aware of his limitations as a spouse, she discusses the struggle she faces as his wife: "He'll give me a great deal of trouble. I know he will. He'll always be wanting my money, and, of course, he'll get more than he ought. . . . And he'll smoke too many cigars, and perhaps drink more brandy-and-water than he ought. And he'll be making eyes, too, at some of the girls who'll be fools enough to let him" (584).

The marriage is portrayed as a happy compromise, the narrator assuring us that "Mrs. Greenow's own marriage was completed with perfect success" because she "took Captain Bellfield for better or for worse, with a thorough determination to make the best of his worst." Bellfield had "had been in luck" to marry her because she would forgive him, gratify his wants, and keep him from ruining them both" (723). This is not a perfect union, but a compromise between pleasure and prudence made by a woman with the experience and self-determination to make her own choice.

Though Arabella is allowed to achieve midlife affect valorized as appropriate to her needs and age in a serious plot, her story resonates with the self-determination and worldly success of the comic widow Barnaby. Martha herself stays within the realm of the transgressive, defying the proprieties as she triumphs over all obstacles put in her way on the midlife remarriage market. As they start life anew, controlling their fates by making their own choices and retaining autonomy, they present new possibilities for women, especially the middle-aged, in a culture that restricts their lives.

In these two widows, the differing feminisms of Frances Trollope and her son are evident. Anthony Trollope had many reservations about female independence, and believed that women's lives were best lived within the confines of marriage. As he says in North America (1862): "The best right a woman has is the right to a husband" (*Autobiography* 1996: 265). Within those limits, however, he gives women new freedoms in the story of Arabella. In her plot, a progressive, gradualist feminism emerges that allows women to exercise the "right" to choose husbands and yet maintain autonomy and control of their own lives in significant ways. Arabella's independence is directly attributable to her likeness to Martha Barnaby. Before she began writing novels, Frances Trollope had learned only too well that women must learn to take care of themselves. In Martha, she expresses a transgressive picquaresque feminism that allows a woman to defy the rules and, even when she appears to be thwarted, ultimately succeed in all her campaigns. Frances Trollope puts to rout strictures on women with hyperbolic intensity in the carnivalesque comedy of the vulgar and sublime widow Barnaby.

NOTES

1. Anthony wrote in his autobiography: "How far I may unconsciously have adopted incidents from what I have read—either from history or from works of imagination—I do not know. It is beyond question that a man employed as I have been must do so. But when doing it I have not been aware that I have done it. I have never taken another man's work, and deliberately framed my work upon it." He goes on to say, "I think that an author when he uses either the words or the plot of another, should own as much, demanding to be credited with no more of the work than he has himself produced" (77–78).

2. Trollope's handwritten "work sheet," Trollope Business Papers, The Bodleian Library.

3. Critics have linked Arabella, along with other of Anthony's female characters, to an underlying feminist discourse in his novels that contrasts startlingly with his personal and public statements about the role of women. He declares in a letter to Adrian H. Joline that "the necessity of the supremacy of man [over woman] is as certain to me as the eternity of the soul" (4 April 1879, Hall, *Letters* 821). He opposed women's right to vote, and in his speech on women's education he confines their learning to "ornament, charity and household management" (Overton 5–6). Though Anthony may be anti-feminist in his public statements and nonfiction writing, he seems to become a feminist when he creates heroines. In novels, he often portrays women who question traditional roles and yearn for a different kind of life, creating what Morse calls an "ongoing fictional dialectic between belief and subversion of Victorian ideals for womanhood" (3). Kincaid argues that "within the novels themselves, the platitudes disappear completely, and the easy answers of both male supremacists and feminists alike are seen to be irrelevant entirely to the dilemma of the woman faced with no satisfying alternatives" (29). Overton posits two Trollopes (that is, two *Anthony* Trollopes), the official, conventional Victorian of public and private discourse, and the unofficial, contradictory novelist—a bifurcation that can best be seen, he argues, in his ideas about the role of women: "He will start out from a bland moralism—that a woman's place is in marriage, or that marriage for ambition is wrong—but these simplifications the novels soon disarm" (7). Though he may profess conventional notions about gender, Anthony cannot seem to escape from his subterranean feminist impulses. Several critics have linked his female characters to an underlying feminist discourse that begins to appear during the 1860s when the debate over women's rights was at its height, which is also when he was composing *Can You Forgive Her?* (Nardin xviii). He met the feminist Kate

Field in 1860 and she became a close friend. Margaret F. King has also established a connection in the 1860s between Anthony Trollope and the Langham Place Circle of feminists through his friendship with Emily Faithfull (307–26).

4. In the 1730s, twenty-four percent of marriages were terminated by the death of a spouse within ten years, and fifty-six percent within twenty-five years, but by the 1850s the numbers had dropped to nineteen percent and forty-seven percent. The trend continued; for the 1880s only thirteen percent of marriages ended before ten years and thirty-seven percent before twenty-five years (Anderson 29).

5. Wrigley and Schofield note that thirty percent of those marrying in the sixteenth century were widows or widowers, and the numbers were still as high in the latter part of the eighteenth century, with fifteen percent of men and twenty percent of women marrying as widowers and widows (258). By the mid-1800s, however, the figures had dropped to only fourteen percent of grooms and nine percent of brides remarrying after the death of a spouse (Anderson 31).

6. In the second half of the nineteenth century, of the total male population, widowers made up four percent at ages 35–44, seven percent at 45–54, and fourteen percent at 55–64, while, for women, the number of widows in similar age ranges were eight percent, fifteen percent, and thirty percent, double the number in every age cohort (Anderson 30). In 1851, the marriage rate per 1,000 of the population of widowers was thirty-six percent at age twenty-five and fourteen percent at age forty, while for widows the rate was fifteen percent at age twenty-five and four percent at forty. The discrepancy continued later in the century—William Farr reports that in 1870–1872, twenty-eight percent of widowers remarried at age twenty-five and fifteen percent at forty, while only sixteen percent of widows remarried at twenty-five and four percent at forty (79–80).

7. Anderson states that "in the mid-nineteenth century 14% of males and 9% of women who married were widowed. The figures fell slowly for the rest of the century, reaching 8.9% and 6.6% respectively in the early 1900s . . . " (31).

8. Heineman notes that Martha differs from Moll Flanders in that she is not either low born or a thorough-going criminal (*Mrs. Trollope* 158).

9. For further discussion of Frances as feminist reformer, see Button (69–86), two books by Heineman (*Frances Trollope* and *Mrs. Trollope*), as well as a book and two essays by Kissel (*In Common Cause,* "More Than Anthony's Mother," and " 'What Shall Become of Us All?': Frances Trollope's Sense of the Future").

10. Martha is actually thirty-five years old at the time of her husband's demise. Neville-Sington notes that the phrase is used by Frances again in both *Hargrave* and *The Lottery of a Marriage* (*Fanny Trollope* 267).

11. Quotes are from the 1995 edition.

12. While Anthony Trollope did not acknowledge the widow Barnaby as the basis for Arabella, he does credit his early, unsuccessful play, *The Noble Jilt,* as the source for *Can You Forgive Her?.* The remarrying widow, Madame Brudo is, in several senses, Anthony's first rewriting of Martha Barnaby. She is like Martha in several ways—manipulative and dishonest, she makes much of her

widow's grief when anyone is around to hear, she claims she will never remarry while obviously angling for suitors, she declares a hypocritical, fabricated love for her niece, she plays her two suitors against each other, and her maid is a go-between in the love affairs. Both Madame Brudo and Martha transgress mourning strictures and remarry too early to satisfy convention. Perhaps the most significant contrast between the two women is that Madame Brudo shows no triumphant self-determination compared to that displayed by Martha. In fact, Madame Brudo argues for female dependence, telling her niece that women "are born to be slaves. They cannot throw off the yoke. 'Tis better for them twice to submit than once to rebel" (182). Another significant difference is that Madame Brudo is simply not funny. George Bartley, the theater manager to whom Anthony sent *The Noble Jilt* for evaluation, responded that no character in the play could "challenge the sympathy of the audience" (Hall, *Trollope* 121). This is evident in Madame Brudo, whose lumbering antics do not entertain, even though the play was intended to be a comedy.

7

Figuring Age and Race: Frances Trollope's Matronalia

Mary Wilson Carpenter

In 1867 Jean-Martin Charcot—who is now known chiefly for his studies on hysteria in women—published a work called *Clinical Lectures on the Diseases of Old Age*. These lectures became the foundational work for the new science of gerontology. Stephen Katz points out that although Charcot's studies on "old age" were based on an exclusively female population, the inmates of the immense Parisian institution of Salpêtrière, Charcot frequently presents his theses and proposals in male terms, but with a critical inflection: "The pathological aged figure is female and the normal adult figure is male" (120).[1] Teresa Mangum similarly proposes that the figure of the aging woman was repeatedly associated with the figure of the child in the nineteenth century. As "childhood" was increasingly specified as the first stage of life, so the last stage became "second childhood" (62–63). Some of the first conduct literature written for those entering this stage of second childhood focuses on women and on the absurdity of their clinging to power that rightfully belonged to adulthood:

A domestic queen, she rules omnipotently. Confident in herself, she cannot bear the rude shock of having advice from her married daughter; nor can she resign the reins, now too heavy for her feeble hands, to a child who, though middle-aged, has never been married, and governed a house of her own. She must interfere; she is rather weak and fancies domestic mishaps are hidden from her; she is irritable and won't be treated like a child. Her memory fails her, and failure is attributed to those around her, and not to her own waning faculties. This state is a pitiable one. Rarely

does the intellect prove sufficiently strong to battle with the growing sense
of infirmity. It is accepted as a boon by those around her,—the melancholy
crisis of *second childhood*. (qtd. in Mangum 41; emphasis added)

Published in *The Argosy* in 1866 under the title "The Art of Growing
Old," this essay graphically represents the growing prejudice against "old
age" that now identified as ageism, and it also demonstrates the characteristic linkage of this prejudice with femininity—a linkage that appears
to have been particularly strong during the increasing specification and
articulation of "old age" in the nineteenth century.

Frances Trollope, who published her first book, *Domestic Manners of
the Americans* in 1832 when she herself was already fifty-three years of
age, was not immune to this cultural ageism. By age fifty-eight she wrote
her son that she felt "my doings are nearly over" (qtd. in Heineman, *Mrs.
Trollope* 153). During her sojourn in America, while still a relatively youthful fifty-year-old, she recounts many instances when she herself was pe-
joratively referred to as "the English old woman." In a conversation with
a "literary man," she felt certain his patronizing smile meant he was thinking, "How the old woman twaddles!"[2] Yet she had published some forty
books before the end of her late-begun writing career, becoming Charles
Dickens' chief competitor in the serialized novel market.[3] Like Dickens,
she combined an interest in social criticism with the desire—and need—
to make money. Her novels and travel books supported her family after
her ill-tempered barrister husband had failed in his practice and in every
other sort of business venture. But she differed from Dickens in one
important point: where his novels are populated by modest, innocent,
beautiful, and above all, *young* heroines, hers are full of strong women
characters, quite a number of them well beyond the appropriate age for
a heroine. In her 1836 novel, *The Life and Adventures of Jonathan
Jefferson Whitlaw*—the first anti-slavery novel to be published in English—
she goes one step farther and creates a heroine who is not only an *old*
woman, but a *black* old woman.[4] In this "female grotesque," Frances
Trollope not only figures age but writes at the intersection of anti-racism,
anti-sexism, and anti-ageism.[5] The novel—supposedly centered on the
white overseer or "confidential clerk," Jonathan Jefferson Whitlaw—actually foregrounds the figure of the seventy-year-old slave woman, Juno,
and not only promotes the sisterhood of black and white women but all
women's potential for independent action. In the process Trollope creates a compelling and stunningly unconventional portrait of an old
woman's power.

As Marilyn D. Button points out, Jonathan Jefferson Whitlaw's
mouthful of a name has a number of significant contemporary resonances:

"Jonathan" derives from "Brother Jonathan," the cartoon figure used by British cartoonists to personify America; "Jefferson," of course, refers to the famous American president whose notorious sexual relations with his female slaves and pleasure in his own children's "slavish" service Trollope had described in her *Domestic Manners* (57); and "Whitlaw" not only suggests someone who does not care a whit about the law (and can be synonymous with the term "felon"), but lacks only one letter to spell out WHITE LAW, as is strongly suggested in its capitalization in the scene in the novel where a white lynch mob is described (74).[6] But the resonances of the classical name Juno chosen for the female character who triumphs in the end are equally significant. Juno Regina was the principal goddess of the Romans, worshipped as the wife and sister of Jupiter and the queen of heaven. She was the patroness of women and the protector of childbirth, and she was also—oddly enough—the guardian of national finances. Her principal festival, appropriately, was called the "Matronalia," because it was dedicated to "mature women," the "matrons" who protected young women and children. Frances Trollope exploits all of these meanings in the representation of her "Juno," and the novel effectively becomes a "matronalia," culminating in the triumphal success of one black and one white matron.

Trollope's abolitionist fiction takes on still more radical implications when read intertextually with *The History of Mary Prince, A West Indian Slave, Narrated by Herself,* published in England in 1831.[7] Put in writing by an English woman, Susanna Strickland, the *History* is said to be "essentially" Prince's own story, "written out fully," though afterward "pruned into its present shape . . . " (Ferguson 55). But this earliest slave woman's narrative, published under the auspices of British abolitionists, is laced with graphic descriptions of floggings and other forms of torture perpetrated on the bodies of Prince and other slaves, while prudishly glossing over the fact of widespread sexual abuse of female slaves by male slave owners, and Mary Prince's probable experience of such abuse.[8] In her correspondence Strickland refers condescendingly to Prince's "simple story" as a "pathetic little history," but as Mary Favret has suggested, it is more honestly described as "violent pornography," shaped or "pruned" by the nineteenth-century obsession with flogging (Ferguson 26; Favret 20). Although it testifies eloquently to Mary Prince's heroic survivorship, it represents the female slave as stereotypically illiterate and "simple" in linguistic capacity, while focusing on the horrifying—and fascinating—spectacle of the tortured black body.

Frances Trollope's abolitionist novel, which incorporates a fictional slave woman's narrative, by contrast represents that slave woman as sharply intelligent, well educated and literary. In doing so, she responds to the question she herself raised in her description of Frances Wright's utopian experiment in Nashoba, Tennessee, where Wright planned to prove that "nature had made no difference between blacks and whites, excepting in complexion . . . by giving an education perfectly equal to a class of black and white children" (*Domestic Manners* 1997: 17). At that time, Trollope had written that "this question of the mental equality, or inequality between us and the Negro race, is one of great interest, and has certainly never yet been fairly tried . . . " (17). In narrating the story of "Juno," however, Trollope provides a historically probable example of how a slave child, educated along with her owner's children, could indeed demonstrate mental equality, or even, as in Juno's case, superiority, especially in the capacity to manipulate language and literature.

Trollope's novel—more liberated in some respects by her Enlightenment sensibility than Strickland's characteristically Victorian narrative—is much more explicit in its representation of the physical relations between white slave owners and black slaves. First, the novel openly describes the sexual exploitation of female slaves and the deliberate production of "yellow" children, and makes a blunt statement about how easily black and white "blood" are mingled and the races made indistinguishable. *Jonathan Jefferson Whitlaw* also testifies to the physical abuse of slaves by their owners, but instead of voyeuristically representing this abuse in terms of its visible effects on the black body, Trollope turns her account to an analysis of slave owner sadism. It is the male slave owner's perverse psychology that comes in for microscopic examination of its diseased tissue, not that of the black body. The narrative also dramatizes the mutually terrible fate of black and white *male* bodies under the murderous violence of institutionalized slavery. Finally, Trollope repeatedly underlines the sisterhood of black and white women in their partnership in oppression and dispossession by white males. And the entirety of this vigorously anti-racist as well as anti-slavery composition is orchestrated under the baton of a woman not only black, but over seventy years of age.

Not until the twelfth chapter, after both the repulsive Whitlaw and his American family and the opposingly virtuous European family, the Steinmarks—surely one of the dullest families in the pages of British literature—have been brought on stage, does Juno make her appearance. Her entrance is that of a witch—an old, black witch conforming to the most conventional stereotypes of witchhood. This performance, we subsequently learn, is deliberate, contrived, and highly skilled. A "discordant laugh" heard from outside the hut, where the viciously sadistic Whitlaw is about to flog the beautiful young slave Phebe, disrupts the "confidential clerk":

The figure which now presented itself at the door might have appalled anyone who beheld it for the first time. A negress, seeming to have been originally of almost dwarfish stature, and now bent nearly double with age, whose head was covered with wool as white as snow, and whose eyes rolled about with a restless movement that appeared to indicate insanity, stood on the threshold of the door, one hand resting on a stout bamboo, and the other raised with its finger pointed as if in mockery of the group within; and again a croaking laugh burst from her. (80)

"This wretched relic of a life of labour and woe" is able to inspire fear, not only in other slaves but in white men, many of whom believe her to have supernatural powers. Although Whitlaw treats "with ribald scorn the prophecies and revelations on which hang the hopes of the world," Juno has already divined that this "confidential clerk" (he is really a spy for Colonel Dart, the owner of Paradise Plantation) trembles "before the mumbled incantations of an old woman" (122). Whitlaw meekly complies with her summons to follow her out of the hut and into the forest.

Here, the narrative interrupts the already interrupted scene of the black female slave about to be flogged by the sadistic overseer—the reader is denied the opportunity to vicariously witness this torture of a beautiful, young, female body—and inserts several chapters about Edward Bligh, a white Christian missionary who preaches to the slaves, his sister Lucy, and their joint concern for Phebe, who they discover has suddenly disappeared. When the narrative returns to Juno and her encounter with Whitlaw in the forest, however, we are first provided with a cameo "slave narrative" of her history. Born and raised in the family of a French Creole, she is permitted the same education as her mistress's children, and she furthers that education, significantly, by "reading of the miscellaneous kind furnished by a New Orleans circulating library" (*JJW* 119). Later, her first male slave owner makes her his intellectual as well as sexual companion and introduces her to "all the most stirring poetry of his country," which happens to be England (119). Juno is represented, then, as both highly intelligent and literate, in stark contrast to the abolitionist representation of Mary Prince and to current European stereotypes about the "inequality" between the European and Negro mind. As Button comments, her mixture of literacy and cunning suggests her kinship to "the trickster figure of African-American folklore" (78), and appears to have been appropriated by Harriet Beecher Stowe for her later anti-slavery novel, *Uncle Tom's Cabin*. But Frances Trollope does not gloss over, as the narrative of Prince does, Juno's sexual exploitation by her various white male owners. Instead, the narrative relates how the "English settler" casually departs for Europe, "taking with him a little yellow girl of eighteen months old"

(119). He bestows Juno on a friend of his, by whom she has eight children. When this man dies, she is sold to the highest bidder and again becomes "the favourite of her owner," and again bears many children. But from the time of the loss of her first child, she never evinces any interest in any of her children or their fathers, and performs her duties "like a well-regulated machine" (119). Next sold to a "widow lady," a "charitable and well-disposed Christian" whom she serves faithfully for more than twenty years, she expects to be willed her freedom when the Christian lady dies, and envisions traveling to England to find the offspring of her first little daughter. Alas, the Christian lady turns out never to have made a will, and Juno finds herself again sold, this time into the services of Paradise Plantation. Now age fifty, she is literally driven insane for a time by this terrible disappointment, but the healthy outdoor work she is given of hoeing and weeding restores her wits in about eighteen months. (It should be noted here that Frances Trollope was a great believer in the benefits of outdoor exercise for the elderly, and happily engaged in mountain hikes at the age of seventy or so herself.)

Juno is thus represented as repeatedly victimized by her white owners, made the object of casual sexual and reproductive exploitation that, after the removal of her first child, she survives by repressing all feeling and functioning only like a machine. Other female slaves on Paradise Plantation are also subjected to sexual abuse—indeed, it is when Phebe is about to be flogged because she will not passively submit to Whitlaw's lust that Juno appears and rescues her, not only by luring him into kissing her rod instead, but by sending him on a fool's errand to New Orleans that she has concocted precisely for this purpose of getting Phebe safely away from him.

When the narrative returns to this scene, the reader is informed that although Whitlaw loathes Juno's "age and ugliness" and hates "her assumption of licence, and even power, above her fellows," he harbors another still stronger sentiment that makes him "bend and servilely crawl" before Juno's "mockings and mysteries" (118). This "wily old woman" knows exactly how to play "upon the terrors which ever lie crouching in the mind of a bad man . . . " (118). Indeed, the narrator launches into hyperbole about Juno's extraordinary command of human psychology:

> A metaphysician might have understood all this wonderfully well, and yet have been puzzled to work the machinery of such a mind as skilfully as Juno did. In truth, she knew to a nicety how far she might carry her tricks with every individual with whom she had to deal; and if all who undertook to rule their fellows studied the ins and outs of human feelings as patiently as old Juno, power as gigantic as Napoleon's might perhaps be

seen to sweep over the earth oftener than once in half a dozen centuries. (118)

It is thus that, with a mixture of dialect addressed to "Massa Whitlaw" and vaguely Shakespearean poetry recited in perfect English, she mystifies Whitlaw to such an extent that he finds himself kneeling on the ground before her and kissing her bamboo rod (124). I would suggest that this is not merely an opportune incident inserted into the plot to amuse the reader as well as old Juno, but a deliberate representation of an abolitionist emblem circulating among British as well as American abolitionists at this time. As Jean Fagin Yellin shows, the originating British medal representing a kneeling, chained black slave and emblazoned with the motto, "Am I Not a Man and a Brother?" had gone through many permutations (3–26). For abolitionist women, it was the image of a kneeling female slave with the caption, "Am I Not a Woman and a Sister?", that spoke most poignantly. These images with their mottoes circulated in various forms, such as medals, cameos, and work-bags, in England during the 1820s and 1830s. One of the variant forms represents the enchained black female slave kneeling before a classically young, white female liberator, identified as the figure of Justice by her pair of scales and branch of palm leaves (18–21). As Yellin points out, this variant has both religious and political implications: "With the inclusion of an empowered white chain-breaking liberator, the enchained black supplicants are seen as powerless" (19). The white figure of Justice, who also bears Christ's sheaf of palm leaves, envisions a peaceful end to slavery brought about by the empowered race, rather than by violent rebellion of the enslaved one.

When contextualized by these circulating images, Whitlaw's act of kneeling and kissing Juno's rod has intensely ironic meanings: here we have the white man whose name abbreviates "white law," kneeling before an old, not a young, woman and a black, not a white, human being. She carries not the peace symbol of the palm branch but a bamboo rod that the kneeling white man kisses in the traditional biblical act of submission. Nor is the tableau incidental to Frances Trollope's subtly contrived plot: as will be shown, it is a prophetic image of the "end" of the narrative.

The novel repeats but also reverses the abolitionist medals in other ways. The black slave Phebe (whose name resonates with the classical meaning of goddess of the moon) is as beautiful, virtuous, and innocent as any of the novel's European heroines, and at the climactic moment in the novel rescues Lucy Bligh from certain death by preventing her from jumping out an open window and running toward the lynch mob, as her brother

Edward already has. Here the *black* woman saves her white "sister." In an even more striking reversal of the abolitionist medal emblem, the novel spectacularizes the paired bodies of black and white men. When the saintly but fanatic Edward is lynched by the mob because he has preached to the slaves, it is black Caesar who catches his body when it is cut loose from its "chain," and then, gently laying the body on the ground, lies down beside it, kissing the "pale lips" and the "dark curls" (348). Where the medals displayed the body of the kneeling black man, the text displays black and white male bodies laid out together. In a sort of "emphasis added," the white men too may be "chained" by the institution of slavery, and it may be the black man left to mourn his white "brother."

The plot repeatedly pits the aging black woman against not one but two youthful white males, both of whom perceive her in terms of cultural conventions about old women. Whitlaw, as we have seen, can be intimidated by Juno's knowing exploitation of his superstitious belief in the "sorcery" and supernatural powers of a woman he imagines as a witch. Edward Bligh, however, the saintly but fanatic preacher who endangers his sister's life as well as his own by his wild fervor for his religious mission, projects his delusions on to Juno, believing her to be possessed by a dangerous "enthusiasm." To the last, Juno reveres Edward's saintliness, but her own clear analysis of slave owner sadism distinguishes her brand of Christianity from his—he exalts the poetry of self-sacrifice to self-destructive extremes, while she tempers self-sacrifice with a self-protection that puts her in a position to defend others.

Moreover, she has observed and penetrated the perverse psychology of men like Whitlaw and his employer Colonel Dart who clearly take pleasure in watching the sufferings of others. This perversity does not arise primarily from sexual desire, in Juno's analysis, but from male narcissism:

> The old woman, amongst many other general conclusions to which her keen observation had brought her, always took it for granted that a man's tenderness towards himself was in exact proportion to his indifference towards others. When she remarked an overseer more careless than ordinary about the accommodation of the gang under his charge, she felt sure that he was particularly well surrounded with snug comforts at home. If he lightly ordered punishment, or looked on with apathy while it was inflicted, she was convinced that he was well-furnished with precautions and consolations for all the aches and pains that flesh is heir to. But if it happened that she marked a fiendish pleasure gleam from the eye while watching the writhing of the victim under torture, then no shadow of doubt was left upon her mind that a species of self-worship, which guarded every avenue to pain, and abandoned every sense to gratification, would be found the only religion—but that carried to fanaticism—which possessed the soul. (163-4)

Juno's more balanced and wiser faith—constituted through her many years of learning how to survive—is also contrasted with the youthful poetic fantasies of her great-grandaughter, Selina Croft, who is brought back to New Orleans by her English father. Through many twists of the plot that are engineered by Juno, though of course contrived by Trollope, Whitlaw discovers that this beautiful young heiress has "black blood," and promptly replaces his proposal of marriage with a proposal that she become his mistress. Selina, who is a devotee of Spenser and other English poets, but who also firmly believes that blacks suffer enslavement because they are descendants of Cain, has already been shocked by Juno's revelation that this ancient black woman is her ancestress. After hearing Whitlaw's degrading proposal, Selina surrounds herself with flowers and commits suicide. It is Juno who finds her, together with the note indicating that the insult of her descent is more than this poetically inclined young woman can bear.

In both Edward Bligh's and Selina Croft's deaths, the text strongly implies the superiority of prose—perhaps especially prose fiction—over poetry. Edward and Selina are both seduced by what the narrative constructs as overly romantic and ultimately self-destructive fantasies produced by English poets and also by the "poetry" of evangelical Christianity. It becomes apparent that the fact that Juno's early education was later supplemented by the New Orleans circulating library, where she doubtless read such "miscellaneous works" as novels, was fortunate. Although she derives solace from reciting poetry to herself, it is notable that she primarily uses it for "trickery and influence" (161).

In the final chapter of the novel, the powers of the aged black woman, derived in part from her greater realism, are dramatically staged. Having once again lured Whitlaw, now the owner of Paradise Plantation, into a spot of her choice through vague promises of information about a slave mutiny, she asks him just three questions about what really happened: "Have you ever caused a negro child to be flogged before the eyes of Colonel Dart SOLELY to promote his amusement by its gestures and its cries?"; "Did you ever cause a negro-woman to be flogged before your eyes till she died, and then report to the colonel that she had died in childbirth?"; and "Did you, or did you not . . . report falsely to the colonel what his nephew said of him, thereby securing the inheritance yourself?" (359). Whitlaw's evasive answers cause one further question to burst from the old woman's lips: "Did Selina Croft and did Edward Bligh owe their early deaths to you?—Monster!—they did!" (359). With these words, Juno raises her bamboo rod and draws from it a whistle, which she blows. Four "powerful negroes" instantly rush from the bushes and beat and stab him to death, a spectacle that Juno watches steadily. Speaking as the figure

of Justice, she has proclaimed Whitlaw's unforgivable cruelty, and condemned him to death. The scene clearly fulfills the "prophecy" of the
earlier moment in the novel when she tricks Whitlaw into kissing her rod:
the black sybil has triumphed over the "whitlaw."

The manner of "burial" also repeats once again the motif of pairing
black and white bodies. Juno now has the other slaves place Whitlaw's
body in the hiding place underground in her own hut. Both Phebe and
Caesar have previously been "buried" alive in this hiding place, but
Whitlaw is now entombed in it. Instead of the black, chained figure kneeling in supplication and asking either "Am I Not a Man and a Brother?"
or "Am I Not a Woman and a Sister?", the bodies of black and white lie
on or under the ground together—slavery brings "death," figurative or
real, to both.

The final ironic reversal of the novel again stages sisterhood between
black and white women—this time both old women. And it is Juno, the
old black woman, who comes to the rescue of Whitlaw's old Aunt Clio.
Clio, who is introduced in the first chapter of the novel, together with
her pregnant sister-in-law Portia, embodies the history of women that her
name suggests: it is the history of women's subordination, often naively
accepted, to male domination. Brought to a spot on the banks of the
Mississippi, which epitomizes the "very perfection of melancholy dreari-
ness," Clio unquestioningly obeys the commands of her brother Jonathan
and labors without sustenance while he fortifies himself with whiskey and
tobacco (he generously offers the two women a small portion of the
former). Ultimately, she cajoles him into allowing her to get out the bag
of corn-cakes and supply poor "Porchy" with something to eat, so that
the young mother, weak with hunger, will be able to sleep. Both women
exemplify the "squalid look of the miserable wives . . . of these men
[wood-cutters on the banks of the Mississippi]" that Trollope had com-
mented on in her *Domestic Manners* (22). Noting the "blueish white"
color of these women and their children, she adds that she had never
witnessed "human nature reduced so low, as it appeared in the wood-
cutters' huts on the unwholesome banks of the Mississippi" (22). In a
later observation, she directly compares the state of such women to that
of slaves:

> If the condition of the labourer be not superior to that of the English peas-
> ant, that of his wife and daughters is incomparably worse. It is they who
> are indeed the slaves of the soil. One has but to look at the wife of an
> American cottager, and ask her age, to be convinced that the life she leads
> is one of hardship, privation, and labour. It is rare to see a woman in this
> station who has reached the age of thirty, without losing every trace of
> youth and beauty. You continually see women with infants on their knee,

that you feel sure are their grand-children, till some convincing proof of the contrary is displayed. . . . The horror of domestic service, which the reality of slavery, and the fable of equality, have generated, excludes the young women from that sure and most comfortable resource of decent English girls; and the consequence is, that with a most irreverent freedom of manner to the parents, the daughters are, to the full extent of the word, domestic slaves. (92–93)

Auguste Hervieu's frontispiece for the first volume of the British edition of *Jonathan Jefferson Whitlaw* illustrates this sisterhood produced by the joint oppression of black and white women by the American male (Illustration 7.1). Titled "A Louisiana Love Scene," the illustration shows Jonathan Whitlaw in an attitude of contemptuous superiority, while a white woman—presumably his wife with a tea towel, a badge of her servitude—stands facing the viewer in an attitude of despair. To her side, a young black female, presumably one of the slaves Jonathan Whitlaw purchases, looks at her with an air of sympathy. Another Hervieu illustration shows Clio in the foreground, holding out the newly born Jonathan Jefferson Whitlaw to his father in such a way as to prominently display the proof of his superiority—his as-yet-undiapered genitalia—while in the background Portia lies on a bed with an expression of deep distress and suffering (Illustration 7.2).

Trollope's anti-slavery narrative thus begins with the depiction of the mutual servitude of white and black women. Admittedly a conservative in terms of the class system in England, which she sees as conferring on English girls the benefits of a benevolent "domestic service," she is nevertheless horrified by the condition of working-class women in America. The narrative clearly distinguishes the horrors of *actual* slavery from that of lower-class white women's domestic slavery, but it repeatedly aligns black and white female characters in parallel positions of the lack of anything close to "equality" or "liberty"—those great "fables" of American democracy. Interestingly, she posits a clear link between the dominance of American men and the premature aging of their overburdened wives. The narrative repeatedly links black and white women metaphorically in shared "sorrow." In a chapter toward the close of the narrative, when black Phebe and white Lucy are both anticipating escape from the American republic and a new life in Europe, their mutual joy and sorrow are described. Phebe feels exquisite enjoyment at the thought that not only she and her lover Caesar will be free, but that their children will be free from "the galling yoke of eternal thraldom" (302). Lucy is similarly happy at the thought of escape from this dangerous land where the institution of slavery ensures the constant threat of violence. But, we are told, "the white and the black girl had each a sorrow at her heart" (302). Lucy fears (rightly)

7.1: "A Louisiana Love Scene" by Auguste Hervieu in Frances Trollope, *The Life and Adventures of Jonathan Jefferson Whitlaw: or Scenes on the Mississippi*. 3 vols. London: Bentley, 1836: Frontispiece.

7.2: "Clio and the newly born Jonathan Jefferson Whitlaw" by Auguste Hervieu in Frances Trollope, *The Life and Adventures of Jonathan Jefferson Whitlaw: or Scenes on the Mississippi*. 3 vols. London: Bentley, 1836: 25.

for the safety of her brother, while Phebe despairs at the thought of leaving her mother and siblings behind in slavery. The two young women walk together in a scene that deliberately recalls their first such walk together through "the dark solitudes of that forest" (302).

In the end, Lucy and Phebe depart for Europe on the same boat, immediately following old Juno's arranged execution of Whitlaw. Juno instructs his executioners to bind up the body, because she has a vault ready for it: "It was my child he killed, and it was my hands that hollowed out his grave" (360). Her act of vengeful justice again signals the kinship of "black" and "white" women: the great-granddaughter this black woman calls "my child" was white. Now at the very end of the narrative, she sets about the task of bringing similar justice to another white woman. Although Whitlaw has willed Paradise Plantation to his Aunt Clio, the will is null and void unless Whitlaw is known to be dead. The honest and faithful Clio, who refuses to believe that "her Jonathan" is not coming back, holds his estate in readiness for his return and will not appropriate a single cent of the inheritance to herself. "The last act of old Juno's life," we are told, "was to settle this knotty point for the good Clio" (364). She therefore arranges, after a suitable interval, for Whitlaw's bones to be found, together with identifying letters, so that his old aunt will be financially secure. This "end" also reverses Juno's own situation earlier in the novel, when her Christian owner failed to leave a will, and therefore failed to give Juno her deserved inheritance of freedom. And it should be noted that Juno thus plays out her role of guardian of finances, although in this case it is not national but matronly finances she protects.

The last paragraphs of the novel, as is customary in nineteenth-century novels, tell us how all the characters "turned out"—all, that is, except Juno. No "end" is laid out for her. She remains the manipulator of other plots, the teller of other stories, the unlikely instrument of justice. Is she the authorial "Other"? Frances Trollope's extraordinary characterization of an old black woman, subject all her life to the ultimate dispossession of the basic human rights of freedom and equality, yet finally the triumphant dispenser of justice both to those who deserved to be punished and to those who deserved to be rewarded, suggests a unique authorial fantasy. Here in a world corrupted by the evil institutions of slavery, sexism, and ageism, it is not the youthful white male who heroically rights the balance. Such a plot would have reinscribed white male privilege even as it—in theory—addressed the wrongs of the very system that instituted that privilege. Instead, it is the old women of the world, black and white, who both inherit and guarantee that just inheritance. The narrative seems to inscribe a coded message: old women of the world, UNITE! No matter what your race or condition, you have more power than you think.

Frances Trollope wrote this novel not only for the anti-slavery forces in America but for herself.

NOTES

1. "Charcot's Older Women" in Woodward, ed. *Figuring Age.* I am indebted to Kathleen Woodward both for my title and for the scope and perspective that her groundbreaking collection brings to age studies.

2. See *Domestic Manners*, ed. Neville-Sington, 72, 79, and 94.

3. Pamela Neville-Sington notes that Charles Dickens "had difficulty coming to terms with the fact that his principal rival was a woman, and one, moreover, who was old enough to be his mother" (*Fanny Trollope* 277). See also chap. 1 of this collection.

4. Although many writers had vividly and compassionately portrayed the condition of slaves, as does Aphra Behn in *Oroonoko, or the History of the Royal Slave* (1688), *Jonathan Jefferson Whitlaw* was the first novel in English written with the avowed intention of opposing slavery and advocating abolition. At the time of its writing and publication, slavery had only recently been abolished in the British Empire, and abolitionist sentiment against the continuing institution of slavery in America ran high. As Helen Heineman points out, the novelist Richard Hildreth "claimed for himself 'the first successful application of fictitious narrative to anti-slavery purposes,'" but his *The White Slave: or Memoirs of Archy Moore* (1836) was published six months after *Jonathan Jefferson Whitlaw* (*Frances Trollope* 143). Frances Trollope's pioneering reform novel belongs with what Ellen Moers terms "the epic age" of women writers, which "did in fact, as much as any literature can, change the world" (14).

5. In "Female Grotesques in Academia," I characterize academic women who are objectified because of their age and femininity as "female grotesques." I borrow the term from Mary Russo's "Female Grotesques: Carnival and Theory," where she refers to women who are both old and pregnant, or "pregnant hags." The term appears peculiarly appropriate to Frances Trollope's Juno, who has endured numerous pregnancies and survives as an aging maternal figure "pregnant" with schemes for helping her own people and outwitting slave owners and overseers.

6. All page references to *Jonathan Jefferson Whitlaw* refer to the Parisian one-volume edition, published in the same year as the British three-volume edition. However, the illustrations by Auguste Hervieu have been reproduced from the latter.

7. Button notes that at least five slave narratives had been published in England by 1836, and that others published in the United States were probably available in England by the time Trollope was writing *JJW* (74, n8). Trollope's own note to her fifth edition of *Domestic Manners* (1839), that "It was not till after I had left the United States that the frightful details of Lynch law reached me. These details are now well known throughout Europe," indicates that her interest in the institution of slavery in the United States was greatly heightened

by her own experience in the country, and that she probably continued to read widely on the subject during the four years between her return and the publication of her anti-slavery novel (quoted in Neville-Sington, *Domestic Manners*, 344, n5).

8. Jenny Sharpe examines the slave woman's sexuality from another perspective, arguing that Mary Prince and others like her, such as Harriet Jacobs, "used their relationships with free men to challenge their masters' right of ownership" (32). For Sharpe, the occlusion of sexual relations between black women and white men in *The History of Mary Prince* is in part a result of Prince's own "voice-agency" or her deliberate self-censorship in order to maintain her resistance to white "ownership."

8

Putting Idiosyncrasy in Its Place: *Michael Armstrong* in Light of Trollope's Early Fiction

Constance Harsh

In turning her attention to the human consequences of the Industrial Revolution, Frances Trollope was by no means alone among nineteenth-century novelists. *Michael Armstrong* (1839–40) may be one of the first pieces of fiction to deal with factory life, but it shares many features with better known works such as Charles Dickens' *Hard Times* and Elizabeth Gaskell's *Mary Barton* and *North and South*. Like them, and like Charlotte Elizabeth Tonna's *Helen Fleetwood*, Benjamin Disraeli's *Sybil*, and Charles Kingsley's *Alton Locke*, Trollope addresses "the condition-of-England question" that consumed Britain from the late 1830s to the mid-1850s. Like these other novels, Trollope finds hope for the future in the special power that can be exercised by a heroine of great courage and insight. Her Mary Brotherton, like such heroines as Margaret Hale and Helen Fleetwood, points the way to a society organized on principles antithetical to exploitative self-interest.

Yet, working with a set of interests her earlier fiction had already set out, Trollope put her own stamp on her contribution to the condition-of-England novel. Like her other novels, *Michael Armstrong* is prone to digression for the sake of striking vignettes. The dramatic pageant at Dowling Hall, as well as Lady Clarissa's efforts to save her valuables from creditors, have about as much to do with the main narrative line as Jonathan Jefferson Whitlaw's pool hustling in New Orleans or the serious fancy-fair in *The Vicar of Wrexhill*. Moreover, typically for Trollope, *Michael Armstrong* features starkly drawn villains who present melodramatic dangers to the heroes. But perhaps the most significant two characteristics on display in this novel and her other early fiction are Trollope's fascination with the grotesque and her ambivalence toward individualism. By negotiating these two related areas in her industrial novel, Trollope demonstrates her ongoing interest in grappling with the drawbacks and allurements of human idiosyncrasy.

Trollope's penchant for depicting the extraordinary was evident even to her earliest readers. Two reviews of *The Vicar of Wrexhill* make clear their distaste for her extravagance. According to the *Athenaeum*, Trollope "scents out moral deformities with a sort of professional eagerness." H. F. Chorley, writing in the *London and Westminster Review* not just of this novel but of her work as a whole, identified "her greatest fault [as] a hankering after the coarse and violent and degrading, as a means of producing effect" (115). Charlotte Brontë may well have had Trollope in mind when she wrote her well-known rejection of industrial sensationalism in *Shirley*: "Child-torturers, slave masters and drivers, I consign to the hands of jailers; the novelist may be excused from sullying his page with the record of their deeds" (61). Indeed, *Michael Armstrong* struck contemporary readers as so shocking as to be a threat to public welfare. The *Athenaeum* took the unusual step of publishing an exceptionally long review of the book after only six numbers had appeared, complaining violently of its potential for sparking violence "among an ignorant and excited population, to which her shilling numbers are but too accessible" (590).

Some of the Gothic horrors of this novel have an obvious relevance to its political theme. For instance, the scene of the hungry Deep Valley apprentices scrambling for hog slops, vividly illustrated by Auguste Hervieu and particularly reprehended by the *Athenaeum* reviewer, plays an important role in illustrating the evils of the industrial exploitation of child labor (Illustration 8.1). This incident provides both an indictment of those in charge of the mill and a warning of the social consequences of its operation. Trollope makes clear the potential this disgusting sight might have for driving an older witness to violence.

Michael Armstrong was a child of deep feeling; and it was, perhaps, lucky for him, that the burning sense of shame and degradation which pervaded every nerve of his little frame, as he looked on upon this revolting spectacle, come upon him while yet too young for any notion of resistance to suggest itself. He felt faint, sick, and broken-hearted; but no worm that ever was crushed to atoms by the foot of an elephant, dreamed less of vengeance than did poor Michael.[1] (184)

8.1: "Make haste young un' or they wont leave a turnip paring for us" by Auguste Hervieu in Frances Trollope, *The Life and Adventures of Michael Armstrong, the Factory Boy*. London: Frank Cass, 1968; London: Colburn, 1840: 184.

In two brief tableaux, both also illustrated by Hervieu, Trollope provides a heartbreaking glimpse of the effects the factory system can have on the family unit: Mr. Bell recalls for Mary Brotherton his encounter with a mother dragging her nearly dead daughter through the snow to work (203; Illustration 8.2); Mary herself comes across a father with the dying son he had carried to the mill lest he lose his pay (276–77). Since one of Trollope's stated goals is to "place before the eyes of Englishmen, the hideous mass of injustice and suffering to which thousands of infant labourers are subjected" (iii), it is important for her to include these scenes and others like them in her narrative. And she explicitly warns readers against facilely concluding that her depiction is unrealistic. After her description of conditions in Deep Valley, she steps aside from the narrative for a moment: "Let none dare to say this picture is exaggerated, till he has taken the trouble to ascertain by his own personal investigation, that it is so. . . . Woe to those who supinely sit in contented ignorance of the facts, soothing their spirits and their easy consciences with the cuckoo note, '*exaggeration*,' while thousands of helpless children pine away" (186). By implication Trollope offers herself as an attractive alternative to such passive critics.[2] The intrepid chronicler of American outrages has turned her attention to England, finding facts whose sensationality is practically proof of their veracity. Moreover, the representation of horror is a staple of the condition-of-England novel. *Alton Locke*'s most revolting scene depicts the rat-eaten corpses of Jemmy Downes' wife and two children (Kingsley 331–32). Disraeli takes his own stab at horrifying his reader by describing the atrocious, unfeminine appearance and occupation of female mine-workers: "Naked to the waist, an iron chain fastened to a belt of leather runs between their legs clad in canvas trousers, while on hands and feet an English girl . . . hauls and hurries tubs of coals up subterranean roads, dark, precipitous, and plashy" (1981: 140). One of Trollope's most grotesque figures, Sally the mad and crippled former factory girl, has close analogs in both *Helen Fleetwood* and *North and South*, in respectively the maimed Sarah Wright and the consumptive Bessy Higgins, like Sally both industrial victims. And, as I have argued elsewhere, even the apparently *outré* persecution that Sir Matthew inflicts on Michael Armstrong at Dowling Hall evokes the danger to the domestic sphere that is so crucial a part of the condition-of-England novel's industrial analysis (Harsh 27, 34). Social problem novels, after all, require the vivid depiction of a problem to make readers take them seriously.

Michael Armstrong, however, seems to evince an interest in grotesquerie that exceeds the requirements of its genre. As Rosemarie Bodenheimer has observed, speaking in particular of the latter part of the novel, "It becomes increasingly difficult to find the line between the expression of

8.2: "I was startled by the sound of a low moaning, and perceived a woman bending over a little girl who appeared sinking to the ground" by Auguste Hervieu in Frances Trollope, *The Life and Adventures of Michael Armstrong, the Factory Boy*. London: Frank Cass, 1968; London: Colburn, 1840: 203.

social outrage and the preemption of factory material for purposes of Gothic horror" (29). Trollope paints Dowling's villainy with so broad a brush that fictional industrialists like Dickens' Josiah Bounderby, however unsavory, seem like models of humanitarianism by contrast. Sir Matthew and his colleagues Dr. Crockley and Parsons take a creepily perverse joy in trying to force Michael to kiss a seven-year-old factory girl in one of the intervals in which she must fall to the ground to avoid machinery. (As Crockley lubriciously urges, "Let us see them sprawling together" [80].) Dowling has an antipathy to Michael that seems to strike even him as aberrant. When Crockley suggests that his friend keep the boy around the house for a couple of months, Sir Matthew demurs, "But if I tell all, I can let you into a secret, Crockley, that would make you change your mind, perhaps. The long and the short of it is, that I can't keep my hands off him." He observes that his reputation would suffer if word got around about "every thing that I may have happened to say and do to him, when his nasty ways have pushed me further than I could bear" (117). Typically enough, Hervieu illustrated a moment of characteristic viciousness, in which Dowling on horseback whips Michael on foot to make him run faster (76; Illustration 8.3). On his deathbed, Sir Matthew experiences an appropriately over-the-top glimpse of his own damnation, as he imagines that he is being smothered by all the factory children he has victimized (364). Other condition-of-England novels depict manufacturers who are misguided or callously indifferent, but often a mill owner is morally salvageable, as in *Mary Barton* and *North and South*. In contrast, Trollope insists on Dowling's irredeemable nature. Dowling seems to suit Trollope's taste for flamboyantly evil characters. The excesses of Trollope's villain in *Michael Armstrong* echo the extravagant villainy of some of her earlier characters. Like Dowling, whom Mary Brotherton anathematizes as "Monster!" (112), Rev. William Cartwright of *The Vicar of Wrexhill* has an air of the unnatural and even the demonic about him—his chuckle, we learn, is "the hosannah of a fiend" (261). Evil monk Isidore Bartone in *The Abbess* has a obsessive desire to destroy Lady Geraldine d'Albano that expresses itself in such dubiously grammatical teeth-gnashing as this: "That air of quiet, firmly-rooted power, which used to act upon my burning hatred, like oil upon flame, now—that I knew, it tottered to its fall, was sweet to me, as a cooling draught to the thirsty traveller" (2: 2). Isidore initiates the most sensational actions of the book: the walling-up of a young woman in a convent for supposedly breaking her vows; and an atmospheric trial before the Inquisition at the Vatican. Colonel Dart, the great plantation owner of *Jonathan Jefferson Whitlaw*, takes pleasure in seeing his slaves whipped; at the opening of one chapter he is revealed "amicably discoursing upon the number of

8.3: "Don't you think I should make a good dancing Master?" by Auguste
Hervieu in Frances Trollope, *The Life and Adventures of Michael Armstrong, the
Factory Boy*. London: Frank Cass, 1968; London: Colburn, 1840: 76.

stripes that a female slave might safely receive without permanent injury to herself or her future progeny" (2: 84). His confidential clerk, the eponymous anti-hero, offers an even more explicit example of sexual sadism. Frustrated in his initial efforts to seduce Dart's slave Phebe, Whitlaw proposes to punish her by stripping and lashing her. When it seems that she may try to run away, he sees her flight as just an additional source of excitement to him: " 'She'd skip handsome over them stumps yonder, I'll engage for her. Go it, my beauty!' he continued, clapping his hands: 'Off with ye! You shall have three minutes' law—upon my soul you shall' " (1: 218). As Helen Heineman has observed, there is a shocking level of specificity in these "dramatized scenes of Whitlaw's erotic brutality" (*Mrs. Trollope* 148).[3]

Yet scenes in both *Michael Armstrong* and other novels suggest that the grotesque is a source of humor and enjoyment for Trollope as well as a means of characterizing depraved individuals. Mary Brotherton seems to model the appropriate reaction to poet Osmond Norval's absurd self-importance as he solemnly ponders how to turn Michael's story into verse: she "sat . . . almost convulsed with laughter, and with her pocket-handkerchief by no means elegantly applied to her mouth" (65).[4] Lady Elizabeth Norris in *The Widow Barnaby* offers a curious example of ridicule by careful design: she holds parties to which she invites only those whose oddities will amuse her; in case they fail, she provides herself with reading material and a table of snacks (1995: 256–57). Both these women, at least in part surrogates for reader and author, demonstrate the enjoyment to be had in human fatuity. More disturbingly, a similar moment in *Jonathan Jefferson Whitlaw* connects the joys of observing outlandishness with the joys of inflicting pain. It immediately follows Colonel Dart's amicable discourse on whipping female slaves. The aged slave Juno suddenly appears at an open window to perplex and mislead Dart for her own purposes, one of which is pleasure: "This queer mixture of fraud, fun, and feeling, never enjoyed herself more than when she saw the savage, bloodthirsty Colonel Dart fawning upon her. . . . She knew—for her comfort—that she had been his torment and his torture for the fifteen years that he had possessed the estate, making him dream by night and meditate by day on plots, poisonings, and assassinations without end" (2: 85). Coming as this does after a reminder of Dart's own sadism, this passage suggests both the appropriateness of Juno's infliction of pain and the similarity of her sadism to his. It also anticipates the denouement of Whitlaw's story, in which Juno will set other slaves upon him to murder him. That part of the book's happy ending is a satisfying, justified act of brutality that Trollope lets go unpunished. Through Juno, Trollope simultaneously exhibits her awareness of the moral dynamics of violent excess and its entertainment value.

More typically, grotesque comedy and horror lie alongside each other in an uneasy yet less troubling relationship. To some extent both qualities are inherent in two of Trollope's most striking anti-heroes, Jonathan Jefferson Whitlaw and Widow Barnaby. The former is both an agent of terror and a boorish object of authorial ridicule who can eloquently observe, "What's freedom for, if we can't do what we like with our own born slaves?" (1: 123). The latter, a far more benign figure, is primarily a source of humor with her outrageous behavior, clothing, and makeup. Nevertheless, her influence is potentially malignant, as when Agnes Willoughby seems seriously in danger of losing her respectability in her aunt's mad dash after Lord Mucklebury (270–72). Sir Matthew Dowling's household in *Michael Armstrong* offers two excellent examples of Trollope's sensibility at work. Michael comes into Dowling's sadistic sights when Lady Clarissa Shrimpton ludicrously exaggerates the heroism of the boy's act of shooing away a threatening cow. After Sir Matthew takes Michael into the Dowling household, cruelty alternates with broad social comedy, most notably in the absurd pageant that celebrates Michael's deed. The humor of this ridiculous spectacle is immediately succeeded by the cruelty of Sir Matthew's punishment of Michael for fluffing his lines— abuse that inspires the eavesdropping Mary Brotherton to action. An even more jarring example of this juxtaposition comes as Dowling dies. As creditors buzz around the household, Lady Clarissa (now his wife) schemes to remove as much as she can from their grasp, and the gossipy Mrs. Gabberly pushes her way in to witness as much of the debacle as she can. Clearly there is humor in their excesses, as there is in the undignified scramble for a dropped wallet that involves Lady Clarissa, Crockley, Parsons, and Mrs. Gabberly. Yet Sir Matthew's ghastly vision of factory children, a solemn warning of the consequences of evil behavior, comes immediately after this scene. Trollope treats both incidents with indiscriminate gusto as though they are equally productive of interest to her readers. It may be just this sort of failure to enforce decorous distinctions between the ridiculous and the sublime that convinced contemporaries of her hopeless vulgarity. In the admittedly different context of *The Vicar of Wrexhill*, H. F. Chorley found the signs of a woman without due reverence—"The coarse distortions of a mind which cannot see or sympathise with any of the pure, or good, or kind, or lofty, or spiritual feelings of human nature" (130). While this comment fails to do justice to Trollope's sincere respect for her own religion, it aptly indicates her unwillingness to temper her relish for the grotesque with a suitable dash of pious conventionality.

If Trollope's fascination with the grotesque inclines her toward an undiscriminating enthusiasm, her ambivalence toward individualism leads her to offer interesting distinctions between forms of self-assertion. At the

heart of *Michael Armstrong* lies a heroic action by a concerned individual—Mary Brotherton's descent into the hell of Deep Valley to rescue a suffering child. As in other condition-of-England novels, a woman
is responsible for the solution to the industrial problem as the novel de-
fines it. Also as in these other novels, some cover is provided for this
unexpected arrogation of traditionally male power. In an address to Mr.
Bell and Nurse Tremlett, Mary defends herself against a possible charge
of impropriety for traveling without a customary retinue:

> Do not set me down in your judgments as a hot-headed girl, indifferent
> to the opinions of society, and anxious only to follow the whim of the mo-
> ment. Did I belong to any one, I think I should willingly yield to their
> guidance. But I am alone in the world; I have no responsibilities but to
> God and my own conscience, and the only way I know of, by which I can
> make this desolate sort of freedom endurable, is by fearlessly, and with-
> out respect to any prejudices or opinions whatever, employing my pre-
> posterous wealth in assisting the miserable race from whose labours it has
> been extracted. (232)

But if such a speech puts Mary in line with other condition-of-England
heroines, it also raises issues that are uniquely important to Trollope in
her early fiction. Mary's orphanhood and her unselfishness help authorize
her self-assertion. Other assertive characters are less justified.

For Trollope, the self-interested individualism of a Widow Barnaby or
a Jonathan Jefferson Whitlaw is fascinating but dangerous. The two novels
in which these characters figure repeatedly make clear that their behavior is at best inappropriate and at worst (Whitlaw) truly evil. Yet Trollope's
repeated designation of each character as the hero of her novel is not
merely ironic. Martha Barnaby is not simply a vulgar woman with mer-
etricious values; she is a figure of great vitality and fun who often earns
the narrator's amused admiration. For instance, despite her misjudgment
of Lord Mucklebury's intentions, Mrs. Barnaby emerges rather well from
their final encounter: having tracked him to London with the thought
of charging him with breach of promise, she resourcefully changes her
approach and meets him only to commission him with purchasing a set
of shells for her (284–85). On many other occasions she is perhaps too
stringently compassed by the negative judgments of the right-thinking
people who always seem to be lurking in this novel. But Trollope is always clearly fascinated by the energy her selfishness brings to her world.
Similarly, even the manifest viciousness of Jonathan Jefferson Whitlaw does
not prevent his becoming a figure of considerable interest and power.
From his infancy he has a talent for acquisition that catches the eye of
Colonel Dart, his future patron (1: 34–35). He has a shrewdness that

lends his rise a positive interest. Perhaps most tellingly, Trollope digresses from her main story for three chapters to follow Whitlaw's adventures as a pool shark in New Orleans. Here, Whitlaw really does become the hero of the piece, working with Crabshawly to win back the money Major Tomlinson and General Holingsworth have stolen from him.

But Trollope's overt allegiance is to unselfishness, as her characterization of her good people repeatedly shows. Indeed, her novels have a consistent commitment to collectivism that is unusual in the English novel. Certainly other condition-of-England novels, like most nineteenth-century fiction, primarily focus on the fate of individuals, who organize themselves into small family units. Although Victorian authors recognize that society is large and multifarious, authors typically imagine their characters finding personal satisfaction in what is known today as nuclear families. To take just the industrial novel as an example, *Sybil, Alton Locke, North and South, Mary Barton*, and *Felix Holt* have at their centers the love story, however complicated, of a single couple. *Michael Armstrong* shares with Trollope's other novels the conviction that happiness consists of collecting all the surviving good characters as a single domestic unit, often a unit in exile. For this novel, this means that Mary, Nurse Tremlett, Michael, Fanny Fletcher, Edward Armstrong, and Martha Dowling wind up living together in a castle on the Rhine. Similarly, the end of *The Abbess* finds a large and heterogeneous group living harmoniously in England—not merely Lady Geraldine and her immediate family, but Lady Juliet's page Morgante, and Camilla di Mondello with her husband and child. *Jonathan Jefferson Whitlaw*'s happy ending involves the entire Steinmark family, joined by Lucy Bligh and the slaves Phebe and Caesar, sailing off to a free, financially comfortable life in Germany.[5] Just as in Trollope's own family circle, which for many years included Auguste Hervieu but not her husband Thomas, a group consisting only of two parents and their children does not suffice for happiness. In each of these novels, conventional marriage plays a role, but marriage is incomplete for Trollope without the addition of a large domestic circle.

Moreover, the experiences of three characters in *Whitlaw* suggest that individuality is problematic even when it is embodied by "good" characters. Selina Croft, the daughter of a wealthy Liverpool merchant, has a number of the qualities of a Trollope heroine: beauty, good manners, and "a kind and generous heart" (2: 298). Yet Selina prefers to read almost nothing but "poetry, for which she had a fondness that approached almost to passion" (2: 288); she has somehow acquired the idea, for which Trollope has no sympathy, that the "marked and hitherto most unhappy race [of slaves] were the descendants of Cain" (2: 298). Within a few chapters Selina will fall victim to her own oversensitivity, committing suicide after learning that she is the great-granddaughter of the slave Juno.

> In common with most young people of a fanciful temperament and poetical turn of thought, she conceived herself somewhat apart from and above the common herd. Neither her fortune nor her beauty created any such feeling, but she had believed herself favoured by Heaven with a soul of higher tone than was usually accorded to mortals. Poor girl!—the descent from these visions to the hateful reality was too violent. (2: 327)

Trollope treats this young woman with a mixture of sympathy and judgment; she figures the young girl's fatal weakness as a conviction that she is somehow a special being.

More intriguing than Selina is her great-grandmother Juno, who embodies the overlap in Trollope's mind of individuality and the grotesque. The first glimpse of Juno anticipates the figure of Sally in *Michael Armstrong*—a woman twisted beyond health and sanity by systematic exploitation: she is a being "seeming to have been originally of almost dwarfish stature, and now bent nearly double with age, . . . whose eyes rolled about with a restless movement that appeared to indicate insanity" (1: 220); she is a "wretched relic of a life of labour and woe" (1: 221). But, just as the hunchbacked body of Betsy Compton in *The Widow Barnaby* hides a keen mind, Juno's appearance is deceptive. She is a canny, well-educated woman who cleverly calculates her words and actions to manipulate the superstitious whites who own her. Her power over Whitlaw and Colonel Dart is impressive. Juno stops the former's attempted rape of Phebe by little more than appearing on the scene: "The moment previous to that at which the palsied and decrepit hag entered, Whitlaw stood fearless and undaunted before Heaven, ready to commit the most hideous crimes in defiance of its laws; but now he stood doubting and unnerved before her, as if awaiting her fiat either to prosecute or abandon his purpose" (1: 224). Juno is a predominantly heroic character, who protects her people and gains the respect of such good individuals as Lucy Bligh and Frederick Steinmark. She very nearly possesses the supernatural abilities to which she pretends. At one point she watches the retreating figure of Edward Bligh and foresees his martyrdom: "She pondered upon his probable destiny, till she herself almost doubted whether the dark future that seemed to open before her eyes were simply the effect of conjecture, or of a revealing of that which was to come, such as was not given to the minds of others" (3: 10–11). Despite all that is positive in Juno's character, however, Trollope evidently is somewhat uneasy about her. Her very success in manipulating others is potentially dangerous: "If all who undertook to rule their fellows studied the ins and outs of human feelings as patiently as old Juno, power as gigantic as Napoleon's might perhaps be seen to sweep over the earth oftener than once in half a dozen centuries" (2: 2–3). Her obsession with being "the ancestress of a very beautiful and glorious race" in England (2: 11) is a type of vanity that leads to tragedy when she abruptly informs Selina of their relationship. The murder of Jonathan Jefferson Whitlaw, however justified (and however unpunished), is presented as a clearly ungodly act in which Bligh's black parisioners refuse to participate. It is significant that Juno does not find a home in the happy German community of the Steinmarks. While her individuality gains her power and respect, it also prevents her from being absorbed into the happy ending.

The well-intentioned missionary Edward Bligh provides another, equally complex example of the problem of individualism. Edward, unlike Selina, has access to the core group of good people who will form a happy unit at book's end: he and his sister Lucy are patrons of Phebe and Caesar, and they become friends with the Steinmark family. Yet Edward's destiny, which nominally takes him to the spiritual leadership of a group of slaves, actually takes him away from his logical home in the central group. Trollope's descriptions of Edward leave no doubt that he is an admirable man of profound faith and integrity. Especially at the beginning of the book, she emphasizes his beauty and piety. An early paean to his sincerity, interestingly enough, explicitly disassociates him from the dangerously self-serving vocation of England's Evangelicals.

> Never did a hope more holy, an ambition more sublime, engross the soul of man. Remote as is good from evil, was the principle which sent him forth, thus self-elected and self-devoted, to raise the poor crushed victims of an infernal tyranny from the state of grovelling ignorance to which they were chained by their well-calculating masters, from that which swells with most unrighteous vanity the hearts of many among ourselves, inclined to separate from the established faith in which they were educated, and to hold themselves apart, as chosen saints and apostles of another. (1: 181–82)

Although Trollope here demonstrates that his self-separation is divinely authorized, her subsequent treatment of Edward suggests that the individuality of his devotion is an ambiguous good. When he sends Lucy off to work as a seamstress, he is at once appropriately protecting her from danger and inappropriately isolating himself: "He had consigned to another the precious charge which his dying father bequeathed to his care; he had left himself alone, surrounded by ignorance and sin, while the one bright spirit that God had given to cheer and sustain him in his thorny path was by his own act banished from the place that Nature assigned her by his side" (2: 40). The narrator goes on to observe that Edward, like Selina, has an "imagination, active to an excess that too surely indicated disease" (2: 41). There is indeed something disordered about

Edward's mind, as both Juno (who shakes her head over him sorrowfully [2: 130]) and Frederick Steinmark (who lectures him on his social withdrawal [3: 228–29]) realize. Trollope's assessment of the multiple factors—unrequited love, loss of position, concern for Lucy, imperfect missionary success—that work on Edward's nature emphasizes the social consequences of his melancholy: "it was all these together, pressing upon a nature too sensitive to bear the slightest item of the list without sinking under it, and too disinterested in its exalted affections to permit itself the consolation of expressing its misery, or asking from the few who loved him the sympathy it would have been almost oppressive to him to find" (3: 189). Part of Edward's sickness is a longing for martyrdom, which finds fulfillment in his utterly pointless death. He leaps from the loft in which he and the women of the group are hidden, not to provide necessary assistance, but to escape the injury to his masculine pride that concealment inflicts. Promptly running to the burning house at Reichland, he helpfully introduces himself to the lynch mob and is immediately hung. His actions constitute at once saintly devotion and solipsistic pathology.

While Trollope clearly has reservations about even the most noble examples of self-separation, she also recognizes that there can be a genuine need for individual acts of self-assertion, particularly in situations in which women encounter male tyranny. The case of Martha Dowling in *Michael Armstrong* demonstrates the dangers of following constituted authority too blindly. Martha, a warm-hearted but overly obedient daughter, is sadly deficient in "moral courage" (225). Even after Mary Brotherton confronts her with her role in convincing Mrs. Armstrong to apprentice Michael into a probably exploitative situation, Martha cannot bring herself to rebel against her father:

> "I love my father, and I hold my duty to him the first and the highest I have to perform on earth."
>
> "Save only what you owe to your own soul, Martha Dowling," replied Mary. "Had you been yourself for nothing in this matter, I might think as you do, that your duty as a child must prevent your interfering in it, though even that, I suspect, would be but doubtful morality. But, Martha! the case is otherwise." (227)

Clearly it is Mary who has the moral high ground at this point; ultimately her words will have their effect on Martha, "sho[oting] with a painful and unwelcome brightness upon the dim and uncertain twilight of her moral perceptions" (292). Martha's mistake has been to see herself only in relationship to her father—as a daughter, not as an autonomous moral being with individual responsibilities. Other novels show a similar acceptance of individualized action. In *The Vicar of Wrexhill*, Rosalind

Torrington takes the initiative to protect Mowbray Park against the influence of Cartwright in the absence of Mrs. Mowbray. But, as with Mary Brotherton, she provides a cover story for her individual self-assertion: confronting the vicar over the offensive extemporaneity of his prayers with Fanny Mowbray, she justifies her intervention by referring to the lessons her late father taught her.[6] *The Widow Barnaby*'s Betsy Compton does not require an excuse for being at odds with her environment: as a "sickly, deformed" (1995: 2) woman, Nature seems to have set her apart. Yet, beyond this individuating circumstance, Betsy chooses to live separately from her brother's superficial and avaricious family, hoarding her own money for most of her life. Trollope shows no sign of disapproving of Betsy's rejection of her sister-in-law and nieces Martha and Sophia; on the contrary, the novel shares in the old woman's enjoyment of her hidden wealth.[7] Lady Geraldine of *The Abbess* has endured years of spiritual isolation as the secretly Protestant head of a Roman Catholic convent. Yet her separation from those around her, however sad, has not twisted her nature: instead, it has facilitated her leadership and enabled her to work for the greater good of the souls with which she has been charged, as her self-justification to her niece Juliet clearly indicates (2: 88).

For Trollope, individuality can evoke admiration as well as fear; her greatest heroines are those who have the courage to set themselves apart from the rest of the world when the occasion demands it. But to consider the four heroic women in the previous paragraph is to see that individual self-assertion is ideally a temporary activity. Each of the four demonstrates her soundness by ultimately choosing community with others rather than isolation. Once provided with the opportunity to live with congenial people, Betsy Compton and Geraldine d'Albano abandon their eminent separation. Once the threat of Cartwright is expunged from Mowbray Park, Rosalind happily unites herself to the Mowbray family. And Mary Brotherton, despite her maintenance of financial power in her select group, chooses to create her own utopian family in Germany rather than remain in England in open hostility to industrialism.

Michael Armstrong, for all its affinities with a genre emerging only at the end of the 1830s, enters into an ongoing yet unspoken project of Trollope's fiction: the investigation and assessment of idiosyncrasy. And of course it is not only in fiction that Trollope makes this part of her agenda. The most obvious appeal of *Domestic Manners of the Americans* lies in its author's pungent descriptions of customs that seemed aberrant and barbaric to English readers. This book reveals what W. H. Chaloner calls her "genius for depicting vulgar people" (159); as Heineman puts it more broadly, "Her surest and best artistic stimulants seem to have been physical discomfort and annoyance" (*Mrs. Trollope* 84). As evidenced by her fiction, Trollope rose to her greatest heights when describing out-rageous people in outlandish situations. When she depicts goodness and happiness, her inspiration perceptibly falls off. Who would not prefer the vulgarity of a Widow Barnaby, or even the depravity of Sir Matthew Dowling, to the sugary tedium of triumphant goodness at the end of most Trollope novels?

Trollope, then, shows a consistent interest in exploring and placing idio-syncrasy in her early work. Savoring extravagance, in both benign and malignant forms, she is capable of delaying her moral judgments in the interests of providing greater enjoyment. Yet her delight in the bizarre is never unbounded. Perhaps questioning the propriety of her own tastes, Trollope establishes limits to her indulgence of the grotesque. She often keeps her grotesque characters under control by foiling their schemes and offering some judgment of their behavior. In most of her novels, idio-syncrasy must be expunged from the world to make possible a collectivist utopia of undifferentiated good people. But the social problem novels *Jonathan Jefferson Whitlaw* and *Michael Armstrong* demonstrate most clearly that Trollope recognizes legitimate power in nonconformity—not just villainy or the guilty pleasure of cheap thrills. These novels do not simply figure outlandishness as the problem; with characters such as Juno and Mary Brotherton, they figure it as necessarily part of the solution. In such novels Trollope not only finds her clearest justification for elabo-rating extraordinary behavior, but perhaps the most balanced use for her ambivalent attraction to individualism. Ultimately, the explanation for the good fit between Trollope's sensibility and the industrial novel lies in the opportunity this emerging genre provides for the simultaneous celebra-tion and excoriation of human idiosyncrasy. If Trollope finds herself time and again drawn back to the enticing energies of monstrosity, the indus-trial novel, like the anti-slavery novel, offers an excuse for enlisting those energies to fight battles that the idealized heroes of conventional romance could not plausibly win.

NOTES

1. All quotations come from the 1840 edition.

2. For an account of Trollope's own research into factory conditions, see Chaloner.

3. Linda Abess Ellis makes a valuable distinction in this regard between Trollope and another contemporary observer of America: "Mrs. Trollope, less interested in propriety than Dickens, incorporates sexual abuse directly into her plot" (111).

4. See also Mary's propensity for making sport of her neighbors and finding new ways to reject suitors (92).

5. Similar collectives, though not quite as striking in nature, dominate the endings of *The Vicar of Wrexhill* and *The Widow Barnaby*. It is interesting that one of the signs of Martha Barnaby's enduring inferiority is her individual destiny: she is too jarringly different to be absorbed into the central group at the novel's close, so she heads off to Australia in the company of one new husband, who is almost immediately replaced by yet another in the final lines of the novel.

6. Rosalind's dialogue is as follows:

> "If you imagine, sir," replied Rosalind, in a voice as tranquil and deliberate as his own, "that I have dared to regulate my conduct and opinions on such a point as this by any wisdom of my own, you do me great injustice. . . . My father, Mr. Cartwright, was one whose life was passed in the situation which, perhaps, beyond all others in the world, taught him the value of the establishment to which he belonged. . . . I hope not to live long enough to forget the reverence which he has left impressed upon my mind for all that our church holds sacred." (1996: 95)

7. However, Betsy is clearly wrong to reject her great-niece Agnes Willoughby. Here, her misperception that Agnes is like her aunt, Martha Barnaby, leads Betsy woefully astray. But, as Betsy needs to be Agnes' *deus ex machina* at the novel's end, rescuing her from the Widow Barnaby, Trollope provides an excuse for the delay of Betsy's generosity that has no particularly important ramifications for Betsy's character. For Betsy, as she recognizes the mistake she has made, "Self-reproach was lost in the sort of ecstasy with which she remembered how thriftily she had hoarded her wealth," which can now benefit Agnes (308). The novel largely shares her reaction.

9

The Intriguing Case of *Hargrave*: A Tragi-Comedy of Manners

Linde Katritzky

Not the least remarkable among Fanny Trollope's impressive qualities is her exceptional versatility. It enabled her to respond to the multiple, often stressful claims of her family and the personal blows and losses she had to sustain, yet to enter also wholeheartedly into the disparate and contrasting worlds and social strata into which she placed her fictional characters. Nothing, for instance, could be further from the sickening "scenes of pitiable wretchedness and revolting squalor, she braved in preparation for the disturbing *Adventures of Michael Armstrong,* nor from the reformatory fervor, with which she branded social injustice in that harrowing tale" (F. E. Trollope 1975: 1: 301), than the opulent and hedonistic high life enjoyed in *Hargrave*.[1] Though Adèle, the older of the newly widowed Mr. Charles Hargrave's two charming daughters, is the offspring of his deceased wife's former marriage, both girls are treated with equal indulgence and lavish attention. Surrounded by admiration and every imaginable luxury, their ease, pleasure, and delicate refinement provide a stark, and perhaps a quite deliberate contrast to the unsentimental realism of the Widow Barnaby, who "cannot afford to let mere feelings interfere with something as momentous as marital decisions" (Heineman, *Frances Trollope* 90). In *Hargrave*, on the other hand, there is not the slightest trace of the vulgarity and coarseness, with which Franny Trollope has variously been charged.[2] Moreover, the plot is constructed with foresight and meticulous attention to detail. Thus her son Anthony's verdict that "she was neither clear nor accurate" and that "of reasoning she knew nothing" (*Autobiography* 1947: 28, 19) may be applicable to some of her work, but should certainly not be taken as a general and authoritative evaluation.

The framework and basic structure of *Hargrave* follow the basic plot of a sentimental romance to such a degree that one otherwise support-ive critic notes: "The novel declines into melodrama" (Heineman, *Mrs. Trollope* 206). Mr. Hargrave devises lavish schemes to arrange wealthy and prestigious matches for his two motherless charges. For his own child, Sabina, he has even set his heart on no less a personage than a German royal prince. She is, indeed, fervently admired by the handsome youth, and her elder half sister, Adèle, is secretly in love with one of the richest and most eligible young Englishmen. Readers thus can hardly doubt a happy end, especially as they get progressively acquainted with the sisters' purity of mind and their touching noblesse of character.

One impediment is, however, clear from the start. Though Charles Hargrave's "education was the same as that of the highest aristocracy," his "handsome fortune had been made in trade; his father having been a highly respected City Banker." Consequently, he "preferred Paris to London for the display of his wealth," expecting not only that there "it went farther and distinguished him more, but also that its origin was less likely to be inquired into." By adding that it may "fairly be doubted if a *nouveau riche* ranks higher in France than in England" (1–2), the authorial voice firmly distances itself from these social conventions. It indicates at the same time that the ambitions of the father and the dreams of the girls undoubtedly will come into conflict with them in Paris during the winter season of 1834–35. There, much of the action will take place in a whirl of lavish festivities and entertainments. Yet, in concordance with the re-quirement of the genre of romance, the mother whom both sisters shared came from the blue-blooded French aristocracy, to which Adèle still be-longs by virtue of her high-born father. A happy ending might therefore be expected after the few usual complications, bound to ruffle the course of true love.

Such complacent reader expectations are, however, confounded throughout the novel. While a felicitous outcome can hardly be doubted, readers are left to guess and worry until almost the last page, because in-novative ideas and unusual circumstances turn a predictable basic plot into an exciting and quite original narration. Set on an international stage, locality descriptions are fresh and penned with vibrant immediacy. De-picting the scenery around Baden-Baden—where Hargrave savors social delights to soothe the pain of his bereavement—enables Fanny Trollope to utilize information collected for *Belgium and Western Germany in 1833*, a travel guide in two volumes, which her publisher, Murray, brought out early in 1834 (F. E. Trollope 1975: 1: 189). It is near Baden-Baden—visited in the course of her researches for that work—that Sabina first meets Prince Frederic. Modestly attired, and looking rather like "something between a hunter of the Alps on the stage and a real *bona fide* German botanist" (179), he stands on a hillside with a "magnificent bird's eye view" of a valley, where half hidden under "blue mysterious vapour" lay the "Mummelsee, or Fairy Lake, of which so many wondrous tales are told" (10).

A more romantic and myth-surrounded location can hardly be found in all of Germany. Sprites and powerful fairies are said to haunt it, and the superstitions that surround it are skillfully manipulated by Fanny Trollope. But her complex novel is not the first literary tribute to the enchanted place. In the picaresque German novel, *Simplicissimus* (1669), the ill-starred hero finds his way there, and here, too, the path is difficult and known to but a few. The fantastic Mummelsee-adventures add transcendent dimensions to this haunting, starkly realistic account of the horrors unleashed by the Thirty-Years War.[3]

In her quite different genre, Fanny also balances myth with reality, delicately and always with the reassurance that the superstitions, which she weaves into her narration, were believed only by the kindhearted but artless locals. Happy in their ignorance and lowly station, they bear out a criticism leveled at *Belgium and Western Germany*, that "much of what she saw in Germany she idealized," and that she "romanticized portraits" in this account of those classes with which she lacked personal contact (Heineman, *Frances Trollope* 46–47). Her well-heeled and well-educated protagonists, on the other hand, are drawn with meticulous perception. Their thoughts and actions are motivated with a familiar ease, gained through thorough firsthand observation of their prototypes. They are, naturally, well aware that fairies can neither exist nor cast spells. Nevertheless, as Prince Frederic explains, "there *are* strange facts connected with the Fairy lake," such as a ruined castle, for instance, hidden most of the time from sight by a "silvery mass of floating mist," but emerging now and again to astonish the beholder. Attached to this information is an explanatory footnote, interesting because it demonstrates Fanny Trollope's conscientious care in constructing and motivating her plot. Additionally it testifies to her sensitivity to reader reaction and to the criticisms, that had met some of her previous reports:

> The locality of this delusive obscurity is selected purposely where no castle stands that the facts of the narrative may not be sifted too closely, and declared to be *personal;* an interpretation which has so often attended the writings of the author, as to render caution necessary. Such delusions,

however, do exist, not only in Germany, but in England. Dover Castle is
sometimes perfectly invisible from the heights to the west of the town, from
whence, at other times it is seen in its fullest glory. (11)

While describing the delightful country rambles, in which the sisters indulge—watched over only by their faithful, utterly devoted servant Roger
Humphries—Fanny Trollope, well versed in the demands her different
genres impose on her, explains that guide writers have to act as "purveyors for all wonder-seeking travelers," while those who look for solitude
purposely seek out places where nobody is likely to follow (7–8). Her
experience as a dedicated traveler equipped her well to describe no less
enthusiastically such lonely rambles, the romantic landscapes of the Black
Forest, or Paris and its glittering, fashionable circles, to which the widower soon returned with his small retinue. Ever adaptable to changing
perspectives, she skillfully uses the experience she had gathered for her
travel account on *Paris and the Parisians,* written after a prolonged stay
in 1835, during the early part of King Louis Philippe's reign. At that time
"political life with its emotions, opinions, and passions" was particularly
exciting and agitated, with even the monarchists divided into supporters
of the reigning regime and those still hoping for the reinstatement of the
Bourbons (T. A. Trollope 1973: 85). Her familiarity with Paris was additionally enhanced by a further visit in 1840. Again she was offered "in-
cessant invitations" to the most brilliant society events, among them "a
very splendid entertainment in honor of the marriage" of Queen Victoria,
arranged by Lord Granville, the British Ambassador (F. E. Trollope 1975:
1: 306–10). Consequently she arranged Hargrave's resplendent festivities with an authority that gives credence to the claim that nobody in all
Paris could surpass his entertainments, as even Prince Frederic has to concede (91). The skill with which she "combined her materials into an amusing whole, and the vividness with which she paints her pictures of . . .
life under the Citizen-King" in *Paris and the Parisians* are justly com-
mended by her daughter-in-law (1: 265–36). But she also turned her
experience into art, energizing the pages of her novel with the same immediacy and freshness of approach.

   If she shares a number of topics with the genre of conventional romance, such as love across social divides, superstitious mysteries and a
fascination with ruins and their faded grandeur, she far supersedes these
well-worn themes by faultlessly superimposing on them an astonishing
detective story. Astonishing not only because her ingenious plot will still
rivet reader attention, but also because it is one of the very earliest excursions into a genre, which since has developed into a universal favorite. A detective story involves a carefully laid trail of clues, which readers

may notice if the author plays fair. But they will not if the author plays well. Fanny Trollope manipulates this intellectual game of hide and seek with such skill that her readers' interest is captivated to the very end, though she leaves the identity of the culprit not in doubt for long.

Readers soon become aware that the "pleasant-tempered Hargrave" (2), generally admired and adored by those who know him best, his family and his retainers, is not quite the character he appears. His ruling passion is vanity, and whether his character will be judged as an absurd and theatrical exaggeration or as a subtle and penetrating case history of megalomania, depends largely on whether Fanny Trollope's assessment of the "effects of vanity in characters where it greatly predominates," will be rejected or accepted. Knowing full well that not everybody will agree with her, she cautions: "Greatly do those mistake who call it a 'little' passion,— it is a great, an absorbing, a tremendous one" (2), especially so in cases as Hargrave's, whose "ambition was as unbounded as his vanity" (39). While his particular obsession is merely focused on personal unlimited wealth and the social acceptance and admiration he craves above all, history is certainly not short on similar examples of delusion of grandeur on a vastly more public and destructive scale. All these megalomaniacs share with Hargrave total lack of sympathy with any other human being than themselves, and like him they resort to "unscrupulous means" to content the "insatiable voracity" of their desires (3). All of them also possess the beguiling charisma, the trait—plausibly explained by an unwavering, egoistic self-admiration, which never lets Hargrave doubt that he, and his visions of the place to which he feels entitled, could in any way be mistaken—which safeguards his reputation in spite of all the mounting evidence against him.

While all Paris is baffled by repeated and particularly daring assaults on successful gamblers, of whom three were robbed of exceptionally large winnings, readers can pick up so many hints, not the least from Hargrave's role as title-hero, that they can be left in little doubt regarding the cunning perpetrator of these sensational crimes. They soon realize that his considerable fortune has been exhausted, but that his "boundless extravagance" (38) continues regardless. He pays in coin, which corresponds to that lost in the robberies. When the shrewd Adèle glimpses by chance that his drawers are stuffed with a much larger supply of ready cash than is compatible with his explanations of how he obtained it, the nagging suspicions that enter her mind serve only to confirm those of readers. It is mainly through her further observations, all of them accidental and obtained without any duplicity or deceit on her part, that the sinister aspects of the congenial Hargrave's true character are gradually revealed. Deeply shocked, her erstwhile filial love for him turns progressively into contempt, but love for her innocent and trusting sister grows only stronger and more mature during this ordeal. Her one overwhelming desire becomes to shield Sabina from a truth that would destroy her. Whether she will succeed, and especially how, is from now on one of the main problems readers will find hard to unravel.

Simultaneously, other questions are raised. No longer can readers wonder whether Mr. Hargrave will succeed with his machinations, but rather, how any respectable young man can ever wish to align himself with a daughter of such a father. As he blissfully continues to lay his matrimonial traps, and lavishly spends in the process, readers are also uneasily aware that his funds cannot last indefinitely. The ploy of robbing successful gamesters cannot be repeated. All Paris is on the lookout for the daring criminal. The salons are buzzing with rumors about him. Thus the outwardly serene Hargrave resourcefully conceives a devilish plot to replenish his resources. Readers can easily sense the drift of his expectations when he invites an immensely rich couple to the next ball, the wife habitually covered in priceless diamonds, while promising to satisfy a pressing debtor with precious stones. These are not handy yet, because they must first be broken from their settings. The main objective of this ingenious detective story is not to determine the person of the culprit, nor even the method of his operation, but to track the chances of two lovely girls to be united with two excellent young men, when such a father stands between them. It is by this unusual stratagem that Fanny Trollope successfully combines detective story and romance, without destroying the intellectual pleasure of conjecture, from which the detective genre derives its singular appeal. That the plan to bring the young couples together originates precisely with this unworthy parent and acts, indeed, as his strongest motivation, adds greatly to the sardonic comedy of manners, which forms a constant sublayer of this multileveled novel.

As a misunderstanding has kept Alfred Coventry away, Adèle has absented herself from the festivities and notes from her lonely bedroom window Hargrave's strange behavior during the glittering ball at which he hopes to ensnare Prince Frederic. No expense has been spared and everybody who matters is there, unanimous in applause for their gracious host. He never looked "so gracefully gay," nor so "eminently handsome," as when receiving his guests with "dignified courtesy and polished ease" (94). Fanny Trollope captures the occasion to perfection: the buzz of preparation, the dazzling result, "the general gorgeous appearance of his magnificent apartments" (90). Nevertheless, she keeps tightly to her stated purpose that "the narrative concerns but a few, and a few only can appear in it" (45). These few she portrays with perceptive sensitivity, explaining every mood and motivation of this chosen circle with credible reasoning.

During the ball Adèle learns that the estrangement with Coventry has in part been occasioned by the conceit of her mother's highborn sister, who had been invited by the widower to join the household, ostensibly to look after her orphaned nieces, but in reality to lend her grand title to the establishment. Partly it was due to differences in French and English manners—a theme that provides Fanny Trollope with various knots in her complex narration, and one that she highlights amusingly in repeated asides. Adèle's (Russian) informant misinterprets her disciplined (French) reaction and hastens to appraise Coventry of her supposed indifference, urging him to depart forthwith for England. Meanwhile she, overcoming the tender French scruples that prohibit her from initiating a serious relationship, pens a conciliatory letter and entrusts the devoted Roger with the delivery, but absolutely on no account to anybody but the intended recipient. Waiting anxiously for his return, she perceives indistinct movements and a tall figure in the garden and hears, as she half believes, a muffled cry. In the first uncertain light of the new morning, startled out of a short slumber, she beholds her stepfather with an implement she cannot distinguish, disappearing rapidly into the shadows. After a while he reappears, carrying a weighty bundle and leaving her in a "tormentingly vague" and painfully puzzling "state of mind" (115).

Still waiting uneasily for Roger, and driven by apprehensive curiosity, she investigates the tangled shrubbery from which her stepfather has emerged, and led by the glimmer of a forgotten diamond, she discovers a buried hammer, a broken gold chain, and a number of settings, "from whence gems had been violently torn," spattered with blood (123). When she finds out that the rich banker's wife has disappeared with all her costly diamonds, Adèle cannot but draw her own dreadful conclusions from the evidence she has uncovered. Only now, and when the reader is already no longer in any doubt, unfolds the proper detective story, with a plot still fresh and surprising, probably because it has been overlooked for so long and consequently has not been copied or reworked. "The principal officer of the Correctional Police in the *arrondissement*" appears at the scene, Mr. Collet, a very early, but fully fledged detective (148). He investigates with brisk efficiency and a sharp and analytical mind, which would not disgrace Sherlock Holmes. All his shrewd questions are exactly to the purpose. No clue escapes him, and from each he draws inferences leading him very quickly to the right conclusion. From now on readers look at the felony from two quite distinct and capably executed perspectives, for "whereas individuals of the species to which Adèle belonged never encounter any trace of crime without a pang of suffering, those of the Correctional Police are rather supposed to receive a throb of pleasure from the same, their sensations greatly resembling those of a sportsman who has succeeded in his pursuit of game" (152).

Mr. Collet is a remarkable literary creation. Thoroughly professional, unimpressed by the opulent trappings of wealth in the Hargrave mansion, or by its owner's charm and impeccable reputation, he trusts nothing but the indisputable facts, on which he builds his case with unimpeachable logic. If Frances Eleanor can be trusted, and the Hargrave manuscript was, indeed, delivered to Mr. Colburn in January 1841, Mr. Collet can owe nothing to Edgar Allan Poe's *Murders in the Rue Morgue*, published in the same year and celebrated as the world's first detective story. Poe, of course, formulated crime and detection "into a *primary* story element,"[4] while Fanny Trollope employed detective elements much in the manner later favored by Wilkie Collins in the *Moonstone*, published in 1868. As the investigations of Charles Dickens' Inspector Bucket are but a subplot in *Bleak House* (1853), the *Oxford Companion to English Literature* (1985) credits Wilkie Collins, a friend of Dickens, with having written the first full-length detective stories in English and having set a mold for the genre that has lasted for a century. Indeed *Moonstone* is widely regarded as "the closest thing to a detective novel produced prior to the appearance of Sherlock Holmes in *A Study in Scarlet*" (1887). Yet Wilkie Collins' incorporation of detective components is very similar to the techniques employed by Fanny Trollope, for "what he did, essentially, was to write a full-bodied novel in the fashion of his time, using detection as a central theme to catalyze the elaborate ingredients" (Cassiday 144; Haycraft 39).

It is by no means impossible or even unlikely that Wilkie Collins was influenced by the much read and widely distributed Fanny Trollope. Besides, he was a friend of her son, Anthony, and had planned a visit to Tom, her eldest son who lived in Florence with her (Glendinning 303, 356). She was not the first writer to turn a sensational jewelry robbery in Paris into literature. E.T.A. Hoffmann, an important force in the German Romantic Movement, had already published his *Das Fräulein von Scuderi*, first as a short story in October 1819, and then as part of a longer work, *Die Serapionsbrüder* (4 volumes), which appeared in 1819–21. Some critics regard this as the first German detective novel, though the interpretation of all available clues leads to an innocent suspect, Olivier Brusson, and the real culprit is only demasked through Olivier's observations and confessions. As the scene is set in Paris during the reign of Louis XIV, and the title-heroine is Madeleine de Scudéry, a French novelist much respected and revered in her time, Hoffmann's short story soon became popular in France, especially as its grim Gothic elements appealed particularly to the taste of the time. The first translation appeared already in 1823, though under the title *Olivier Brusson,* somewhat altered and without mention of the author. But as the favorable resonance continued, other versions soon followed.[5]

Fanny Trollope could have been indebted for her plot to the same source as Hoffmann, the *Causes Célèbres* (Volume I), a renowned collection of criminal cases compiled by the French advocate François Gayot Pitaval (1673–1743), and much used as literary quarry (XV: 239). It is, however, quite likely that she was familiar with a translation of Hoffmann's short story. It may be pure coincidence that Adèle's family name is de Cordillac, while the sinister and doomed character in Hoffmann's tale is called Cardillac. But there are other parallels, which seem to indicate a creative affinity. Exactly as in the case of Hargrave, the high esteem in which Cardillac is generally held prevents any suspicion from attaching to him, his obvious closeness to the crimes notwithstanding. As happens to the hapless and honest Roger, Cardillac's virtuous, innocent assistant, is therefore accused and nearly convicted, and neither of them will confess to the truth: Olivier will not, for love of his employer's daughter. Nor will Roger Humphries, who falls under suspicion because he is spotted returning furtively to the mansion during the early hours of the fatal ball and is found in possession of some of the coins. He cannot exonerate himself because he will not part with the letter entrusted to him. He returns with the letter, having failed to deliver it. Especially noteworthy is the shared motive of sparing a loving daughter the pain of recognizing in her father a notorious and disgraced villain. In *Das Fräulein von Scuderi*, Olivier will rather die than burden his betrothed with his horrid secret. In *Hargrave* it is Adèle, who hardly hesitates a moment before sacrificing all her scruples to shield her beloved Sabina from similar disclosure. Last, not least: the ingenious solution through which Sabina is saved from ever being tainted by the transgressions of her father, though set into completely different circumstances, is basically the same, which allows Cardillac's daughter to live happily ever after. In marked contrast to the gruesome felonies of Hoffmann's demonic criminal, Hargrave's assaults are planned and executed with all the impeccable foresight and precision, with which he arranges his sumptuous entertainments. As his victims are gamblers and a banker, who can well afford to replace his wife's precious adornments, his egoistic transgressions accord throughout with his refined sensibilities, and as he never physically harms his victims, the comic elements of the novel blend in without giving offense.

It is no mere coincidence that, like the events in *Das Fräulein von Scuderi* and *The Murders in the Rue Morgue*, the criminal incidents in *Hargrave* take place in Paris, for in that metropolis the first well-organized European police force was established. The "Brigade de Sureté" was organized in 1812, initially only with four men and with Eugène François Vidocq (1775–1857) as its chief, a colorful character. He had turned from thief, forger, highwayman, and even escaped galley-slave to informer and law enforcer, as which he had already worked for several years. Claiming that his criminal past enabled him to penetrate the devious mind of any lawbreaker, he applied and proclaimed modern analytical detection methods with singular success. He was suspended in 1825, as his checkered career attracted much controversy, and it was even suspected that he might have staged himself some of the sensational cases he solved so brilliantly. His somewhat romanticized reminiscences, *Mémoirs de Vidocq,* appeared anonymously in four volumes in 1828–29, and his exploits influenced many outstanding writers of his day, notably Victor Hugo, Balzac, and Alexandre Dumas, with all three of whom he established friendly relations. Obviously, he also left his mark on Fanny Trollope's Mr. Collet.

The example of the Sureté was duplicated in London. Sir Robert Peel (1788–1850), appointed Home Secretary in 1828, began to transform the ragged London police into the respected Metropolitan Police, later known after their location as Scotland Yard. It was not until this force became truly disciplined and effective that the English detective novel came into its own. The considerably earlier Mr. Collet was fashioned on the French model and thus belongs to the very earliest representatives of a genre, in which women of the rank of an Agatha Christie, Dorothy Sayers, Margery Allingham, Ngaio Marsh, or Ruth Rendell were to excel. Pamela Neville-Sington calls it, therefore, an outright "Parisian detective novel," noting that "political intrigue abounds in Fanny's detective novel" (*Fanny Trollope* 224n, 296). Mr. Collet is remarkable not only for his early appearance in literature, or for the analytical logic, with which he penetrates straight to the root of a baffling problem, but also for being left empty-handed at the end, his perfectly coordinated policework having been frustrated by the astute measures of an inexperienced girl.

Adèle, still struggling against her own conclusions from the same evidence that quickly convinced Mr. Collet of Hargrave's guilt, has noted his penetrating investigation with growing apprehension. Entirely possessed by the idea of saving Sabina, she resolves that her "father must be snatched from the horrible fate that was preparing for him" (157). Consequently, she arranges a hasty escape, thus circumventing the clever trap Mr. Collet has set with professional precision. She throws him off the scent by informing her noble aunt that their flight to England is imperative, as Charles Hargrave had become involved in a politically sensitive plot concerning the reinstatement of Charles X. His apprehension would result in ruin and disgrace for the entire family. Nothing could have been more calculated to fuel the imagination of her aunt, who forthwith set rumors in motion, which grew in the retelling, embellished and aggrandized until Charles Hargrave emerged a veritable hero. In these gossip-scenes Fanny Trollope displays with advantage her sardonic humor; she shows a shrewd understanding of a society that lives for pleasure and self-indulgence, craves gossip and sensationalism, but fiercely rallies around its own privileged members. Scant information is freely enlarged; the few known facts are twisted to fit the most gallant version of events. An acquaintance of the Hargrave family epitomizes the general attitude of society: of "the three conflicting histories which had reached him, he certainly could not be said completely to believe either; but of the three, the one which he had received on the vilest authority was that which appeared to him most likely to be true." Furthermore, "the only statement to which he paid absolutely no attention, was the true one" (225). Mr. Collet's shrewd professionalism notwithstanding, the reputation of Charles Hargrave emerges unscathed from all criminal scandals.

The aunt is a truly comic figure in her spreading of falsehoods, mostly fabricated, and yet fervently believed by herself. She is a wholehearted part of the superficial high-life, but her kindhearted and sincere nieces have never really been seduced by its glamour. Adèle's sudden transformation from compliant submissiveness into a capable and resourceful manager therefore entails no arbitrary change in her characterization. To forestall any reproach on these lines, Fanny Trollope inserts one of her perceptive authorial explanations: "When a woman of strong feelings is placed in a situation sufficiently exciting to make her thoroughly and entirely forget the weakness of her frame and the habitual cowardice of her nature, she becomes as dauntless as an Alexander. Adèle de Cordillac at that moment wholly lost sight of self, and this, together with an important object to be achieved, suffices to make a hero" (157). Fanny Trollope herself had amply demonstrated the feasibility of such a transformation. She was not completely unprepared for this change, having read widely and wisely, and acquired comprehensive knowledge of the ways of the world through judicious use of literature. Astute observations and a gift to turn personal experience into general use complemented this theoretical education. Hence her books are so enlivened by pertinent remarks on human nature and its hidden traits that Pamela Neville-Sington, for instance, extracts a number of them from *Hargrave* to elucidate in her biographical appraisal Fanny Trollope's own state of mind and that of her affairs.[6]

Frequent apt quotations and references to literature demonstrate Fanny Trollope's comprehensive study and remarkable memory. Not all of her literary allusions will now be readily understood; but from those that are still common currency, it is clear that she is not just quoting choice sentences, as can be picked up here and there without much trouble, but that she was incorporating the essence of her reading matter into her own work, blending it with her own experience and opinions.

Thus she repeats Alexander Pope's dictum that "a little learning is a dangerous thing" (*An Essay on Criticism*), only to add that this "was very well said and truly; but a great deal is still more so, if it be received into the memory of one whose judgment does not keep pace with his powers of apprehension" (197). She refers to the protagonist of Alain-René's *Le Diable Boiteux* (1707), who floats over Madrid at night, sardonically observing the dark secrets of its inhabitants, when she notes: "The eye of an Asmodeus, in looking down upon the crowded haunts of men, can descry what is passing among them with much greater rapidity than he can record it" (45). Changes in mood and attitude of her two sisters are compared to those of Goldsmith's Olivia and Sophia, the daughters of the Vicar of Wakefield (69). Hargrave, she reports, acquired his exquisite command of etiquette, his winning ways and urbanity, precisely as recommended by Lord Chesterfield in the *Letters to his Son* (96), written from 1737 onward and later published against the Earl's will. Though Chesterfield wrote privately, and directed his advice specifically to a son, well known for his studious, kindly nature and uncouth manners, his emphasis on behavior has often been censured. Hargrave's behavior, conforming so exactly and exclusively to the precepts Chesterfield attempted (in vain!) to instill into his unpolished son, burlesques Chesterfield's refined ideal. The "stifled sigh, a melancholy smile, and an unexplained shake of the head, which seemed as pregnant with meaning as that of my Lord Burleigh" (274) refers to Sheridan's *The Critic*, where this Lord Treasurer under Queen Elizabeth appears too weighed down by pressing cares to utter a word, and merely shakes his head sorrowfully.

Similarly, an entire passage in *King Lear* is relevant, when Roger, falsely accused and stubbornly refusing to reveal the true nature of his errand, is likened to "a very foolish, fond old man" (246). The somewhat irrational mixture of Roger's confusion and resistance to authority are precisely expressed, as Shakespeare continues: "To deal plainly, / I fear I am not in my perfect mind. / Methinks I should know you and know this man; / Yet I am doubtful" (4.7). To describe the social triumphs of the undistinguished banker's wife, entirely due to her stunning diamonds, Fanny Trollope adapts a quote from *Hamlet* (4.5): "When sorrows come, they come not single spies, but in battalions." She replaced "sorrows" pointedly with *honours* (77) and shows her ability to apply the lessons learnt from literature to different circumstances. Shakespeare is quoted and integrated far more frequently than any other writer. Besides *Hamlet* (e.g., 170, 178) there are also references to act 1, scene 4 of *King Henry VIII* (79), *Othello* (126), and *The Tempest* (303). Heroines who share her high regard of Shakespeare are characterized by this trait as especially worthy and intelligent. In *Michael Armstrong*, for instance, Martha

Dowling, who of all her race "was the only one whose heart was not seared and hardened by the ceaseless operation of opulent self-indulgence," carried with her "a volume of Shakespeare," with which she enriched her idle moments (53, 72). Correspondingly, as soon as an opportunity becks, "the delighted Sabina made herself mistress of Shakespeare," contending herself in her exile from Paris with "one huge volume of ill-printed columns" (263). Obviously, she is an avid and thoughtful reader, conversant with Goethe and Walter Scott (256). Adèle, not less erudite than her younger sister, "bought an English Bible" (263). Her previous thoughts on religion and her conversion to Protestantism (191–92) do not merely help to characterize her as a reflective and independent personality, they also introduce a topic cleverly, partly propounding some of Trollope's own convictions. These repeatedly spill over into her creative art, as witnessed by her *Vicar of Wrexhill* (1837), and a decade later *Father Eustace: a Tale of the Jesuits* (1847). Simultaneously, the conversion enables Adèle to preserve her fiercely guarded secret, having no need to go to confession, which surely would have deflated all the spiritual pretensions of her stepfather. Thus, a credible solution is possible at the end of the novel, in spite of the perplexing dilemmas that plague its heroines until almost the last page.

Adèle is one of the literary models through whom Fanny Trollope can most freely express her ideal of femininity: "high-minded and truth-loving" in spite of her "innocent ignorance" (172); filled with "much gentle courage" (174), "wise and good" as well as "boldly enterprising" (187); and when challenged by emergencies, resolute, efficient, and "generous-hearted" (265). Responsible, discerning, and disciplined, she pursues what she regards as right regardless of possible consequences, "sternly bending all the strength and power of her mind upon the tremendous task" (266). The realistic and experienced Fanny Trollope knows full well that such independence of mind can be sustained only by independence of means. Consequently, she has endowed the young woman with a considerable private fortune, inherited from her deceased father. Indeed, "Mademoiselle de Cordillac's pecuniary independence of her stepfather was perfectly well known" (17).

Adèle needs all her exceptional qualities to accomplish her determined designs for shielding Sabina from recognizing the depravity of her father and to rescue the faithful Roger from the clutches of the law. Additionally, she has to clear away the misunderstandings arisen between herself and Alfred Coventry: That it is she who converts to Protestantism, while Charles Hargrave adopts Catholicism purely for reasons of social convenience. This is not merely a necessity for sustaining an intricate plot. It also indicates Fanny Trollope's own predilection, which she confirms in a short aside confirming her belief in the superior benefits of Anglo-Catholic Protestantism, with its "rational, pure, and natural principle," for "the moral and social condition of man" (199). Yet she is no bigot. The Catholic priest, who befriends the beleaguered family in their exile and acts as confessor to Sabina and her father, is a thoroughly sympathetic character. His simple and sincere spirituality is in stark contrast to the overpowering hypocrisy of Hargrave, whose contorted religious aspirations are fueled by self-deceiving ambition and vanity.

Every detail of *Hargrave* breathes contemporary concerns. Each one fits into the overall picture with scrupulous concern for probability of the facts as well as of the various different personalities. The story holds together by an impeccable internal logic, to which the author draws repeated attention—for instance, in the few notes she provides—as if to refute any accusations regarding her supposed disability to construct a tight and logical plot. Her novel recalls a time, which has passed, and places, which no longer exist in the form she experienced them herself. But her vivid and faithful descriptions recapture that lost past and allow her readers to participate for a while in a world now lost forever. A reviewer in the *Athenaeum* found the story line highly improbable, but nevertheless had to concede that "in defiance of our testimony against the probabilities of the book," readers "will find it difficult to lay it aside, when once they have taken it in hand."[7] No doubt readers will find this prediction as true in our time as it was then, for Fanny Trollope's art and creativity transcend biographic and historic interest, render her literary legacy still relevant today, and should secure it an honored place among the great Victorian novels that are still read and remembered.

NOTES

1. Page numbers in the text refer to Stroud 1995 edition. F. E. Trollope relates that the manuscript was ready and delivered to "Mr. Colburn in January 1841, by the hand of Mrs. Trollope's brother Henry Milton." After a delaying controversy, caused by Mrs. Trollope having published "another novel ('The Blue Belles of England') with a rival publisher, in serial form," the matter was settled. Mr. Colburn published and paid the agreed "six hundred and twenty-five pounds." *Hargrave* "had a very good success, and reached a second edition in 1843" (1975: 1: 321–23).

2. For example, in the *Widow Barnaby* "the vulgar folks are a little too vulgar" (F. E. Trollope 1975: 1: 294). As quoted by Victoria Glendinning: Emily Tennyson found Fanny Trollope "not at all coarse as one would expect from her works" (208).

3. H. J. Ch. Grimmelshausen, *Der Abenteuerliche Simplicissimus teutsch*, vol. 1 bk. V, chap. XII–XVII (Frankfurt/M: Deutscher Klassiker Verlag, 1989).

4. Heineman, *Frances Trollope* 321 and Bruce Cassiday 95.

5. B. Geldges et al. 152, 158–60, 273–74.

6. See 100, 178, 211, 222, 225.

7. Qtd. in Heineman, *Mrs. Trollope* 207, 292 n2: unsigned review of *Hargrave, Athenaeum* 806 (1843): 333–34.

10

Fanny Who?

Linda Abess Ellis

I am in conference with my seminar professor. Sitting in his small office, looking through a grimy window toward a gray winter sky, I imagine myself in the south of Italy. I suggest doing my paper on nineteenth-century travel literature. "Oh, I do hope you'll include Mrs. Trollope," he responds, cheerfully sending me on my way.

To a graduate student, a professor's "hope" becomes an imperative. Before long, I see the wisdom of his suggestion. As I read a bit of Frances Trollope's work, somewhat superficially at first, my casual remark turns into an obsession. The semester project leads to further investigations, involving obscure sources and remote libraries, each discovery more delightful than the one before. When I share my enthusiasm with colleagues, however, the most common response I hear is "Fanny who? Any relation to Anthony?"

Mrs. Trollope's name now prompts a modest degree of recognition. She no longer fits the "almost-unknown-woman-author" profile that I studied over a decade ago. I credit N. John Hall's collection of Trollope letters, his biography of Anthony, and recent full-length biographies of Frances Trollope by Helen Heineman, Teresa Ransom, and Pamela Neville-Sington for arousing interest among Trollope (i.e., Anthony) lovers. Trollope's unconventional life, the most compelling feature of these studies, has always intrigued readers: our small local library has five biographies of Frances Trollope. Unfortunately, of her works, only *Domestic Manners of the Americans* is readily available.

Pamela Neville-Sington, in the most recent of these biographies, takes a fresh approach to her subject, telling Trollope's life story through passages from the works. Reading these passages removed from their original contexts inspires me to reread some of my favorites among her books. Thus, only days after finishing Neville-Sington's account, I find myself in the recently refurbished Rose Main Reading Room of the New York Public Library. While waiting for my number to light, I write notes to myself, think about dinner plans, study my fingernails. When 322 finally appears on the board, I go to the window and receive my gift: three cardboard preservation boxes, each holding a single volume of *Jonathan Jefferson Whitlaw*. The front of each box has instructions for handling the fragile pages within. The old book smell that comes out as I open the box thrills me; I wish the Levengers would package it in aerosol cans.

Despite the library's attention to preservation, these brittle pages need careful, conscious handling. Little splinters crack off whenever I absently turn the page. Soon, however, I become less mindful. My attention drifts from the physical book, first into the story contained in these dusty boxes, then back to Trollope herself. After a few minutes, I become oblivious to this great hall, and my thoughts jump back and forth between Mississippi and Bruges, until I see both at once: an aged black American woman who cunningly triumphs over a cruel plantation owner and his sadistic overseer, and a not-so-young white English woman whose indomitable spirit triumphs over bankruptcy, failed marriage, and her children's deaths. Trollope began this book while finishing *Paris and the Parisians in 1835*, simultaneously struggling, both emotionally and financially, to keep her family together. As I continue reading this dark work, I am struck by the contrast between the world of *Whitlaw*, whose dramatic descriptions of plantation life include an attempted rape and a lynching, and the lively, elegant scenes Trollope describes in *Paris and the Parisians in 1835*. Trollope's narrative ability again astounds me, as I follow her lighthearted, playful narrator through fashionable Paris.

Historians and literary critics read *Domestic Manners of the Americans* in light of Frances Trollope's experiences, treating, for instance, her rejection by many residents of Cincinnati as a potential explanation for her animosity toward Americans. For me, such knowledge of Frances Trollope's personal predicaments does add to the appeal not only of *Domestic Manners*, but also of all her novels and travel accounts. *Paris and the Parisians*, glittering with the excitement and joys of Paris, takes on a new dimension when I try to imagine the depths of her despair as she achieves this authorial voice. Less dramatic, yet also interesting, are the biographical details surrounding *A Visit to Italy*. Reading *Italy*, her fifth travel book, with the knowledge that within a few years Trollope would be making Florence her permanent home, makes me wonder: had she made this voyage with the notion of leaving Penrith? Might she have examined the places she visited as potential locations for a new residence? In the back of my mind, as I read these accounts, is my image of Frances Trollope as an accomplished, experienced storyteller; thus I expect manipulation of her experiences as she shapes her observations for publication.

In his autobiography, Anthony pays homage to his mother's "power of dividing herself into two parts" (1947: 24). During the spring of 1835, she somehow divided herself into even more parts. Her husband, Thomas Anthony, having overdosed on calomel for many years, was rapidly failing, and her daughter Emily was in the last stage of tuberculosis. During the few months she lived in Paris, she found time to consult with doctors about Emily and Thomas Anthony, both growing weaker; to research her new travel book; to entertain her cousin, Fanny Bent; and to connect with old friends; all the while deep in grief following the recent death of her son, Henry. I try to imagine her feelings as she walked along the grand boulevards near their temporary quarters on the Rue de Provence. There were seven of them: Trollope, her husband Thomas Anthony, her son Tom, and her daughters Emily and Cecilia, Fanny Bent, and Auguste Hervieu, who would illustrate this new book. The fifty-five-year-old Trollope was responsible—financially and emotionally—for all.

I find little trace of her private meditations in the resulting book, *Paris and the Parisians in 1835*. Trollope may have deliberately avoided showing her own despair, as she well knew that their livelihood depended on the success of the book. Thus, despite her grief for Henry and her fears for her daughter and husband, Trollope achieves a cheerful, gossipy tone, emphasizing the pleasures of Parisian society. The narrative voice is that of a storyteller, quite similar to the narrative voice of her novels. Her finances still precarious, she writes with potential income in mind, recognizing that her readers expect a witty, entertaining account of her stay.

Paris has a chatty, informal tone, with chapters written as letters addressed to "My Dear Friend," letters filled with anecdote and description of local customs, often with comments on the differences between these customs and those in England. Trollope builds on the successful formula she had used in both the first part of *Domestic Manners* and in *Belgium and Western Germany in 1833*; her material is, for the most part, anecdotal rather than statistical. Passions on both sides of the reform controversy in Britain had contributed to the success of *Domestic Manners*; another attempt at political commentary must have seemed useful. Thus, in these fictitious letters, Trollope claims that because the political situation in France deserves attention, the purpose of her trip is an investigation into "the wisest way in which the French nation . . . can be governed" (xvi). To lighten the tone and to supply the domestic details her readers expect, she does a substantial amount of this investigation in combination with some sort of entertainment, all of which, with the exception of the opera, she professes to find exceedingly enjoyable. The narrator, filling her time with cheerful activities, seems carefree. Political discussions take place in pleasant settings, such as in the Tuileries Gardens or in glamorous drawing rooms. Her narrator is a cultured, well-mannered visitor, able to discuss arts and politics in fashionable circles.

Trollope finds entertainment "sitting in the Tuileries Gardens and studying costume" or examining "specimens of the various and strongly-marked divisions of people." Her narrator is a meticulous observer, relating clothing and carriage to politics. She attempts to identify the political sympathy of various subjects by their appearances, as if in a playful guessing game, which her remarkably astute narrator consistently wins. Describing men, women, and children in the park, she pays careful attention to each small detail, and points out differences between the British and French ways of dress. French women, she says, have "an air of quiet, elegant neatness," while the children look like "miniature maskers." Her narrator appears to be enjoying herself, relishing her excursions in the gardens. I have to look again and again at these details to find signs of mourning, signs that Trollope had more pressing concerns than next season's wardrobe. Eventually I think I see a small clue, reading about the fashion of dyeing beards and moustaches: "At a little distance the young men have really the air of having their faces tied up with black riband as a cure for the mumps." She says no more, however, refusing to dwell on this offhand observation, making no further connection between young men and disease.

Quickly moving on to a discussion of "unclean" "working-classes" enjoying the Gardens, Trollope uses her characteristic sarcastic tone to show what "mob rule" is likely to bring to England: "The [former] obligation to appear clean in the garden of the king's palace was an infringement on their liberty, so that formality is dispensed with; and they have now obtained the distinguished and ennobling privilege of being dirty and ill-dressed as they like" (73–76). Intending *Paris* for the same audience that had made *Domestic Manners* successful, she preserves the anti-democratic, anti-republican attitude appreciated by British readers who were nervous about potential reforms. Several letters later, Trollope describes young students, complaining: "The silly cant of republicanism has got among them; and till this is mended, continued little riotous outbreakings of a naughty-boy spirit must be expected." She goes on the express her gratitude that English "great schools are tory to the heart's core" (150).

Trollope uses French politics as a unifying theme for *Paris and the Parisians;* she gives almost every letter a political dimension. She draws on her activities as examples to support the conservative stance that had made her travel books so popular. Thus, she finds a political agenda even in her discussion of arts and literature. She devotes Letter IX to "Literature of the Revolutionary School" as yet another illustration of the pernicious effects of the new regime, contrasting the "puny literary reputations of the day" with the great writers of previous generations. She explains the present-day "extraordinary lack of great ability": "The oil which feeds the lamp of revolutionary genius is foul, and such noxious vapours rise with the flame as must needs check its brightness" (51–54).

For readers wanting to know even more of the perils attendant on any change in the British political system, Trollope devotes a ten-page "Postscript" to her analysis of the French political situation. Here, one finds her most strongly worded pronouncements since the publication of *Domestic Manners* as she continues to play on her audience's fears of class warfare:

> A self-regulating populace is a chimera, and a dire one. The French have discovered this already; the Americans are beginning, as I hear, to feel some glimmerings of this important truth breaking in upon them; and for our England, spite of all the trash upon this point that she has been pleased to speak and to hear, she is not a country likely to submit, if the struggle should come, to be torn to pieces by her own mob. (1997: 410)

When not discussing politics, Trollope projects a refined, genteel traveler, as if to counter critics who had called her coarse and crude. She underscores her sensitivity, her inability to endure crude or rude behavior, poor hygiene, or unattractive fashion. The streets of Paris, she finds, have neither gas lighting nor macadam paving. Instead of tidy British drains, she discovers "a gutter in the middle of the streets expressly formed for the reception of filth." Trollope expresses horror at the French practice of throwing "nuisances and abominations of all sorts" from doors and windows. As a result, a simple stroll often becomes unpleasant: "Happy indeed is it for the humble pedestrian if his eye and nose alone suffer from these ejectments . . . a look, wholly in sorrow and nowise in anger, is the only helpless resource should he be splashed from head to foot" (79).

Most of *Paris,* however, shows a gay, glittering city. Trollope's account of her revulsion at French standards of cleanliness seems calculated more to show her ladylike side than an attempt to show her unhappiness. These letters read as if written by a sensitive, well-bred English woman who cannot abide indecencies, whether of rude behavior, dirty streets, sloppy dress, or, most distressing, revolutionary sympathies.

On another visit to the New York Public Library, I ask for two more preservation boxes. I settle in with Trollope's fifth travel book, *A Visit to Italy*. I read, knowing that during the year before this trip, Trollope had planned and began building a new home near Cecilia at Penrith while working on three novels. After returning from Italy, she and Tom lived in the new house for only a few months, then sold it to her daughter and son-in-law and moved to Florence. I wonder about her thoughts as she traveled through southern Europe. Was she thinking about a warmer climate? Or just a change of pace? Having published eighteen books in the last ten years, and at the age of sixty-two finally seeing her dependents (with the exception of Tom) at last on their own, Trollope may have approached this trip more with a sense of relief than of necessity.

Italy, also in the form of letters, infused with Frances Trollope's characteristic immediacy and spirit, gives me a new smile with every fragile page I turn. Almost every chapter/letter has a paragraph or two of ecstatic, florid description, followed by a qualification, an explanation that all is less lovely than it seems. Each reversal comes as a surprise to me, as I remember that, before very long, she and Tom would make their permanent home in Italy. I wonder why she must find fault everywhere they go.

Trollope begins her account of Genoa with an elaborate description, praising that city's

> splendid individuality among the cities of the earth . . . her palaces, with their marble terraces, their hanging-gardens . . . the unspeakable brightness of the sea that bathes her shore . . . the bold hills that are her buckler to the north, with the innumerable villas, which seem to smile upon her . . . the overflowing fertility of the golden garden in which she lies basking.

I am wholly unprepared for Frances Trollope's forlorn declaration in the very next paragraph that she "would rather look at Genoa as a sight to be seen than as a home to live in" (1: 43). If a new home were on her mind, Genoa clearly would not serve.

The "noble" and "majestic" landscape of Turin proves not only unhealthy, but also prone to natural disasters. Trollope observes that "pulmonary affections of the most fatal kind are frequent at Turin . . . intermitting fevers are also common" (1: 19–20). Health dangers abound in other cities as well. In Florence "there is a vile malaria in the beautiful cascina precisely at the hour when all the English world resorts thither in order to inhale as much of the air as possible" (1: 201).

As in *Paris*, the dangers she cannot, will not, abide are offenses, not of the natural world, but cultural ones—she judges harshly when she describes ordinary behavior that differs from British norms. Trollope paints Italians with the stereotype of southern laziness, reinforcing popular conception, and managing, at the same time, to make a connection with the southern states of America. Children on the beach at Sestri de Levante, she says, are:

> All old enough to be profitably employed, either in learning, or in labour, but all lying about in the sun, in more complete inaction and idleness than I ever watched elsewhere, except, perhaps in the negro-breeding farms in Virginia, where the children, preparing for the southern market, are permitted to fatten in very perfect idleness. (1: 57)

This connection, with its implications for the moral character of the Italians, goes far beyond typical presentations of southern laziness. It echoes the narrator of the popular *Jonathan Jefferson Whitlaw*, who calls slave children "one of the most popular speculations," having observed them on each plantation, "lying about . . . all well fattened and fed" (2: 153–54). I suspect, however, that she planted these echoes to boost sales rather than to suggest that Italians have little regard for the humanity of their children.

If Trollope's account of the expatriate English colony in Florence reflects the actual situation she found, it seems strange that she would soon join them. She finds her fellow British subjects rejected by the more "distinguished" Italians. She continues: "I confess it is a matter of surprise to me, to hear of so many English families in the middle station of life, who appear to have settled themselves down among a people who positively fly before them" (1: 290). Her accounts of the delights of Florence mitigate these observations, however, and help to explain her later choice and eventual pleasure living there.

Trollope treats Italy's glorious landscapes, so unlike anything familiar to her English readers, with similar ambivalence. She uses drama and danger, conventional components of landscape description, to advertise her own stamina. The Alps especially intrigue her, for in dangerous mountain passes she is able to portray genuine danger combined with an appreciation of the sublime. Her description of crossing the Alps begins with an account of sharing a carriage with an Italian woman who tries to frighten Trollope "with a series of terrific adventures which had befallen sundry of her acquaintance who had ventured to cross the mountain." Trollope, however, in her persona of intrepid traveler, finds "extreme enjoyment" in the "frightful desolation" of the "colourless desert," the "grim uniformity" where "death lies crouching beneath the bright smooth surface." She admits to a

> species of excitement . . . that to my mind must always neutralize the sensation of fear, or rather convert it into an emotion of the most delightful

kind, produced by a mixture of real sublimity, fanciful mystery, excited curiosity, and positive atmospheric exhilaration. (1: 13–17)

The common perception of Trollope as indefatigable, well into her sixties, owes much to *A Visit to Italy*.

Trollope portrays herself not only as an adventurous traveler, but also as a sophisticated one. The writer of these letters from Italy is an authority on painting, sculpture, music, and literature, perhaps in yet another attempt to counter personal attacks from reviewers who continued to find her behavior vulgar and unladylike. She describes visits to galleries and churches, concerts and operas, judging the execution of paintings, the effects of architectural details, and the quality of musical performances. During her visit to Michelangelo's home in Florence, a museum tended by the Buonarroti family, Trollope admires "the earliest efforts of Michael Angelo, both in painting, and sculpture" (2: 4). The museum contains a "collection of autograph manuscripts [which] form the most precious part of the relics thus preserved; because they are likely to bring us into the closest acquaintance with the heart and mind of their immortal author" (2: 2). She describes the contents of several letters and poems, finding them interesting and amusing, demonstrating by her discussion both her literary good taste and her fluency in Italian.

Like many of today's travelers, Trollope finds the arts of Florence particularly fascinating. She devotes ten rapturous pages to the "precious pictures" of the Pitti Palace, her visits there spoiled only by limited visiting hours (1: 112–18; 156–60). Maintaining that her taste and judgment equal that of "wiser folks," she declares she will dispense with guidebooks and, instead, "blunder on, approving or not approving, without any reference to 'foregone conclusions'" (1: 139).

In her persona as a sensitive, cultured traveler, she finds music, as well as art and literature, enchanting. While in Florence, she visits "Europe's umwhile wonder and delight, Madame Catalani Valabrique" and is greatly moved by a private performance. "I felt," she says, "as if some magical process was being performed upon me . . . unconsciously, my eyes filled with tears" (1: 161–62). Italian opera fares less well. At a performance in the "splendid" opera house at Genoa, she says, "The orchestra was pretty fair, but the singing very indifferent" (1: 44). From Florence, Trollope reports: "We have seen a beautiful Opera-house, the Pergola, and heard an indifferent Opera so badly performed there that I feel no great inclination to go again" (1: 264).

Perhaps because I know of Trollope's affection for Italy, little in this book strikes me as representing genuine displeasure. In contrast with *Domestic Manners*, Trollope treats hardships lightly, making fun whenever possible. Her party faces problems that seem more discomfiting and inconvenient than genuinely dangerous, thus more easily dismissed. At Borghetto, for instance, where the scenery again overwhelms her, she recommends leaving "the bad coffee, and the not-too-splendid room where it is served," instead using the time more profitably for "seeing all that can be seen without doors" (1: 58). On an excursion from Florence, her enjoyment of punting on a canal in the gardens of the Poggio di Cajano, a nearby palace, might have been spoiled by "some millions of mosquitoes [who had] taken it into their heads to seek pastime there as well as ourselves." Her party "did not, however, dispute the matter long with them, but yielding to the majority betook ourselves to our rustic dinner-table, where we found all of the consolation we could desire" (1: 174).

Again, as in her earlier travel books, Trollope finds ways to air her well-known political views. Her audience expects to find such commentary, and Trollope includes the requisite analysis of the Italian system. This time, however, critics found her too kind, lacking her usual "caustic manner" (qtd. in Neville-Sington, *Fanny Trollope* 305). Some of the old sarcasm is gone; nevertheless, Trollope still finds opportunities for re-affirmation of the British way of life. After conversation with an unnamed (and perhaps imaginary) "gentleman . . . well acquainted with what is going on both before and behind the scenes," she makes a rather strong statement, one calculated to please the audience that adored *Domestic Manners*, declaring

> that the Constitution of ENGLAND when guarded with common prudence from the democratic innovations which have of late years buzzed about it . . . like stray wasps from a nest set in motion at a distance . . . is the only one which appears to be formed in reasonable, honest, and holy conformity to the freedom of man as a human being, and to the necessary restraint inevitable upon his becoming one of a civilized, social compact. (1: 167)

I am musing on this wasps' nest metaphor as I hear an announcement that the library will close in fifteen minutes. I put *A Visit to Italy* back in the cardboard boxes and return them to the window. I remind myself that this lighthearted, enthusiastic traveler wrote, as she had advised Harriet Garnett also to write, with "popular taste" in mind (qtd. in Neville-Sington, *Fanny Trollope* 362). Neither Trollope nor I see a contradiction between her anti-democratic, anti-reform travel books and her justly celebrated reform novels.

11

Frances Trollope's "Modern" Influence: Creating New Fictions, New Readers, a New World

Susan S. Kissel Adams

Frances Trollope is the antithesis of the stereotype of the nineteenth-century woman writer. We are told that such women authors tended to write "domestic novels" based on their "limited experience" of life; that few great nineteenth-century male writers (and even fewer female writers) felt at home living in or writing about London; that women writers lacked the "relentless drive" needed to write serial novels; that they often wrote under pseudonyms (such as Currier, Ellis, and Acton Bell or George Eliot); and that Charlotte Brontë's *Jane Eyre* became, in 1847, the first heroine who saw men as equals and insisted on her rights (Pool 134, 105, 47). Such generalities ignore the fictional creations of Frances Trollope, one of the most popular novelists of the 1830s–1850s. Her life and works not only refute the stereotypical pattern outlined above; they helped to change it. Her fiction was a modernizing force—one we are only now beginning to appreciate.

Frances Trollope was a woman of the world. While she lived in London and its environs for many decades of her adult life (into her sixties), she also toured, and sometimes lived in, other parts of the world: America, Belgium, France, Ireland, West Germany, Austria, and, in her final decades, Italy. She traveled by rail, foot, horseback, steamboat, carriage; in her fifties and sixties, climbed mountains and tall buildings; went down into salt mines and catacombs; dodged pirates in the Gulf of Mexico; investigated factories in the north of England; and talked to royalty, slaves, and people in many walks of life, in many societies, throughout the world.

She wrote travel books about her experiences, the most famous of which remains her first one, *Domestic Manners of the Americans* (1832), published when she was fifty-three years of age. Over the next twenty-four years, she published five more travel books and thirty-five novels under her own name, seven in serial form, often publishing several works in one year—getting up early in the morning to write for two or three hours, as would become her son Anthony's practice (Neville-Sington, *Fanny Trollope* 352, 269). To say she was energetic is an understatement. Her courage and stamina as the sole support of her family, from her fifties into her seventies, have been remarked on by virtually all who have studied her career. Most importantly, these same qualities are revealed in her fiction: her strong, intimate, authorial voice; her compassionate but independent heroines; and her innovative subject matter advocating social reform of the nineteenth-century factory system, evangelicalism, slavery, and the institution of marriage.

Her heroines follow her lead, moving through a wide world extending from the fashionable drawing rooms of London; to scenes of street riots in Paris; to the wilderness hardships of frontier America; to idyllic surroundings in Germany; to quiet seaside pastimes in Brighton, England; to the dark factories of Great Britain's industrial north. Hers are not at all stereotypical nineteenth-century heroines: "kind, gentle, unaspiring, unassertive, and intellectually feeble" (Siefert, Preface). Instead, they are the predecessors of those heroines whom Carolyn Heilbrun, in *Toward a Recognition of Androgyny*, calls "modern," a historical phenomenon she locates in the 1880s–1920s (91)—one that Susan Morgan extends further back to origins in the novels of Walter Scott and Jane Austen (11). Although Morgan does not consider Frances Trollope's heroines in her study, *Sisters in Time*, they belong to her "[nineteenth-century] great age of the British novel and great heroines in the fiction of men and women" (4), to those works that suggest that "women did have a strong voice in shaping Victorian culture"(10), ones in which fictional heroines are linked to "historical process" (12) and "connectedness, the feminine, mercy and forgiveness [are seen as] . . . progressive models of human relations" (17). Certainly, in the fiction of Frances Trollope, bright, youthful heroines insist on reshaping their worlds to build more socially inclusive, egalitarian communities, from Lucy Bligh in *The Life and Adventures of Jonathan Jefferson Whitlaw* (1836); to Annie Beauchamp in *The Barnabys in America: or, Adventures of the Widow Wedded* (1843); to Mary Brotherton in *The Life and Adventures of Michael Armstrong, the Factory Boy* (1840); on to Frances Trollope's last novel and its heroine, Clara Holmwood, in *Fashionable Life; or Paris and London* (1856). Each heroine seeks to "feminize" an overly masculinized society, working to bring together the two sexes, as well as differing classes and races, in cooperative communities. This literary pattern in Frances Trollope's popular fiction became one that Charles Dickens, Elizabeth Gaskell, Anthony Trollope, and Harriet Beecher Stowe, among others, followed as well—a paradigm equating civilization's progress with greater feminine influence and leadership.[1]

In creating her courageous, outspoken, determined, young heroines, Frances Trollope was also creating new readers and new tastes as well. That she did so was yet another indication of her independent spirit and remarkable courage, for at every turn she faced the barbs of critics who called her "vulgar" and labeled her creations "unladylike" (Ellis 51). Yet Frances Trollope continued, undeterred, to create strong, young heroines, as well as determined, defiant, and admittedly unladylike middle-aged and elderly ones (the Widow Barnaby and such formidable spinsters as the Misses Lucy and Christina Clark of *One Fault*, 1840). She also created realistic portraits of unpleasant subjects other novelists before her, both male and female, had tended to avoid. She believed that fiction should "become an instrument for the improvement of society" and, "if she considered anything to be outside her 'proper sphere,' it would have been the bland, sentimental lady-like three-decker produced by her fellow women novelists" (Ellis 52). As Linda Abess Ellis explains, "although she clearly enjoyed her popularity and deliberately shaped elements of her work to appeal to her potential audience, she just as frequently violated the tastes and prejudices of her time" (135).

And so Frances Trollope wrote about rape (in *The Life and Adventures of Jonathan Jefferson Whitlaw*, 1836) and the sexual exploitation of women by clergymen (in *The Vicar of Wrexhill*, 1837). She exposed child exploitation and the abusive factory system (in *The Life and Adventures of Michael Armstrong, the Factory Boy*, 1840) as well as the brutality of slave owners, overseers, and ordinary white Americans (in *The Life and Adventures of Jonathan Jefferson Whitlaw*, 1843; *The Barnabys in America: or Adventures of the Widow Wedded*, 1843; and *Refugee in America*, 1832). She revealed the hardships and inequities of marriage for woman (*One Fault: a Novel*, 1840; and *Mrs Mathews; or Family Mysteries*, 1851) and the plight of the fallen women (*Jessie Phillips: a Tale of the Present Day*, 1843). In doing so, she paved the way for other novelists to follow in her footsteps—for Charles Dickens and Elizabeth Gaskell many years later to write about the industrial exploitation of workers, the former in *Hard Times* (1854) and the latter in *Mary Barton* (1854) and *North and South* (1855); for Harriet Beecher Stowe to write about slavery in *Uncle Tom's Cabin, or, Life Among the Lowly* (1852); and her son Anthony to write about the fallibility of the clergy in his Barchester series of novels (after his mother's *The Vicar of Wrexhill*, 1837 and *Uncle Walter, a Novel*,

1852, had introduced this subject); and for Anthony also to write about fallen women in *The Vicar of Bullhampton* (1870) and *An Eye for an Eye* (1879, after his mother's ground-breaking *Jessie Phillips*)—and, in so doing, find it no longer a taboo subject for fiction (George Watt 104).[2]

Frances Trollope defied fashion in the 1830s, helped to create it in the 1840s and 1850s, and went out of fashion again in the latter decades of the nineteenth century. Teresa Ransom summarizes her career in this way:

> Her novels discussed such unmentionable subjects as the rights of un-married mothers, child exploitation, slavery and women's emancipation; she also dared to suggest that women should be given the vote, and be allowed to stand for parliament, the church, and the legal profession. Her readers were both amused and scandalized by her novels, but as Victorian morality tightened its grip, Fanny's books fell from favour among the Es-tablishment. She was loved by her readers, who waited with impatience for the next Mrs. Trollope novel; but she was castigated as vulgar and too daring by most contemporary critics. Such publicity only increased her sales. (*Fanny Trollope* xvii)

Thus, through her heroines and her works, Frances Trollope helped to create the modern age—although, in doing so, her works became unfash-ionable in the Victorian period and her stands (on behalf of fiction, authors, readers, and society) passed without acknowledgment and were lost.

However, it was an age that most certainly had been affected by her writing and the controversies her fiction had engaged in—an age of con-stant social debate and reform in which Frances Trollope played a vital part. A few of the changes that would follow close on the heels of Frances Trollope's novels dealing with labor, slavery, and women's issues are: the Matrimonial Causes Act of 1857; the *English Women's Journal,* 1858; the Society for the Promotion of the Employment of Women, 1859; the beginnings of the British suffrage movement in the 1860s (Harsh 116; 169); the new Divorce Law of 1857 (Pool 154); the Little Poor Law of 1844, one year after the publication of *Jessie Phillips,* reinstating the right of unmarried mothers to sue fathers for the maintenance of their children (Neville-Sington *Fanny Trollope* 311–12); the British Ten Hour Law of 1847 to help address the plight of those factory workers laboring fourteen- to sixteen-hour days, a law she had advocated in *Michael Armstrong* over seven years earlier; and the end of slavery in the United States at the end of the Civil War in 1865, almost thirty years after her anti-slavery *Jonathan Jefferson Whitlaw* was published. None of these events or changes can be traced directly to Frances Trollope's influence—but her fiction helped to arouse public interest and feeling about issues such as women's rights, slavery, labor reform, and the plight of fallen women under the New Poor Law of 1834, all abuses her fiction exposed as needing reform.

Frances Trollope lived in an age of "unprecedented change" in the early nineteenth century, a time during which the population of England and Wales had doubled by 1851, undergone vast industrialization and urbanization, and begun widespread social, religious, and parliamentary reform (Gilmour 2). It was a time, also, when the novel and novelist were to become increasingly influential, acting often as the "social conscience of the age" (39). As Mr. Bold proclaims in Anthony Trollope's *The Warden* (1855), "if the world is to be set right, the work will be done by shilling numbers" (206). This is a lofty goal, to set out to better the world, sometimes undertaken in an overly zealous or misdirected manner (as is the case with John Bold's attack on *The Warden*'s benign and innocent Mr. Harding). Nevertheless, early nineteenth-century novelists, foremost among them Frances Trollope herself, did set out to achieve a better world through their fictional exposés. For who else could make sense of all the changes taking place, document them, sort out the good from the bad, or deal with the resulting social uncertainty and sense of unrest, if not society's chief observers and commentators, its writers and novelists? And who could better do so than Frances Trollope herself, a mature woman who had seen so much of the world, experienced instant success with her first book, yet endured a difficult marriage, raised two daughters and three sons (only to bury three of those children, along with her husband as well, late in her life), all the while suffering two bankruptcies and undergoing vicious critical reviews throughout her writing career?

In serial novels such as *Jessie Phillips*, *Michael Armstrong*, *The Widow Married*, and *The Barnabys in America*, Frances Trollope used her intimate, interactive relationship with her reading public to enlarge her readers' worlds; warn them about wrongdoings in society at home and abroad; shape their sense of propriety, good taste, and morality in a rapidly changing culture; and befriend them in their times of social anxiety, personal suffering, and political unrest. As Jennifer Hayward explains, serial writers such as Charles Dickens (and Frances Trollope, she might have added):

> provided information, showing readers how to act in social situations. Novels introduced disparate classes to each other, showing the increasingly juxtaposed "two nations" [of the rich and the poor] how others actually lived and thus helping to promote mutual understanding and to catalyze social change. Novels explored difficult social issues and attempted to move toward solutions. Novels helped to make coherent a radically new social and physical landscape; by organizing random, apparently senseless social relations and economic facts into narrative trajectories, authors imposed a

shape on inchoate and therefore terrifying changes . . . novels helped dis-
placed populations orient themselves by representing and thereby rendering visible their lives. (29–30)

Hayward shows how Charles Dickens and other serial writers also helped
readers take lower class characters seriously (31).

Frances Trollope did so, as well, through her depictions of slaves (Juno,
Phebe, and Caesar in *Jonathan Jefferson Whitlaw*), factory workers (Fanny
Fletcher and Michael and Edward Armstrong in *Michael Armstrong*), or
fallen women (Jessie Phillips in the novel by the same name), portraying
them as important, individualized characters. Frances Trollope, too, forged
relationships across class and racial barriers: when Mary Brotherton rescues Michael, Edward, and Fanny from the factory system (then educates
them and marries Edward), Martha Maxwell helps the ill-fated Jessie
Phillips, and Lucy Bligh helps the mistreated slaves Phebe and Caesar
escape and begin again in Germany at the end of *Jonathan Jefferson
Whitlaw*. Frances Trollope creates models of new communities, imagining "an egalitarian society [Britain] could not yet bring into being" (Harsh
169), where lower classes and upper classes intermingle, as in the ending
of *Michael Armstrong*, or women of different social backgrounds come
together to form a civilized community in Frances Trollope's last novel,
Fashionable Life; or Paris and London (1856).

Frances Trollope affirms everyday, ordinary lives, as she admits in her
introduction to *One Fault* (1840):

> The persons of the story I am about to tell were neither of high rank, nor
> of distinguished fashion; and, worse still, the narrative cannot by possibility
> be forced to become one of romantic interest. Ordinary every day human
> beings, and ordinary every day events are my theme. . . . That they shall
> be such men and women as I have seen and known, is the only fact con-
> cerning them that can be urged as an apology for introducing them at all.
> (1: 1–2)

At the same time, Frances Trollope points the way to better lives, private and public, for her ordinary characters through the model societies
they form in *Michael Armstrong*, *Jonathan Jefferson Whitlaw*, and other
works. And she is not afraid to give her readers the benefit of her own
personal experience and insight into human relationships and life. Thus,
she ends *One Fault* by stressing something she had learned through her
own long, disappointing, and difficult marriage, "To all mothers and all
daughters, with most kind wishes for success in all their projects; together
with a friendly request that they will bear in mind one important fact;
namely, that all ill-tempered men who may make large settlements, do
not die at the age of twenty-six years" (3: 312).

Nor was Frances Trollope's relationship with her readers merely one-sided. In part because of reader demand for her beloved heroine, the Widow Barnaby, Frances Trollope became the first novelist to develop two sequels starring her middle-aged female rogue, a pattern Anthony Trollope would follow in his two famous, six-part series of Barsetshire and Palliser novels. On the other hand, Frances Trollope would also cancel a sequel she had planned to write to *Michael Armstrong*, explaining in her Preface to its publication as a one-volume novel in 1840 (following its serial publication the year before) that she feared her work might have fed public unrest and led to rioting and unruliness she wished neither to condone nor encourage. Further, in her conclusion to *Jessie Phillips*, Frances Trollope acknowledges once more the effect of readers on her writing:

> The story of Jessie Phillips would have wandered less widely from what was intended, when the first chapters were written, had not the author received, during the time it was in progress, such a multitude of communications urging various and contradictory modes of treating the subject, that she became fearful of dealing too closely with a theme which might be presented to the judgment under so great a variety of aspects. The result of the information which has been earnestly sought for by the author, and eagerly given by many, appears to be that a new Poor Law, differing essentially from the old one, was absolutely necessary to save the country from the rapidly coroding process which can eat like a canker into her strength. . . . It appears evident that much of the misery so justly complained of might yet be remedied, were a patient and truly tolerant spirit at work *in all quarters* upon the subject. (3: 323–24)

In an age when newspapers were expensive, when serial fiction had become increasingly accessible and popular, fiction inspired a "multitude of communications" that Frances Trollope received in response to evolving episodes of *Jessie Phillips*. Novels such as hers produced a "powerful effect" on public opinion (Pool 2). Frances Trollope tried to use that effect for the betterment of society. With her help, by 1838 "the door of serious subject matter was opening," and serial novels began educating the public about important social issues. By mid-century the status of both novel and author had been raised—and a vast middle-class reading public developed (29, 100). If the price for being involved in so much change was to be called names and insulted by critics, it was a price Frances Trollope was willing to pay, not only because she needed to support her family, but also because she felt she had something important to say.

It is significant that Frances Trollope did not begin her writing career until she was fifty-three years of age. The authorial voice in her first work is very similar to her last—that of a mature woman who has seen the world. Her experience not only had led her to feel confident in breaking new ground in her fiction's subject matter and in creating independent, worldly, rebellious heroines, but in approaching her readers naturally, directly, and intimately. She addresses her reading public much as she describes effective parents interacting with their children in *The Vicar of Wrexhill*:

> It would be nearly impossible to convey in words an adequate idea of the difference which exists in a household where the parents make a secret of all things of important interest, and where they do not. . . . Without this easy, natural, spontaneous confidence, the family union is like a rope of sand, that will fall to pieces and disappear at the first threat of any thing that can attract and draw off its loose and unbound particles. . . . Let no parent believe that affection can be perfect without it; let no mother fancy that the heart of her girl can be open to her if it find not an open heart in return. . . . It is not in the nature of things that confidence should exist on one side only; it must be mutual. (1837: 82–83)

Herein lies the origin and essence of "the Trollope style" (Ransom, *Fanny Trollope* xviii)—Frances Trollope's "easy, natural, spontaneous confidence" passed down from mother to son, the same voice Anthony Trollope would adopt to address his readers in the latter part of the nineteenth century. It is an approach based on openness, trust, mutuality, respect, and care.

What Frances Trollope developed, and her son Anthony made lastingly famous, was a narrative style based on warmly expressed concern for the reader's personal, moral, intellectual, and social development. As has been said of Anthony Trollope's narrator, his fiction "requires that the listener trust the narrator . . . that author and reader should move along together in full confidence with each other . . . he has persuaded us to put our faith in the personality behind the authorial voice" (Fredman 39–40). Not only were both authors committed to creating readers who could understand the underlying seriousness of their critiques of society, but also readers who could learn from their fictional examples how to better "read" the increasingly complex world they inhabited. Their works have much to do with decoding a rapidly changing culture, as we will see in Frances Trollope's *Uncle Walter; a Novel* (1852) and Anthony Trollope's subsequent *The Warden* (1855) and *Barchester Towers* (1857).

Frances Trollope's novels advocate reading as a way of learning about the world—especially for young, inexperienced, socially confined women. In *Uncle Walter*, the young heroine is able to defy her prestigious, powerful father and escape the matrimonial schemes of her mother, in part because she is well-read. With the sympathetic Mr. Caldwell, her Uncle Walter, and the spinster Wiggensville sisters, Kate Harrington reads and discusses modern literature and contemporary thought, grappling with the problems of her age and the changing society she lives in. It is a difficult task, especially, as Uncle Walter says, at a time in history when the "age of treatises on universal knowledge is past. We have no admirable Crichtons now, who know everything; but we have specialties who, each in their own way [further the state of human knowledge]" (3: 40). Kate cannot possibly learn all there is to know, but she can find out about a larger world, extend the narrow boundaries of her life, and train her mind to discern truth from falsehood, good from bad, appearance from reality, in a complex society. Through reading informative nonfiction and realistic novels, Kate can escape the fate of those docilely led by others—by persons such as her own brother, James Harrington, "who have far more indulgence for ignorance linked with submission, than for information if allied to independence" (3: 171).

Information can lead to freedom—its absence to virtual enslavement. Through reading, Kate can learn the necessity of escaping the designs of her mother, a woman to whom "it never occurred . . . to open a volume in Kate's room, any more than in her own" (1: 37)—a woman of great respectability and position who, nevertheless, led a most narrow, ignorant life. As Frances Trollope's narrator informs her readers in *Uncle Walter*,

> [it] must be confessed that Lady Augusta added that deep-seated vulgarity of mind which is the inevitable product of a life spent in looking up to that on which we ought to look down, reverencing that which deserves no reverence, mistaking small things, and small people, for great things, and great people, and in contracting all thoughts and all feelings within the narrow circle of a paltry, yet arbitrary conventionalism. (1: 70)

Frances Trollope's fiction attempts to help readers discern the truly admirable from the only seemingly so, the really vulgar from that which, because it is unconventional, often is labeled as such (Frances Trollope's fiction, itself, for instance). She acts as interpreter and guide for readers attempting to find their way through a deceptive, difficult, ever-changing world. As she warns, "The words of very decent, well-behaved people, like the Doctor [Kate's father], often require translating into plain English, in order to be fully intelligible even to their own hearts" (1: 132). She offers her services as a translator experienced in the world's languages and customs (as she most certainly was), including those of the new, multifaceted, urbanized, industrialized, bureaucratized Britain.

Frances Trollope moves her readers beyond surface appearances to underlying realities. Describing Lady Augusta Harrington's preparations for a coming-out party for Kate, she exposes the lady's "operations" as being handled as carefully as "a landing-net [by] an angler" to ensnare the wealthy Lord Goldsmith for her daughter (1: 195). The narrator guides her readers through a profusion of wax-lights and flowers, elegant musicians, and lavish supper buffet delicacies, exposing the reality underlying contemporary fashion:

> any one unaccustomed to such things might really have supposed that they were going to enjoy themselves exceedingly, if they had taken a review of the preparations before the arrival of the actors who were destined to fill the scene. Our readers, however, are, of course, not so rustically ignorant, and so wholly unaccustomed to fashionable parties, as to suppose anything so preposterously ridiculous, and so utterly unlike the truth. *They* know, unless indeed they are absolutely, and altogether nobodies, how much, and how little, of real enjoyment is to be hoped for, when space enough for one hundred is to be occupied by three. (1: 193–94)

Frances Trollope's "somebodies," the bright and thoughtful readers she creates through her confidences, are those who can discern "the truth"— not those who are taken in by the fashionable, heartless marriage game.

As the kindly Uncle Walter (newly arrived back in England after many years away in Australia) immediately discerns, British society reveals its double standard when "no language [is] strong enough to upbraid the degraded creature who sells herself, when the price paid is to save her from starvation, . . . [then] smile[s] upon and approve[s] the very same act, when not the necessaries, but the luxuries of life are the legalized payment" (1: 309). This is the same kind of hypocrisy that leads Kate's father, the Reverend Henry Harrington, "Doctor of Divinity, Warden of All Saints' College in the University of Oxford, Prebendary of the Cathedral Church of Glastonbury, and Rector of a large and wealthy parish at the west end of [London]" (1: 4), to preach against "irreligious apple-women and rebellious news-vendors" in the public parks on the Sabbath while ignoring the more "lordly sabbath-breakers [*sic*]" on foot or lolling about in elegant carriages, making it "abundantly clear to the great unwashed that their rulers were only humbugging them when they enacted Sabbath Observance Bills, and harangued against the wickedness of all popular Sunday recreations" (1: 3, 2). Those of high rank inside and outside the Church of England, those who are successful, fashionable, and rich, who operate as the moral arbiters of nineteenth-century society, are not necessarily right; in fact, Frances Trollope shows, they may be quite dishonest and immoral.

Trollope's audience must learn to "read" others carefully and learn that what nineteenth-century society labels right or wrong, good or bad, mad or sane, may prove very much the opposite. As the astute Uncle Walter understands, "The world would have denied that the mind of Lady Juliana was in a state to deserve the appellation of *insane*, but a large portion of it would have admitted that it was *unsound*. Walter did not sufficiently recognize the difference between tweedledum and tweedledee; yet it lawfully divides the inmates of a mad-house from those who put them there" (1: 155). Without condescending to her readers, with care and respect for their welfare, Frances Trollope mentors them in more careful and correct "readings" of a shifting, topsy-turvy world. What matters most, she suggests, is the underlying motivation of human beings, the connection between their hearts and their heads, not their social station in life. In the case of Lady Augusta Harrington, ignorance and heartlessness combine with high social standing. Kate's elegant "coming out" party is not an act of love; instead, it "owed its origins in no respect and in no degree to any feelings of kindness, hospitality or friendship whatever, but wholly and solely [to] . . . vanity and ostentation, stimulated, however, by the hope that every penny expended would be repaid by a *quid pro quo* of one sort or other" (1: 168). It would be a profound mistake for Kate to follow in her mother's footsteps, just as it would be for the reader to seek mere "respectability" and follow fashion as mindlessly and coldly as Lady Augusta has done. Kate defies her parents, with Frances Trollope's full approval, renouncing Lord Goldstable with his "income of eighty thousand a-year," to follow the dictates of her heart and mind and join with her intellectual companion, friend, and fellow reader, Mr. Caldwell (a man rejected by her parents because he will have "to work for the means of existence," 1: 288, 291).

Social position, class rank, success in society, the admiration of the contemporary world—none of these should fool Frances Trollope's readers into making easy assessments when shaping the patterns of their lives. This is her view, as it would become her son Anthony's as well. For Anthony Trollope, too, is concerned with helping his audience learn to "read" the world aright. In *The Warden*, published three years after his mother's *Uncle Walter*, Anthony Trollope continues Frances Trollope's exposé of the clergy in this, his first successful novel, and the wonderful Barsetshire series to follow. More importantly, Anthony Trollope continues his mother's concern with enabling his audience to "read" discerningly and oppose conventional judgments of the world, even if they are advocated by the loftiest church personages or the highest legal advisers in the land. Readers of *The Warden* are shown that they must be wary of clergy such as the Reverend Dr. Theophilus Grantly, Archdeacon of Barchester, and Rector of Plumstead Episcopi, a man of stature in the world but not a man to be fully admired. He is a deceptive and secretive man who hides his own reading, locking away his volume of Rabelais from his wife, a woman "entitled to all such knowledge" (109) in the judgment of that more open and honest man, someone the reader can trust as an "intimate": the narrator.

Anthony Trollope cautions us to understand, "Dr. Grantly was by no means a bad man; he was exactly the man which such an education as his was most likely to form; his intellect being sufficient for such a place in the world, but not sufficient to put him in advance of it" (20). It is the hope of Anthony Trollope, as of his mother before him, that readers will educate themselves more fully (in part, through realistic fiction such as theirs) in such a way as to develop minds and hearts that will put them "in advance" of the world, not make them mere creatures of it, or, worse, its dupes. What society claims as Dr. Grantly's virtues, in fact, are often his faults: his "rigid constancy," his "overbearing assurance of the virtues and claims of his order," and his "strong confidence in the dignity of his own manner and the eloquence of his own words" (20–21). In sum, the narrator of *The Warden* finds that Dr. Grantly:

> was a moral man, believing the precepts which he taught, and believing also that he acted up to them; though we cannot say he would give his coat to the man who took his cloak, or that he was prepared to forgive his brother even seven times. He was severe enough in exacting his dues, considering that any laxity in this respect would endanger the security of the church; and, could he have had his way, he would have consigned to darkness and perdition, not only every individual reformer, but every committee and every commission that would even dare to ask a question respecting the appropriation of church revenues. (21)

In short, Dr. Grantly is representative of the "church militant" (64), doing battle for the Church of England wherever he goes, opposing any reform of the Church, right or wrong—not a forgiving, patient, thoughtful, or generous man. As with Dr. Pessimist Anticant (Thomas Carlyle), Dr. Grantly is revealed as failing to recognize the truth the narrator shares with his reader, "'Tis a pity that he should not have recognized the fact, that in this world no good is unalloyed, and that there is but little evil that has not in it some seed of what is goodly" (194). Dr. Grantly's training has not taught him to read well the ambiguities, paradoxes, and subtleties either of the world or of himself.

A much less fine figure of a man, of a much lower ecclesiastical standing, small of stature, nearly sixty years old, is the novel's protagonist, the Reverend Mr. Septimus Harding. Of this man, warden of Hiram's Hospital, the narrator must admit:

> Mr. Harding's warmest admirers cannot say that he was ever an industrious man; the circumstances of his life have not called on him to be so; and

yet he can hardly be called an idler. Since his appointment to his precentor-ship, he has published, with all possible additions of vellum, typography, and gilding, a collection of our ancient church music. . . . He has greatly improved the choir of Barchester. . . . He has taken something more than his fair share in the cathedral services, and has played the violoncello daily to such audiences as he could collect, or . . . to no audience at all. (8–9)

Only modest claims can be made, it seems, about Mr. Harding's achievements. As to whether he is entitled to the full sinecure of his office as hospital warden, a sum John Bold claimed was far greater than the original hospital benefactor intended, Mr. Harding is unsure. He knows that "many others—indeed all others of his own order—would think him right; but it failed to prove to him that he truly was so" (39). Mr. Harding lacks the assurance of a Dr. Grantly—a man who knows he is right—just as he lacks the prestige and aura of the Archdeacon, who "looked heavy, respectable, decorous, and opulent, a decided clergyman of the Church of England, every inch of him" (250).[3]

When Mr. Harding visits Sir Abraham Haphazard about John Bold's case against the hospital wardenship, he finds in the person of the attorney general another great personage of the world, a man who seems:

a machine with a mind. His face was full of intellect, but devoid of natural expression . . . a man to be sought for on great emergencies, but ill adapted for ordinary services; a man whom you would ask to defend your property, but to whom you would be sorry to confide your love. . . . He never quarrelled with his wife, but he never talked to her, he never had time to talk, he was so taken up with speaking. (230)

Here is another of Anthony Trollope's men of the world—another man of great intellect, but a man insufficiently developed so as to be "in advance" of the world. He is a man with a mind, but no heart, a truly "manly" man, like Archdeacon Grantly. Such men, men who are not intimate with their wives, who speak (in public) but do not converse or confide (even in private with their intimates), are no more admirable in Anthony's fiction than in his mother's. Those men who are to be admired have integrated the feminine into their characters, as with Mr. Harding and his friend the bishop: "There was a gentleness about the bishop to which the soft womanly affection of Mr. Harding particularly endeared itself, and it was quaint to see how the two mild old priests pressed each other's hands, and smiled and made little signs of love" (113). Like Frances Trollope's sensitive men, Uncle Walter and Mr. Caldwell, Mr. Harding and the bishop are gentle men of feeling who deserve the reader's respect.

Sir Abraham, of course, is incapable of admiring such a man as Mr. Harding. In fact, when Mr. Harding defies Sir Abraham's counsel that "a man is never the best judge of his own position," countering with the argument that "a man is the best judge of what he feels himself" (235), and informing Sir Abraham that he will resign the wardenship (even though John Bold has dropped the case), Sir Abraham judges Mr. Harding as "contemptible . . . he hardly knew how to talk to him as a rational being" (234). And yet Mr. Harding, aware Sir Abraham "regarded him as little better than a fool . . . did not mind; he and the attorney-general had not much in common between them; he knew also that others, whom he did care about, would think so too; but [his daughter] Eleanor, he was sure, would exult in what he had done, and the bishop, he trusted, would sympathize with him" (238). Mr. Harding, a coward and fool in the eyes of everyone but his daughter and aged friend, is the true man of honor and courage in *The Warden*.

Anthony Trollope's readers must learn to be as discerning as Frances Trollope's—to look beyond labels and public personas in nineteenth-century British society to discern true character in order to distinguish an Uncle Walter from a Reverend Henry Harrington, a Mr. Harding from a Dr. Grantly or a Sir Abraham Haphazard. Nor should his audience form judgments based simply on reading the increasingly accessible and powerful daily newspapers, such as the *Jupiter* (alias the "Thunderer," the *Times*). Its articles have been written by men such as Tom Towers, men who equate public power and prestige with private morality ("How could a successful man be in the wrong?", Tom asks himself; 202). Tom Towers confidently argues with John Bold in *The Warden*, taking "such high ground that there was no getting up on to it. 'The public is defrauded,' said he, 'whenever private considerations are allowed to have weight'" (204). The narrator comments, "Poor public! how often is it misled! against what a world of fraud has it to contend" (204). It is Anthony Trollope's responsibility and his concern to lead readers through Britain's deceitful, modern ways.

The chastened John Bold has been taught to read properly by *The Warden*'s heroine, Eleanor Harding. John learns from Eleanor not to ignore his own feelings about Mr. Harding or his observations of Mr. Harding's compassion and decency toward Hiram Hospital's twelve pensioners in order to promote general, sweeping reforms of the Church of England. Eleanor cautions her suitor, "If those who do not know [my father] oppose him, I shall have charity enough to believe that they are wrong, through error of judgment; but should I see him attacked by those who ought to know him, and to love him, and revere him, of such I shall be constrained to form a different opinion" (87). Later, in his interview with Tom Towers, John Bold proves he has learned his lesson from Eleanor Harding. He leaves the offices of the *Jupiter* thinking,

> I know he got his information from me. He was ready enough then to take my word for gospel when it suited his own views, and to set Mr. Harding up before the public as an imposter on no other testimony than my chance conversation; but when I offer him real evidence opposed to his own views, he tells me that private motives are detrimental to public justice! Confound his arrogance! What is any public question but a conglomeration of private interests? What is any newspaper article but an expression of the views taken by one side?
> Truth! it takes an age to discern the truth of any question! (204–5)

What matters finally in *The Warden* is simply that twelve old men at Hiram's Hospital have been well and truly cared for over the years by the gentle and good Mr. Harding.

At the end, after "justice" has been done, many of these old men, some of them illiterate, begin to rejoice:

> The one hundred a year to each of them was actually becoming a reality. . . . But other tidings soon made their way into the old men's rooms. It was first notified to them that the income abandoned by Mr. Harding would not come to them. . . . Mr. Harding's place would be at once filled by another. That the new warden could not be a kinder man they all knew; that he would be a less friendly one most suspected; and then came the bitter information that, from the moment of Mr. Harding's departure, the twopence a day, his own peculiar gift, must of necessity be withdrawn. (270–71)

Their ignorance has led them to follow others' "readings" of their situation, resulting in new "dissensions" among them and a "now comfortless hospital" (281). In *The Warden*, ignorance leads to dependence on others on the part of those who cannot read, and those who do read must be sure to do so very carefully in order not to be misled as well. The reader must discern the motives of reports read in the newspapers and demand that fiction, too, be "truthful" to the world they know. For the problem with the novels of "Mr. Popular Sentiment" (Charles Dickens), "a very powerful man" of the age, the narrator explains, is that "his good poor people are so very good; his hard rich people so very hard; and the genuinely honest so very honest" (206). Truth is not so easy to discern, as Anthony Trollope's readers know full well; readers must continue to be wary of those writers and books they allow to influence their views and lives.

Ordinary men and women (such as readers themselves) are capable of great courage and heroism in the works of both Frances and Anthony Trollope. They may be ordinary daughters who stand up against misguided, even immoral, fathers and mothers, as with Kate Harrington in *Uncle Walter*. They may be gentle, graying men, such as Frances Trollope's Uncle Walter and Anthony Trollope's Mr. Harding, defying and exposing the heartlessness of the great and godly around them. Or they may simply be men who, as Anthony Trollope says of Mr. Harding, "had that nice appreciation of the feelings of others which belongs of right exclusively to women" (*Barchester Towers* 2: 265). At the conclusion of *Barchester Towers*, Anthony Trollope pays Mr. Harding the greatest compliment of all:

> The Author now leaves him in the hands of his readers; not as a hero, not as a man to be admired and talked of, not as a man who should be toasted at public dinners and spoken of with conventional absurdity as a perfect divine, but as a good man without guile, believing humbly in the religion which he has striven to teach, and guided by the precepts which he has striven to learn. (2: 271)

Mr. Harding is well intentioned, if admittedly (as he himself anxiously comprehends) fallible—striving to be and do the best that is humanly possible. That is all that could be asked of anyone—so Anthony Trollope assures the equally fallible, ordinary men and women who are his readers.[4]

Anthony Trollope's fiction reveals great sympathy for humankind, as does his mother's—especially for the mistreated. Their common concern is justice, asking readers to redefine those who are good and bad, respectable and not respectable, moral and immoral. Yet, at the same time, they show that justice is complex and difficult to attain; not all reform and change are for the good. As Frances Trollope says in *Jessie Phillips*, those who often are "deeply interested in [the poor's] welfare," as with her "amiable Assistant Poor Law Commissioner" (as opposed to those such as Anthony's Mr. Slope in *Barchester Towers* who only pretend to be), can find themselves thwarted by reform legislation itself as they attempt to do "the most good that the circumstances permitted":

> Once, when it was very clearly evident that, by advancing the sum of two pounds five and sixpence, he had actually kept a family of seven persons from coming upon the parish at all, he had been officially declared, though with great civility, to have been altogether wrong. As his general conduct, however, was not such as exactly to justify dismissal, he was permitted to retain his appointment; but . . . his judgment [was set] aside, whenever it appeared to lean towards common sense . . . and [he was] . . . remov[ed] . . . from one place to another with more than usual rapidity, which in a

very satisfactory degree prevented the possibility of his being useful any
where. (3: 322–23)

Frances Trollope's Assistant Poor Law Commissioner in *Jessie Phillips* is
yet another kindly Mr. Harding come to modern, arbitrary, bureaucratic
judgment!

It takes understanding and compassion, as well as knowledge of individual cases and situations, to prevent the repeated mistreatments, private and public, suffered by a Jessie Phillips. If, as Frances Trollope says,
she has been "too weak, too erring . . . yet . . . it [is] a thing to wonder
at that she, and the terribly tempted class of which she is the type, should
seem so very decidedly to be selected . . . as a sacrifice for all the sins of
all their sex. . . . There is no chivalry in the selection, and to the eyes of
ignorance, like mine, there is no justice" (*Jessie Phillips* 3: 316–17). In
addition, social remedies, abstractly conceived and mechanistically applied,
may only add to a community's distress: "The constantly increasing evils
arising from the attempt to generalize regulations upon points so essentially requiring variety of modification, as well as the radical mischief and
obviously demoralizing effect of substituting central in the place of local
authority, are already so strongly felt that it were a sin to doubt their
ultimate reform" (3: 324–25). In the novels of both mother and son, ill-
conceived reform laws are seen as doing more harm than good.

Frances Trollope, well-known reformer and instigator of change, advises caution, close study, knowledge of individual circumstances, and
human feeling whenever formulating new policy (as her son also does in
The Warden). Justice can only be done by good people desiring to do
good things in the world about them. These will be people who can
"read" discerningly, not merely from appearances or conventions, the true
motives and characters of themselves and others. The increasingly complex, duplicitous, modern world of the nineteenth-century requires readers
who can look beyond titles, clothes, and public speeches and who understand that, because something is new, it is not necessarily better—not
necessarily social progress. Anthony Trollope joins his mother in warning
readers to beware of social fashion:

A man is sufficiently condemned if it can only be shown that either in
politics or religion he does not belong to some new school established
within the last score of years. He may then regard himself as rubbish and
expect to be carted away. A man is nothing now unless he has within him
a full appreciation of the new era; an era in which it would seem that neither honesty nor truth is very desirable, but in which success is the only
touchstone of merit. We must laugh at everything that is established . . . or
else we are nought. (*Barchester Towers* 1: 116)

Change can be good: more widespread literacy, education, reading; less abusive marriages between people of differing social classes; and new laws protecting fallen women and child laborers. As Frances Trollope's Mr. Bell advises in *Michael Armstrong*, "each new use we learn to make of the still much-unknown creation around us, ought to be welcomed with a shout of praise. . . . It is not from increased, or increasing science that we have any thing to dread, it is only from a fearfully culpable neglect of the moral power that should rule and regulate its uses, that it can be other than one of God's best gifts" (205). What is to be feared is not what is new, but, instead, what is the same old, familiar evil: greed, selfishness, and human hypocrisy, poised to exploit social unrest and change.

Frances Trollope played a significant role in bringing about reform in the nineteenth century. She promoted causes of social justice and worked to create a better society through her fiction. She engaged in redefining the words "respectable," "moral," "good," and "genteel" in her period. In doing so, she contributed to the rise of the middle class, elevating and affirming her "ordinary" readers, suggesting that social rank should matter less than compassion and civility of human character. And she helped to create a vast reading public, shaping its tastes through her popular fiction. Because of her courageous lead, other authors of the age found themselves able to tackle new subjects and adopt important social stands already advocated through her groundbreaking works. Frances Trollope paved the way for novels such as Charles Dickens' *Hard Times*, Elizabeth Gaskell's *Mary Barton* and *North and South,* Harriet Beecher Stowe's *Uncle Tom's Cabin*, and, as we have seen, Anthony Trollope's *The Warden* and *Barchester Towers*—helping to alter the nature of literary protagonists and literary heroism. Through her courageous fictional heroines, Frances Trollope also sought to alter existing relationships in the nineteenth-century between men and women, whites and blacks, rich and poor, employers and employees, husbands and wives, the powerful and the powerless.

Frances Trollope possessed a clear vision and deep moral concern for humanity. Hers was a modernizing and progressive influence, enlightening her audience during a time of rapid change, enabling them to "read" their society more discerningly. At the same time, she was never an advocate of change for change's sake, working, instead, for change for humanity's betterment. Witty, compassionate, and wise—her voice proved worth listening to (as evidenced by the popular success of her novels with the reading public and the responsive fictional works of her son Anthony and other, important nineteenth-century authors, besides). A century-and-a-half later, more new readers are finding her fiction refreshingly accessible—and her voice, one that continues to delight, enlighten, and inspire modern-day readers.

NOTES

1. See my discussion of this literary paradigm in chapters 6 and 8 of *In Common Cause*, 75–93, 115–45.

2. See Chapter 8 of my *In Common Cause*, 115–45, discussing Frances Trollope's influence on each of these authors and works in more detail.

3. Both Frances Trollope and Anthony Trollope present fictional portraits of the implacable male (Mr. Harding's opposite), based on the personality of the difficult Thomas Anthony Trollope they knew at home as husband and father. See Pamela Neville-Sington, *Fanny Trollope* 44 and 358; Ransom, *Fanny Trollope* 133; and George Watt 41, for several discussions of a few of the earnest, serious, brooding, and/or ill-tempered male characters who "know they are right" in the novels of Frances and Anthony Trollope.

4. Anthony Trollope also makes clear that his most wicked characters, such as Mr. Slope in *Barchester Towers*, are not beneath the reader's contempt. Mr. Slope is, instead, a man in need of softer, kinder, more gentlemanly (i.e., more feminine) ways (62). Anthony Trollope's unscrupulous and domineering female characters (Signora Neroni and Mrs. Proudie in *Barchester Towers*) also are shown to be deserving of the reader's fair judgment, tolerance, and compassion. These women delight as well as scandalize, as with Frances Trollope's innovative protagonist, the Widow Barnaby, of her earlier trio of Barnaby novels.

Bibliography

WORKS BY FRANCES TROLLOPE

The Abbess; a Romance. 3 vols. London: Whittaker, Treacher, 1833.

The Attractive Man. 3 vols. London: Colburn, 1846.

The Barnabys in America: or Adventures of the Widow Wedded. Illust. John Leech. 3 vols. London: Bentley, 1842.

Belgium and Western Germany in 1833; including Visits to Baden-Baden, Wiesbaden, Cassel, Hanover, the Harz Mountains, etc. 2 vols. London: Bentley, 1836.

Blue Belles of England. 3 vols. London: Saunders, 1842.

Charles Chesterfield; or the Adventures of a Youth of Genius. Illust. H. K. Brown. 3 vols. London: Colburn, 1841.

Domestic Manners of the Americans. Illust. Auguste Hervieu. 2 vols. London: Whittaker, Treacher, 1832.

———. Ed. Donald Arthur Smalley. New York: Alfred Knopf, 1949.

———. Barre, MA: Imprint Society, 1969.

———. Ed. and Introd. Herbert Van Thal. London: Folio Society, 1974.

———. Ed. Oxford: Oxford UP, 1984.

———. Ed. and Introd. by Pamela Neville-Sington. London: Penguin, 1997.

Fashionable Life; or Paris and London. 3 vols. London: Hurst, 1856.

Father Eustace; a Tale of the Jesuits. 3 vols. London: Colburn, 1847.

Gertrude; or Family Pride. 3 vols. London: Hurst, 1855.

Hargrave; or the Adventures of a Man of Fashion. 3 vols. London: Colburn, 1843. Introd. Teresa Ransom. Stroud: Sutton, 1995.

Jessie Phillips: a Tale of the Present Day. Illust. John Leech. 3 vols. London: Colburn, 1843.

The Laurringtons; or Superior People. 3 vols. London: Longman, 1844.

The Life and Adventures of a Clever Woman. Illustrated with Occasional Extracts from her Diary. 3 vols. London: Hurst, 1854.

The Life and Adventures of Jonathan Jefferson Whitlaw: or Scenes on the Mississippi. Illust. Auguste Hervieu. 3 vols. London: Bentley, 1836.

———. Paris: Baudry's European Library, 1836.

The Life and Adventures of Michael Armstrong, the Factory Boy. Illust. Auguste Hervieu, R. W. Buss, and T. Onwhyn. 3 vols. London: Colburn, 1840.

———. Frank Cass & Co., 1968.

The Lottery of Marriage; a Novel. 3 vols. London: Colburn, 1849.

The Mother's Manual: or Illustrations of Matrimonial Economy. An Essay in Verse. Illust. Auguste Hervieu. London: Treutel, Würtz and Richter, 1833.

Mrs Mathews; or Family Mysteries. 3 vols. London: Colburn, 1851.

The Old World and the New; a Novel. 3 vols. London: Colburn, 1849.

One Fault; a Novel. 3 vols. London: Bentley, 1840.

Paris and the Parisians in 1835. Illust. Auguste Hervieu. 2 vols. London: Bentley, 1836.

Petticoat Government; a Novel. 3 vols. London: Hurst, 1850.

The Refugee in America: a Novel. 3 vols. London: Whittaker, Treacher, 1832.

The Robertses on their Travels. 3 vols. London: Colburn, 1846.

A Romance of Vienna. 3 vols. London: Bentley, 1838.

Second Love; or Beauty and Intellect. 3 vols. London: Colburn, 1851.

"Signs of the Times. The Righteous Rout." Unpublished manuscript. Trollope Family Papers. The University of Illinois at Urbana-Champaign.

The Three Cousins. 3 vols. London: Colburn, 1847.

Town and Country; a Novel. 3 vols. London: Colburn, 1848.

Travels and Travellers; a Series of Sketches. 2 vols. London: Colburn, 1846.

Tremordyn Cliff. 3 vols. London: Bentley, 1835.

Uncle Walter; a Novel. 3 vols. London: Colburn, 1852.

The Vicar of Wrexhill. Illust. Auguste Hervieu. 3 vols. London: Bentley, 1837.

———. New York: AMS P, 1975.

———. Stroud: Sutton, 1996.

Vienna and the Austrians. Illust. Auguste Hervieu. 2 vols. London: Bentley, 1838.

A Visit to Italy. 2 vols. London: Bentley. 1842.

The Ward of Thorpe Combe. 3 vols. London: Bentley, 1841.

The Widow Barnaby. 3 vols. London: Bentley, 1839; Phoenix Mill, England: Sutton, 1995.

The Widow Married; a Sequel to the Widow Barnaby. Illust. R. W. Buss. London: Colburn, 1840.

The Widow Wedded; or The Adventures of the Barnabys in America. London: Ward and Lock, 1843.

The Young Countess; or Love and Jealousy. 3 vols. London: Colburn, 1848.

The Young Heiress; a Novel. 3 vols. London: Hurst, 1854.

Young Love; a Novel. 3 vols. London: Colburn, 1844.

SECONDARY SOURCES CITED

Anderson, Michael. "The Social Implications of Demographic Change." *The Cambridge Social History of Britain 1750–1950*. Ed. F.M.L. Thompson. Vol. 2. Cambridge: Cambridge UP, 1990. 1–70.

Auerbach, Nina. *Communities of Women: An Idea in Fiction*. Cambridge, MA: Harvard UP, 1978.

Austen, Jane. *Jane Austen's Letters*. 3rd Ed. Ed. Deirdre Le Faye. Oxford: Oxford UP, 1995.

Ayres, Brenda. *Dissenting Women in Dickens' Novels: Subversion of Domestic Ideology*. Westport, CT: Greenwood P, 1998.

Bawer, Bruce. *Stealing Jesus: How Fundamentalism Betrays Christianity*. New York: Three Rivers P, 1997.

Bloom, Harold. *The American Religion: The Emergence of the Post-Christian Nation*. New York: Simon and Schuster, 1992.

Bodenheimer, Rosemarie. *The Politics of Story in Victorian Social Fiction*. Ithaca, NY: Cornell UP, 1988.

Boone, Joseph Allen. *Tradition Counter Tradition: Love and the Form of Fiction*. Chicago: U of Chicago P, 1987.

Boswell, James. *The Life of Samuel Johnson, LL.D.* Chicago: U of Chicago P, 1952.

Brontë, Charlotte. *Jane Eyre*. Ed. Q. D. Leavis. Toronto: Penguin, 1966.

———. *Shirley*. Eds. Herbert Rosengarten and Margaret Smith. 1849. Oxford: Oxford UP, 1981.

Brown, Ford K. *Fathers of the Victorians: The Age of Wilberforce*. Cambridge: Cambridge UP, 1961.

Button, Marilyn. "Reclaiming Mrs. Frances Trollope: British Abolitionist and Feminist." *College Language Association Journal* 38 Sept. 1994: 69–86.

Carlyle, Thomas. "Chartism." 1839. *Thomas Carlyle: Critical and Miscellaneous Essays*. 5 vols. New York: AMS P. 4: 118–204.

———. "Signs of the Times." 1829. *A Carlyle Reader: Selections from the Writings of Thomas Carlyle*. Ed. G. B. Tennyson. Cambridge: Cambridge UP, 1984. 31–54.

Carpenter, Mary Wilson. "Female Grotesques in Academia: Ageism, Antifeminism, and Feminists on the Faculty." *Antifeminism in the Academy*. Eds. Vèvè Clark, Shirley Nelson Garner, Margaret Higonnet, and Ketu H. Katrak. New York: Routledge, 1996. 141–65.

Cassiday, Bruce, ed. *Roots of Detection. The Art of Deduction before Sherlock Holmes*. New York: Ungar, 1983.

Chaloner, W. H. "Mrs. Trollope and the Early Factory System." *Victorian Studies* 4 Dec. 1960: 159–66.

Charcot, Jean-Martin. *Clinical Lectures on Senile Chronic Diseases*. Trans. William S. Tuke. New York: Arno P. 1979.

[Chorley, Henry Fothergill]. "Works of Mrs. Trollope." Rev. of *The Vicar of Wrexhill*. London and Westminster Review 28 Oct. 1837: 112–31.

Coke, E. T. *A Subaltern's Furlough: Descriptive of Scenes in Various Parts of the United States . . . during the Summer and Autumn of 1832*. London, 1833.

Corrigan, Philip, and Derek Sayer. *The Great Arch: English State Formation as Cultural Revolution*. Oxford: Basil Blackwell, 1985.

Countryman, L. William. *Dirt Greed and Sex: Sexual Ethics in the New Testament and Their Implications for Today*. Philadelphia: Fortress P, 1988.

Cullen, Michael J. *The Statistical Movement in Early Victorian Britain: The Foundation of Empirical Social Research*. New York: Barnes & Noble Books, 1975.

Cunningham, John William. *The Velvet Cushion*. London, 1814.

Cunnington, Phillis, and Catherine Lucas. *Costume for Births, Marriages and Deaths*. London: Adam & Charles Black, 1972.

De Lauretis, Teresa, ed. *Feminist Studies/Critical Studies*. Bloomington: Indiana UP, 1986.

Dickens, Charles. *Hard Times* (1854). New York: Harper and Row, 1965.

———. *The Letters*. Pilgrim Edition. Eds. M. House, K. Tillotson, and G. Story. Oxford: Oxford UP, 1965.

Disraeli, Benjamin. *Sybil; or, The Two Nations* (1845). Ed. Thom Braun. London: Penguin, 1980.

———. Ed. Sheila M. Smith. Oxford: Oxford UP, 1981.

Douglas, Ann. "Introduction: The Legacy of American Victorianism: The Meaning of Little Eva." *The Feminization of American Culture*. New York: Anchor P, 1988. 3–13.

Douglas, Mrs. Frances. *The Gentlewoman's Book of Dress*. London: Henry and Co., 1890.

Dyos, H. J., and Michael Wolff, eds. *The Victorian City: Images and Realities*. 2 vols. London: Routledge, 1973.

Ellis, Linda Abess. *Frances Trollope's America: Four Novels*. New York: Peter Lang, 1993.

Farr, William. *Vital Statistics: A Memorial Volume of Selections from the Reports and Writings*. London: Office of the Sanitary Institute, 1885.

Favret, Mary. "Flogging: The Anti-Slavery Movement Writes Pornography." *Essays & Studies* 51 (1998): 19–43.

Ferguson, Moira, ed. *The History of Mary Prince, A West Indian Slave, Narrated by Herself*. Rev. ed. Ann Arbor: U of Michigan P, 1997.

Finlayson, Geoffrey. *Citizen, State, and Social Welfare in Britain 1830–1990*. Oxford: Clarendon P, 1994.

Fredman, Alice Green. *Anthony Trollope*. New York: Columbia UP, 1971.

Gallagher, Catherine. *The Industrial Reformation of English Fiction: Social Discourse and Narrative Form, 1832–1867*. Chicago: U of Chicago P, 1985.

Gaskell, Elizabeth. *Mary Barton* (1854). London: Dent, 1969.

———. *North and South* (1855). London: Oxford UP, 1973.

Geldges, B. et al. *E.T.A. Hoffmann. Epoche—Werk— Wirkung*. München: Beck, 1986.

Gilmour, Robin. *The Novel in the Victorian Age: A Modern Introduction*. London: Edward Arnold, 1986.

Glendinning, Victoria. *Anthony Trollope*. New York: Penguin, 1994.

Green, Katherine Sobba. *The Courtship Novel, 1740–1820: A Feminized Genre.*
   Lexington: UP of Kentucky, 1991.

Greg, W. R., ed. "Why are Women Redundant?" *Literary and Social Judgments.*
   New York: Holt, 1876. 274–308.

Guy, Josephine M. *The Victorian Social Problem Novel: The Market, the Individual
   and Communal Life.* New York: St. Martin's P, 1996.

Hall, N. John, ed. *The Letters of Anthony Trollope.* Stanford, CA: Stanford UP,
   1983.

———. *Trollope: A Biography.* Oxford: Clarendon P, 1991.

Harrison, Brian. *Peaceable Kingdom: Stability and Change in Modern Britain.*
   Oxford: Clarendon P, 1982.

Harsh, Constance. *Subversive Heroines: Feminist Resolutions of Social Crisis in the
   Condition-of-England Novel.* Ann Arbor: U of Michigan P, 1994.

Haycraft, Howard. *Murder for Pleasure: The Life and Times of the Detective Story.*
   New York: D. Appleton-Century Co., 1941.

Hayward, Jennifer. *Consuming Pleasures: Active Audiences and Serial Fictions
   from Dickens to Soap Operas.* Lexington: UP of Kentucky, 1997.

Heilbrun, Carolyn G. *Toward a Recognition of Androgyny.* New York: Harper
   and Row, 1974.

Heineman, Helen. "Frances Trollope in the New World." *American Quarterly*
   21 (1969): 544–59.

———. *Frances Trollope.* Boston: Twayne, 1984.

———. *Mrs. Trollope: The Triumphant Feminine in the Nineteenth Century.*
   Athens: Ohio UP, 1979.

———. *Restless Angels: The Friendship of Six Victorian Women.* Athens: Ohio UP,
   1983.

———. *Three Victorians in the New World: Charles Dickens, Frances Trollope and
   Anthony Trollope.* New York: Peter Lang, 1992.

Henriques, Ursula. "Bastardy and the New Poor Law." *Past and Present* 37
   (1967): 103–29.

Hildreth, Richard. *The White Slave: or Memoirs of Archy Moore.* Boston: John H.
   Eastburn, 1836.

Hoffmann, E.T.A. *E.T.A. Hoffmann's Werke.* 15 vols. Ed. Georg Ellinger. Ber-
   lin: Deutsches Verlagshaus Bong, n.d.

Hogarth, William. *Engravings by Hogarth.* Ed. Sean Shesgreen. New York:
   Dover, 1973.

Hollis, Patricia, ed. *Pressure from Without in Early Victorian England.* London:
   Edward Arnold, 1974.

Hooker, Richard. *Of the Laws of Ecclesiastical Polity.* 2 vols. London: Dent, 1964.

Horstman, Allen. *Victorian Divorce.* London: Croom Helm, 1985.

Jalland, Pat. *Death in the Victorian Family.* Oxford: Oxford UP, 1996.

Jameson, Fredric. *The Political Unconscious: Narrative as a Socially Symbolic Act.*
   Ithaca, NY: Cornell UP, 1981.

Katritzky, Linde. *A Guide to Bonaventura's "Nightwatches."* New York: Peter
   Lang, 1999.

——. *Johnson and the Letters of Junius.* New York: Peter Lang, 1996.

——. *Lichtenbergs Gedankensystem.* New York: Peter Lang, 1995.

Katz, Stephen. "Charcot's Older Women: Bodies of Knowledge at the Interface of Aging Studies and Women's Studies." *Figuring Age.* Ed. Kathleen Woodward. Indianapolis: Indiana UP, 1999, 112–30.

Kestner, Joseph. "Men in Female Condition of England Novels." *Women and Literature* 2 (1982): 77–99.

——. *Protest and Reform: The British Social Narrative by Women, 1827–1867.* Madison: U of Wisconsin P, 1985.

Kincaid, James R. *The Novels of Anthony Trollope.* Oxford: Oxford UP, 1977.

King, Margaret F. "'Certain Learned Ladies': Trollope's *Can You Forgive Her?* and the Langham Place Circle." *Victorian Literature and Culture* 21 (1993): 307–26.

Kingsley, Charles. *Alton Locke, Tailor and Poet: An Autobiography.* 1850. Oxford: Oxford UP, 1983.

Kissel Adams, Susan S. *In Common Cause: The "Conservative" Frances Trollope and the "Radical" Frances Wright.* Bowling Green, OH: Bowling Green State U Popular P, 1993.

——. "More Than Anthony's Mother: Frances Trollope's Other Contributions to British Literature." *Kentucky Philological Review* 20 (1989): 12–17.

——. *Moving On: The Heroines of Shirley Ann Grau, Anne Tyler, and Gail Godwin.* Bowling Green, OH: Bowling Green State U Popular P, 1996.

——. "'What Shall Become of Us All?': Frances Trollope's Sense of the Future." *Studies in the Novel* 20 (1988): 151–66.

——, and Margery Rouse. *The Story of the Pewter Basin and Other Occasional Writings: Collected in Southern Ohio and Northern Kentucky.* Bloomington, IN: T.I.S. Pub., 1981.

L'Estrange, A. G. *The Life of Mary Russell Mitford.* 3 vols. London: Richard Bentley, 1870.

Lewis, C. S. *English Literature in the Sixteenth Century Excluding Drama.* Oxford: Clarendon P, 1954.

Mangum, Teresa. "Little Women: The Aging Female Character in Nineteenth-Century British Children's Literature." *Figuring Age.* Ed. Kathleen Woodward, Indianapolis: Indiana UP, 1999, 59–87.

McCord, Norman. "The Poor Law and Philanthropy." *The New Poor Law in the Nineteenth Century.* Ed. Derek Fraser. New York: St. Martin's P, 1976. 87–110.

McKeon, Michael. *The Origins of the English Novel 1600–1740.* Baltimore: Johns Hopkins UP, 1987.

Merrifield, Mrs. *Dress As a Fine Art.* London: Arthur Hall, 1854.

Miller, D.A. *Narrative and Its Discontents: Problems of Closure in the Traditional Novel.* Princeton, NJ: Princeton UP, 1981.

Milton, John. *Paradise Lost and Selected Poetry and Prose.* Introd. Northrop Frye. New York: Holt, 1951.

Moers, Ellen. *Literary Women: The Great Writers.* New York: Oxford UP, 1985.

Morgan, Susan. *Sisters in Time: Imagining Gender in Nineteenth-Century British Fiction*. New York: Oxford UP, 1989.

Morris, R. J. "The Middle Class and British Towns and Cities of the Industrial Revolution, 1780–1870." *The Pursuit of Urban History*. Eds. Derek Fraser and Anthony Sutcliffe. London: Edward Arnold, 1983. 286–306.

Morse, Deborah Denenholz. *Women in Trollope's Palliser Novels*. Ann Arbor: UMI Research P, 1987.

Mullen, Richard. *Birds of Passage: Five Englishwomen in Search of America*. London: Duckworth, 1994.

Murray, Douglas. "Gazing and Avoiding the Gaze." *Jane Austen's Business: Her World and Her Profession*. Eds. Juliet McMaster and Bruce Stovel. Basingstoke: Macmillan, 1996. 42–53.

Nardin, Jane. *He Knew She Was Right: The Independent Woman in the Novels of Anthony Trollope*. Carbondale: Southern Illinios UP, 1989.

Neville-Sington, Pamela. Introduction. *Domestic Manners of the Americans*. By Frances Trollope. New York: Penguin, 1997.

———. *Fanny Trollope: The Life and Adventures of a Clever Woman*. New York: Viking, 1997.

———. *Paradise Dreamed: How Utopian Thinkers Have Changed the Modern World*. London: Bloomsbury, 1993.

Overton, Bill. *The Unofficial Trollope*. Sussex: The Harvester P, 1982.

Owen, David. *English Philanthropy, 1660–1960*. Cambridge, MA: Belknap P of Harvard UP, 1964.

Pool, Daniel. *Dickens' Fur Coat and Charlotte's Unanswered Letters: The Rows and Romances of England's Great Victorian Novelists*. New York: HarperCollins P, 1997.

Poovey, Mary. *Making a Social Body: British Cultural Formation 1830–1864*. Chicago: U of Chicago P, 1995.

Prochaska, F. K. *Women and Philanthropy in Nineteenth-Century England*. Oxford, 1980.

Ransom, Teresa. *Fanny Trollope: A Remarkable Life*. New York: St. Martin's P, 1995.

———. Introduction. *The Widow Barnaby*. By Fanny Trollope. Phoenix Mill, England: Alan Sutton, 1995. v–ix.

Rev. of *Jessie Phillips*. *John Bull* 23 (1843): 732.

Rev. of *The Life and Adventures of Michael Armstrong, the Factory Boy*. By Frances Trollope. *Athenaeum* 615 (10 Aug. 1839): 587–90.

Rev. of *The Vicar of Wrexhill*. By Frances Trollope. *Athenaeum* 517 (1837): 708.

Russo, Mary. "Female Grotesques: Carnival and Theory." *Feminist Studies/ Critical Studies*. Ed. Teresa De Lauretis. 213–229. Rpt. in *The Female Grotesque: Risk, Excess, Modernity*. Ed. Mary Russo. New York: Routledge, 1995. 53–73.

Sadleir, Michael. *Trollope: A Commentary*. London, Oxford UP, 1927.

———. New York: Farrar, 1947.

Savage, Gail L. "'Intended Only for the Husband': Gender, Class, and the Provision for Divorce in England, 1858–1868." *Victorian Scandals: Representations of Gender and Class.* Ed. Kristine Ottensen Garrigan. Athens: Ohio UP, 1992.

Sharpe, Jenny. "'Something Akin to Freedom': The Case of Mary Prince." *Differences* 8:1 Spring 1996: 31–56.

Siefert, Susan. *The Dilemma of the Talented Heroine: A Study in Nineteenth Century Fiction.* Montreal, Canada: Eden P, 1978.

Smith-Rosenberg, Carroll. "Woman and Religious Revivals: Anti-Ritualism, Liminality, and the Emergence of the American Bourgeoisie." *The Evangelical Tradition in America.* Ed. Leonard I. Sweet. Macon, GA: Mercer UP, 1997. 199–231.

Stevenson, John Andrew. "Fly Not Yet." Bodleian Ballads Catalogue: Harding B 11 (4274). 8 Dec. 2000. http://bodley.ox.ac.uk/cg.

Stone, Lawrence. *The Family, Sex and Marriage in England 1500–1800.* New York: Harper and Row, 1977.

———. *Road to Divorce: England 1530–1987.* Oxford: Oxford UP, 1990.

Stowe, Harriet Beecher. *Uncle Tom's Cabin, or, Life Among the Lowly* (1852). New York: Harper and Row, 1965.

Thackeray, William Makepeace. Rev. of *The Vicar. Fraser's Magazine* 17 (1838): 79ff.

Tillotson, Kathleen. *Novels of the 1840s.* London: Oxford UP, 1954.

Todd, Barbara J. "The Remarrying Widow: A Stereotype Reconsidered." *Women in English Society 1500–1800.* London: Methuen, 1985.

Tompkins, Jane. *Sensational Designs: The Cultural Work of American Fiction, 1790–1860.* New York: Oxford, 1985.

Trollope, Anthony. *An Autobiography.* Introd. Bradford Allen Booth. Berkeley: U of California P, 1947.

———. Gloucester: Alan Sutton, 1987.

———. Ed. David Skilton. London: Penguin, 1996.

———. *Barchester Towers* (1857). New York: Oxford UP, 1989.

———. *Can You Forgive Her?* 1864–65. *The Electronic Text Center.* Ed. David Kiton. 1994. Folio Society Ed. London: the Folio Society, 1989. U of Virginia. 8 March 2001. <http://etext.lib.virginia.edu/>.

———. *An Eye For An Eye.* 2 vols. London: Chapman and Hall, 1879.

———. *The Letters of Anthony Trollope.* Ed. N. John Hall. 2 vols. Stanford, CA: Stanford UP, 1983.

———. *The Noble Jilt.* London: Constable & Company, 1923.

———. *The Vicar of Bullhampton.* 1870. Oxford: Oxford UP, 1933.

———. *The Warden.* 1855. New York: Oxford UP, 1989.

Trollope, Frances Eleanor. *Frances Trollope: Her Life and Literary Work from George III to Victoria.* 2 vols. London: Bentley, 1895.

———. Vol. 1. London: Bentley, 1895. AMS Edition, 1975.

Trollope, Thomas Adolphus. *What I Remember.* 2 vols. London: Bentley, 1887.

———. New York: Harper, 1888.

———. Ed. Herbert van Thal. London: William Kimber, 1973.

von Grimmelshausen, Hans Jacob Christoffel. *Werke Ed.* Dieter Breuer. Frankfurt: Deutscher Klassiker Verlag, 1989. Vol. 1. *Der Abenteuerliche Simplicissimus teutsch.* Bk. V. Ch. XII–XVII. 489–517.

Wallins, Roger. "Mrs. Trollope's Artistic Dilemma in *Michael Armstrong.*" *Ariel* 8.1 (1977): 5–15.

Watt, George. *The Fallen Woman in the Nineteenth-Century English Novel.* London: Croom Helm, 1984.

Watt, Ian. *The Rise of the Novel: Studies in Defoe, Richardson and Fielding.* Berkeley: U of California P, 1957.

"*The Widow Barnaby.*" Rev. *The Athenaeum.* 584 (1839): 9–10.

"*The Widow Barnaby*, by Mrs. Trollope." Rev. *The London Times.* 24 Jan. 1839: 5.

Woodward, Kathleen, ed. *Figuring Age: Women, Bodies, Generations.* Indianapolis: Indiana UP, 1999.

Wrigley, E. A., and R. S. Schofield. *The Population History of England 1541–1871: A Reconstruction.* Cambridge, MA: Harvard UP, 1981.

Yeazell, Ruth Bernard. *Fictions of Modesty: Women and Courtship in the English Novel.* Chicago: U of Chicago P, 1991.

Yellin, Jean Fagin. *Women and Sisters: The Antislavery Feminists in American Culture.* New Haven, CT: Yale UP, 1989.

BIOGRAPHIES

Bigland, Eileen. *The Indomitable Mrs. Trollope.* London: James Barrie, 1953.

Ellis, Linda Abess. *Frances Trollope's America: Four Novels.* New York: Peter Lang, 1993.

Hall, N. John. *Trollope: A Biography.* Oxford: Clarendon, 1991.

Heineman, Helen. *Mrs. Trollope: The Triumphant Feminine in the Nineteenth Century.* Athens: Ohio UP, 1979.

Johnston, Johanna. *The Life, Manners, and Travels of Fanny Trollope: A Biography.* New York: Hawthorne Books, 1978.

Neville-Sington, Pamela. *Fanny Trollope: The Life and Adventures of a Clever Woman.* New York: Viking, 1997.

Ransom, Teresa. *Fanny Trollope: A Remarkable Life.* New York: St. Martin's P, 1995.

Trollope, Frances Eleanor. *Frances Trollope: Her Life and Literary Work from George III to Victoria.* 2 vols. London: Bentley, 1895.

Index

About the Contributors

BRENDA AYRES is Associate Professor of English at Middle Georgia College in Cochran, Georgia. She is the author of several published articles, poems, short stories, and *Dissenting Women in Dicken's Novels: Subversion of Domestic Ideology* (Greenwood, 1998). Besides this collection of criticism on Frances Trollope, she has been the editor of *The Emperor's Old Groove: The Disneyfication of Our Children* and *Silent Voices: The Extant Victorian Women's Novel.*

MARY WILSON CARPENTER is an Associate Professor of English at Queen's University in Kingston, Ontario. She is a Victorianist who also works in age studies. She has published "Female Grotesques in Academia: Ageism, Anti-Feminism, and Feminist on the Faculty" in *Antifeminism in the Academy* as well as "Eco, Oedipus, and the 'View' of the University" in *Diacritics.* In addition, Dr. Carpenter has published *George Eliot and the Landscape of Time* and many articles on Victorian writers and feminist theory.

LINDA ABESS ELLIS has taught composition and literature at the Elizabeth Seton campus of Iona College, Pace University, and Westchester Community College. Ellis wrote *Frances Trollope's America: Four Novels.* Inspired by Fanny Trollope's voyages through France and Italy, Dr. Ellis and her husband travel as much as possible.

ANN-BARBARA GRAFF is currently a lecturer in English at the University of Toronto. In her doctoral thesis, she explored the intersection of Darwinian evolutionary discourse and liberalism in Victorian works of literature and politics. Her publications include a biographical sketch of Frances Trollope in *Nineteenth Century British Women Writers*.

CONSTANCE HARSH is Associate Professor of English at Colgate University in Hamilton, New York. She is the author of *Subversive Heroines: Feminist Resolutions of Social Crisis in the Condition-of-England Novel* and has written on the novels of George Gissing.

KAY HEATH is an assistant professor at Virginia State University. Her chapter is from her dissertation, "Aging By the Book: Textual Constructions of Mid-life in Victorian Britain."

HELEN HEINEMAN wrote Trollope's biography, *Mrs. Trollope: The Triumphant Feminine in the 19th Century*. She also wrote Trollope's biography for the Twayne *English Authors Critical Biography* (1984), and included a critical study of Trollope in another book, *Restless Angels: The Friendship of Six Victorian Women* (1983), as well as in *Three Victorians in the New World: Charles Dickens, Frances Trollope and Anthony Trollope* (1992). Dr. Heineman is president of Framingham State College in Massachusetts.

PRITI JOSHI is an assistant professor of English at the University of Puget Sound. She is currently working on a manuscript tentatively titled *Producing the Middle-Class: Discourse of the Poor, 1840–1860*. Dr. Joshi has also published "The Dual Work of Wastes in Edwin Chadwick's *Sanitary Work*" on the Dickens Project: *Our Mutual Friend* Web site.

LINDE KATRITZKY is Adjunct Professor at the University of Florida, graduated from the University of Munich, Germany, and holds an MA in German and a PhD in English from the University of Florida. She lived many years in England and has published articles on literature, the Enlightenment, and English/German cultural relations in international journals. Her monographs include *Lichtenbergs Gedankensystem, Johnson and the Letters of Junius*, and *A Guide to Bonaventura's "Nightwatches."*

SUSAN S. KISSEL ADAMS is Professor of English at Northern Kentucky University. She has written *In Common Cause: The "Conservative" Frances Trollope and the "Radical" Frances Write* and *Moving On: The Heroines of Shirley Ann Grau, Anne Tyler, and Gail Godwin*. In addition, she has coedited, with Margery Rouse, *The Story of the Pewter Basin and Other Occasional Writings: Collected in Southern Ohio and Northern Kentucky* and has published a number of articles on nineteenth- and twentieth-century American and British authors.

DOUGLAS MURRAY coedited with Margaret Anne Doody the Oxford World's Classics *Catharine and Other Writings of Austen*. He has published numerous articles on eighteenth-century literature (particularly Jane Austen) and is interested in the Church-of-England novel. Murray is Professor in the Department of Literature and Language at Belmont University in Nashville, Tennessee.

PAMELA NEVILLE-SINGTON has published the most comprehensive biography on Trollope to date. *Fanny Trollope: The Life and Adventures of a Clever Woman* (1997) thoroughly integrates Fanny's work with a discussion of Fanny's life. Besides incorporating reader response, Neville-Sington also situates Trollope in literary history by identifying what writers influenced her and what writers, in turn, she influenced. A recognized expert on Fanny, Dr. Neville-Sington has edited and written the introduction and notes to Trollope's *Domestic Manners of the Americans* (1997). She is also the author of *Paradise Dreamed: How Utopian Thinkers Have Changed the Modern World* (1993).